The Man Who Invented
CHRISTMAS

To: ....

From: ....

Mr. Fezziwig's Ball

(engraving by John Leech, 1843)

The Man Who Invented
CHRISTMAS

HOW CHARLES DICKENS'S
A Christmas Carol
RESCUED HIS CAREER AND REVIVED
OUR HOLIDAY SPIRITS

LES STANDIFORD

WITH
CHARLES DICKENS'S *A CHRISTMAS CAROL*

B\D\W\Y
BROADWAY BOOKS
NEW YORK

Published in the United States by Broadway Books,
an imprint of the Crown Publishing Group, a division of
Penguin Random House LLC, New York.
crownpublishing.com

Broadway Books and its logo, B \ D \ W \ Y, are trademarks of
Penguin Random House LLC.

Originally published in hardcover in the United States by Crown,
an imprint of the Crown Publishing Group, a division of
Penguin Random House LLC, New York, in 2008.

Library of Congress Cataloging-in-Publication Data
Standiford, Les.
The man who invented Christmas : how Charles Dickens's
A Christmas Carol rescued his career and revived our holiday
spirits / Les Standiford. — 1st ed.
Includes bibliographical references.
1. Dickens, Charles, 1812–1870. Christmas carol. 2. Christmas
stories, English—History and criticism. 3. Christmas—England—
History—19th century. 4. Christmas in literature. I. Title.
PR4572.C69S73 2008
823'.8—dc22   2008014978

ISBN 978-1-5247-6246-9
Ebook ISBN 978-1-5247-6326-8

Printed in the United States of America

BOOK DESIGN BY BARBARA STURMAN
Cover image: Motion Picture © 2017 Bleecker Street Media LLC.
All rights reserved.

10 9 8 7 6 5 4 3 2 1

2017 PAPERBACK EDITION

This book is dedicated to the real Sam Weller,

Who taught me the book trade

in a worldly temple in Salt Lake City,

And to Mitchell, and Rona, and Otto, and Marshall

And so many good book people everywhere.

God bless them, every one.

CONTENTS

The Man Who Invented Christmas

CONTENTS

A Christmas Carol   229

Behold I do not give lectures or a little charity,
When I give I give myself.

—WALT WHITMAN

NATIVITY

In London, in 1824, it was the custom to treat a debtor little differently from a man who had reached into a purse and stolen a similar sum. In this case, he was a father of seven, and though he was gainfully employed, it was not gainful enough. His debt was to a baker, a man named Karr, who lived in Camden Street, and the sum was forty pounds, no small amount in those days, when an oyster was a penny, a whole salmon a pound and six, and a clerk who worked for a tightfisted miser in a countinghouse might not earn as much in a year.

Accounts were tallied, the sheriff was consulted, and men were sent in consequence. Our father—John his name, and thirty-seven—was taken by the sheriff's men to what was called a "sponging house," a kind of purgatory where those who could not meet their obligations were afforded some few days to seek relief from their creditors' charges, intervention from a person of influence, or possibly a loan from family or friends.

In this instance, help was not forthcoming. Two days passed with no good word, and then our John, officially an insolvent debtor, was passed along to the Marshalsea, imprisoned alongside smugglers, mutineers, and pirates. "The sun has set on me, forever," he told his family as he left.

One who tried to help was a son of John, who, then twelve, took a job, at six shillings a week in a tumbledown factory-house that sat on the banks of the River Thames. One day long afterward the boy would speak of the place, "Its wainscoted rooms and its rotten floors and staircase, and the old grey rats swarming down in the cellars, and the sound of their squeaking and scuffing coming up the stairs at all times, and the dirt and decay of the place, rise up visibly before me, as if I were there again."

His job was to fill small pots with shoe blacking, and tie them off with paper, and then to paste on each a printed label. The boy worked ten hours a day, standing near a window for better light and where any passersby might see him, with a break for a meal at noon, and one for tea later on. And though the place was grim and the work was numbing, and this had put his childhood to an end, he worked on. For his father was in prison. For a debt of forty pounds. For his family's bread.

"My whole nature was so penetrated with the grief and humiliation of such considerations," the boy would one day write, "that even now . . . I often forget in my dreams that I have a dear wife and children; even that I am a man; and [I] wander desolately back to that time of my life."

While these words testify to the force of a childhood blow, they also offer reassurance that there would one day come a lightening of his circumstances. That the boy would not spend forever in his dismal occupation, nor would his father stay forever in the Marshalsea, though there were three long months there, with our young man visiting his father in a tiny room behind high spiked walls, and where, the boy recalls, they "cried very much."

And where his father told him "to take warning by the Marshalsea, and to observe that if a man had twenty pounds a year, and spent nineteen pounds nineteen shillings and six-pence, he would be happy; but that a shilling spent the other way would make him wretched." These words of caution, and lament, and more, and then at 10:00 p.m. the warning bell would toll and our young man of twelve would walk out into the foggy London night, five miles toward home, and some hours of oblivion before the scurrying, and the squeal-ing, and the little pots of blacking came again.

The boy's name was Charles, of course, and his family's name was Dickens, and most who have commented on the life of the famed author have observed that those sorry experiences of his youth, described in a scrap of autobiog-raphy never published during his lifetime, constitute the most significant of his formative years. All art grows out of its maker's loss, it has been said—and if that is so, Dickens's loss of his childhood was to become the world's great gain.

Dickens, who is generally considered one of the most accomplished writers in the English language, published twenty novels in his lifetime—he died in 1870—and none of them has ever gone out of print. His personal experience of harsh working conditions and a deep sympathy for the poor inform much of his writing, and more than one scholar has made a life's work out of tracing the parallels between the author's life and his fiction. The number of academic books, dissertations, monographs, and articles devoted to Dickens and such lengthy works as *Oliver Twist* and *David Copperfield*, *Bleak House* and *Great Expectations*, is, practically speaking, beyond counting.

But perhaps the best known and certainly the most beloved of all Dickens's works has received relatively little study. Though *A Christmas Carol* abounds in references to Dickens's life, and is the very apotheosis of his themes—and though it is exquisitely crafted, often referred to as his most "perfect" work—critical attention has been scant.

Perhaps it is because the book is short, fewer than 30,000 words; perhaps it is because of its very popularity, its readership said at the turn of the twentieth century to be second only to the Bible's; or perhaps it is because of the difficulty or the irrelevance of analyzing what is simply very good. Dickens's contemporary, William Makepeace Thackeray, as scathing a critic as ever walked the streets of London, once said of it, "Who can listen to objections regarding such a book as this? It seems to me a national benefit, and to every man or woman who reads it, a personal kindness."

Perhaps the most surprising thing about the story behind this well-known story, however, is the pivotal role it played both in Dickens's career and in cultural history itself. At the time he sat down to write his "slender volume," Dickens's once unequaled popularity was at a nadir, his critical reputation in a shambles, his bank account overdrawn.

Faced with bankruptcy, he was contemplating giving up on writing fiction altogether. Instead, he pulled himself together and, in six short weeks, wrote a book that not only restored him in the eyes of the public but began the transformation of what was then a second-tier holiday into the most significant celebration of the Christian calendar.

However, as many an old storyteller has put it, we have gotten a bit ahead of ourselves.

Part One

MEAN SEASON

1.

On the evening of October 5, 1843, thirty-one-year-old Charles Dickens sat on a stage in the smoke-laden city of Manchester, surely unaware that on this evening a process would begin that would change his life—and Western culture—forever. At the moment he was simply trying to pay attention as fellow novelist and junior member of Parliament Benjamin Disraeli completed his remarks to their eager audience.

Dickens and Disraeli, along with political firebrand Richard Cobden, were the featured speakers for this special program, a fund-raiser for the Manchester Athenaeum, the industrial capital's primary beacon of arts and enlightenment. Designed by Charles Berg, architect of the Houses of Parliament, the Athenaeum's headquarters (as well as its mission) was greatly revered by culture-starved workingmen and the more progressive of the city's leaders. But a lingering downturn in the nation's economy—part of the industrial revolution's ceaseless cycle of boom and bust—had sent the Athenaeum into serious debt and placed its future in doubt.

Hoping to turn the tide, Cobden, a Manchester alderman and also an MP, had joined with other concerned citizens to lay plans for a bazaar and "grand soirée" in the adjoining Free Trade Hall. A popular and vociferous op-

ponent of the onerous Corn Laws, which imposed stiff duties on imported grain and inflated the profits of England's
landowners at the expense of a citizenry often unable to buy
bread, Cobden could always be counted upon to draw an
audience. But with the addition of popular authors Disraeli
and Dickens to the bill, the promoters hoped for a bonanza
of shopping and new subscriptions that would secure the future of the Athenaeum once and for all.

Disraeli—the man who would go on to serve nearly forty
years in his nation's government, including two stints as
prime minister, propelling his country into such epic undertakings as the annexation of Cyprus and the building of the
Suez Canal—was at that time simply the socially conscious
son of Jewish parents, a budding politician who had left the
study of law to write a series of popular romances.

The evening's headliner, however, was Dickens, who
had become perhaps the world's first true celebrity of the
popular arts. The author of *Sketches by Boz, The Pickwick
Papers, Oliver Twist, Nicholas Nickleby,* and *The Old Curiosity Shop* was far and away his country's best-selling author,
acclaimed as much for his themes—the passionate portrayals
of the misery of the poor and the presumption and posturing
of the rich—as for his spellbinding powers as a storyteller.
And yet, for all his accomplishments, Dickens sat upon that
Manchester stage a troubled man. True, he had risen from
a poverty-stricken childhood of his own to enjoy unimagi-
nable success and influence. But what preoccupied him on
that evening was how rapidly—and how unaccountably—his
good fortune had fled.

In fact, an account of Dickens's rise from his miserable days in a London boot-blacking factory up until the time of his appearance in Manchester reads like melodrama:

His education was first interrupted at the age of twelve, when his father—a naval pay clerk who always struggled to meet his obligations—was imprisoned for debt (in time, the rest of the family, including Dickens's mother, Elizabeth, and his three younger brothers and sisters finally joined his father in Marshalsea). Though he was able to resume school briefly after his father was released, the family's fortunes plunged again, and at fifteen, young Charles was taken from school and apprenticed as a law clerk. Though he found the work there only slightly less dismal than the bottling of boot polish—and though he quickly came to loathe the hypocrisy of a labyrinthine and self-serving legal system—he formed a lifelong commitment to the distinction between "justice" and "the law."

In 1829, at the age of seventeen, Dickens took a job as a court stenographer, and five years later, at twenty-two, began writing for a British newspaper, the *Morning Chronicle,* which dispatched him across the country to cover various elections. Along the way, Dickens discovered an interest in and facility for writing of the foibles, eccentricities, and tragedies embedded in the nation's legal and political machinations; his keen eye and caustic wit enabled him to place a number of pieces in periodicals, a practice that not only supplemented his income but gratified his ego as well.

Of his first publication, a sketch titled "A Dinner at Poplar Walk," in the December 1833 issue of *Monthly Magazine*, Dickens recalls the purchase of "my first copy of the magazine in which my first effusion—dropped stealthily one evening at twilight, with fear and trembling, into a dark letter-box, in a dark office, up a court in Fleet Street—appeared in all the glory of print; on which occasion by-the-bye,—how well I recollect it!—I walked down to Westminster Hall, and turned into it for half-an-hour, because my eyes were so dimmed with joy and pride, that they could not bear the street, and were not fit to be seen there."

While many of his first "outside" publications took the form of rudimentary short stories, Dickens began to make a name for himself with his nonfiction work for the *Chronicle,* especially the series of "Street Sketches" that offered readers for the first time a vivid and empathetic view of ordinary London life. Pieces such as "Brokers and Marine Store Shops," "The Old Bailey," and "Shabby-Genteel People," not only fascinated the readers of Dickens's time but foreshadowed the dramatic style of today's so-called new journalism. As the critic Michael Slater notes, "Already in these sketches Dickens is experimenting, very effectively, with that blending of the wildly comic and the intensely pathetic that was to win and keep him such thousands of devoted readers in after years."

This success in the *Morning Chronicle* led its publisher, George Hogarth, to invite Dickens to fashion a similar piece for the launch of a new publication, the *Evening Chronicle*. Soon Dickens was contributing regularly to the new publication and others, signing off as "Boz," and creating something of a stir in London literary circles. In October of 1835, the publisher John Macrone offered Dickens one hundred pounds for the rights to publish a collection of *Sketches by Boz,* a handsome sum for a young reporter making just seven pounds per week.

Writers' use of pseudonyms for the publication of literary items was a standard affectation of the time, and more than a small amount of gossip arose among those "in the know" as to the true identity of such widely read figures as Fitzboodle, Titmarsh, and Mr. C. J. Yellowplush. Dickens was fond of passing along to friends the contents of a hush-hush note he had received informing him in no uncertain terms that the writer behind the moniker of "Boz" was none other than his friend and fellow essayist Leigh Hunt.

It was not until advertisements for *Sketches* were placed that the true identity of "Boz" (taken from a childhood nickname for Dickens's youngest brother, Augustus) was revealed, and for several years afterward, Dickens maintained the good-natured and popular affectation. Friends called him Boz, and Dickens often referred to himself in the third person as Boz. (Later he would be fêted at the "Boz Ball" during a tour of the United States, and as late as 1843, his novel *Martin Chuzzlewit,* though acknowledging its author as Charles Dickens, still carried the notation "Edited by Boz" on its title page.)

Sketches was published in February of 1836 and met with unqualified success. Suddenly, Dickens saw himself validated as a spokesman for the underclass and an appointed foe of buffoonery, unwarranted privilege, and chicanery. One paper lauded him as "a kind of Boswell to society," and another called the sketches "a perfect picture of the morals, manners, and habits of a great portion of English Society." John Forster, who would one day become Dickens's great friend, adviser, editor, and first biographer, wrote in the *Examiner* that Dickens had excelled particularly in his portraits of the ludicrous and the pathetic, all rendered in an "agreeable, racy style."

The success of *Sketches by Boz* led the publishers Chapman and Hall to contact Dickens regarding a project they had been turning over for some time. An artist named Robert Seymour had approached them with an idea for a serial publication on sporting life, with his own woodcuts to be accompanied by someone else's lively text. Given what he had accomplished in *Sketches,* Dickens was just the man to add spice to this endeavor, the publishers told him, and offered him fourteen pounds per month to take the project on.

Dickens, however, was initially cool to the idea. He objected that "although born and partly bred in the country I was no great sportsman, except in the regard of all kinds of locomotion; that the idea was not novel, and had been already much used; that it would be infinitely better for the plates to arise naturally out of the text [instead of the other way around]; and that I should like to take my own way, with a freer range of English scene and people, and I was afraid I should ultimately do so in any case."

Given their admiration for *Boz,* Chapman and Hall agreed to see it Dickens's way—he was to be the dog, with

Seymour the tail—and once that was settled, Dickens was off and running. As he would write later, "My views being deferred to, I thought of Mr. Pickwick, and wrote the first number."

What Seymour had conceived of as a kind of extended set of cartoons profiting at the expense of Cockney sportsmen became something much richer in Dickens's hands. He and Seymour met face to face only once, on April 17, 1836, "to take a glass of grog" in Dickens's words, and to discuss a few changes Dickens thought necessary for the plates that would go in the second issue of what was now being called *The Posthumous Papers of the Pickwick Club*, by Boz. Seymour, quite well known in his own right, must have seen which way the winds were blowing, but still he seemed agreeable enough. He made the changes Dickens asked for . . .

. . . and then, on April 20, after dashing off a note to his wife—"best and dearest" of her kind—Seymour killed himself.

Seymour made no mention in that letter of his own career's downward trajectory, nor was there any bitter lament to the effect that the master of a project had become its slave. It is one of history's undeniable ironies, however, that the demise of one artistic career would mark the meteoric rise of another.

With Seymour gone, Dickens was forced to arrange for another artist, Halbot Browne, to draw the plates for *Pickwick*. Now a married man (he and Catherine Hogarth had proclaimed their vows on April 2), Dickens also negotiated a raise with Chapman and Hall to twenty pounds per month, with the understanding that he would expand each issue of *Pickwick* from twenty-six to thirty-two pages.

It was something of a leap of faith for Chapman and Hall to continue the project, for the sales of the first issue were fewer than five hundred copies, and the second and third did only marginally better. By the fourth issue, however, Dickens was in full control of the publication. Beginning with that number, he began the transformation of Mr. Pickwick from a fool into a benevolent, incomparable comic protagonist, served and advised by the faithful Sam Weller, whose pungent asides to his earnest but bumbling master have provided the inspiration for mordant comics to this very day: "now we look compact and comfortable, as the father said ven he cut his little boy's head off, to cure him o' squintin."

As the magazine's original harmless buffoonery was replaced by such often dark and pointed humor, the stock of the Pickwick Club rose in the eyes of the public. Sales for the fourth number jumped to 4,000. By the eleventh, 14,000 copies were sold. And by the end of the run, in November of 1837, more than 40,000 readers were lining up for installments. The era of Dickens as a true literary star had begun.

Entire volumes have been devoted to the impact of Dickens's immense popularity upon publishing, and he is generally credited as being single-handedly responsible for transforming an industry. In many ways, he would influence publishing as profoundly as the steam engine or the blast furnace would redirect manufacturing. The publishing industry had evolved markedly, however, over the past century, from the moment the startling new form of the novel made its debut. While modern critics debate just which publication constitutes the starting point of the genre, all are agreed that nothing quite like the works of Defoe (*Robinson Crusoe,* 1719), Fielding (*Tom Jones,* 1729), and Richardson (*Clarissa,* 1740) had come before them. This form of writing, a rendering of imaginary characters involved in a compelling narrative taking place in a world that seemed almost real, all of it designed primarily for the entertainment and not the edification of its audience, proved extremely popular among the British reading public.

In contrast to previous publishing staples—the Bible, schoolbooks, hymnals, instruction manuals, and the like—novels were ephemeral, meant to be consumed and discarded. Thus was created an ongoing demand for new works, not only for works of literary quality but also for a long line of adventure stories, gothic tales, and romances of all sorts. The "silver fork" novel, set against the backdrop of British high society, was one of many such subtypes popular in the decades immediately preceding Dickens's ascent, with Disraeli's *Vivian Grey* (1827) being one of the more notable in the genre. It has been estimated that between 1815 and 1850, some 3,500 novels were published in an effort to fill the demand.

And while these novels were generally printed in small editions of 1,000 to 2,000, some reached higher levels. Sir Walter Scott, who published his first novel, *Waverly,* in

1814, and who would bring out a new book nearly every year until his death in 1832, was the first writer whose success suggested that one might actually make a career solely as a novelist. His *Ivanhoe* sold out its initial printing of 10,000 within a few weeks of its publication in 1819, an unprecedented number. By Dickens's time, no book had again reached such heights, but that did not keep publishers from hoping, of course.

Initially, publishers sold their books directly to the public, working primarily by mail order. Advertisements were placed in newspapers and magazines, which were delivered by post and newsboys in London and throughout the country, and readers ordered what appeared interesting. In time, newspapers and magazines began to compile their own lists of new and recommended books, and by the mid-1700s, critical reviews were appearing on a regular basis to guide readers in their choices.

Most of the publishing companies in the 1700s were small family enterprises, and in order to dispose of unsold stock threatening to crowd them out of their homes and small offices, many firms opened shops on the premises to serve a walk-in trade. Others, such as Chapman and Hall in 1830, began business as booksellers who also intended to produce many of their own wares. These vertically integrated enterprises, in which editing, printing, marketing, and sales often went on under the same roof, persisted well into the middle of the nineteenth century, though there were a few stand-alone bookshops that sold stationery, magazines, newspapers, and notions, as well.

By the early 1800s, significant change had come to publishing. The industrial revolution not only encouraged specialization in manufacturing but in general business practice as well. The goals and methods for the successful design, manufacture, wholesaling, and retailing of any product are quite distinct, after all, and it is no different in the editing, printing, distribution, and retailing of books. Thus, those vertical publishing enterprises began to fragment, according to the strengths and interests of those involved.

By 1800, for instance, the Longman family had begun its move out of retailing and into publishing exclusively; by the 1820s the firm would further limit its scope to education, a focus that endures to this day. In the 1840s, William Henry Smith, the son of a West End stationer and erstwhile wholesaler, laid the foundation for contemporary chain retailing, when he established the first network of bookstalls at the nation's railway stations, his enterprise known then and now as W. H. Smith.

The epicenter of book retailing in London had shifted as well. While printing and publishing businesses remained in the central city, retailers followed the migration of the upper and middle classes toward the affluent western neighborhoods of Covent Garden, St. James's, and Chelsea. By Dickens's time, there were two dozen or more shops catering to the carriage trade in the western suburbs, including that of John Hatchard whose Piccadilly bookstore, opened in 1782 and still in operation, became the largest of its kind in all London.

Another modern practice also made its appearance in London about the same time. Bookseller James Lackington, though claiming to act in the interests of the book-buying public, had wisely concluded that selling a great many books at a small margin was more profitable than selling a very few at a high margin. Soon he was purchasing large quantities of unsold stock from publishers, marking them at a steep discount, and watching them fly out the door of a shop that he called the Temple of the Muses—thus was the business of "remaindering" begun. Though Lackington incurred the wrath of many fellow retailers before he died in 1815, publishers privately hailed him for offering a way that they might recoup some of the losses they had incurred by betting too heavily on the wrong literary horse.

While the retail book trade was largely propped up by the tacit mutual agreement not to discount the cover price of books, Dickens was a champion of the free-market system and an opponent of any form of price-fixing. Of course, he had reason to be laissez-faire regarding price wars because he derived most of his writing income early in his career not from book sales but from contracts that paid him for a regular production of words.

Most of his works were composed and published in twenty weekly or monthly installments, sold in magazine format—sometimes as part of an established magazine—for a shilling. His pay went from fourteen pounds an issue for *Pickwick* to £150 for *Nicholas Nickleby* to £200 for *Martin Chuzzlewit,* for instance (with bonuses tied to circulation and various republications). When a novel was completed, the publishers would typically bind up the whole in a three-volume set called a "three-decker" and offer it for thirty-one shillings sixpence, a hefty sum for a reader used to paying a shilling at a time for his reading pleasure.

In fact, the primary market for the three-decker was the sizable network of commercial lending libraries in the country, a market that benefited from Dickens's enormous popularity. The largest of these syndicates might order up as many as 2,500 copies of a three-volume set of a later Dickens novel—and, indeed, commercial libraries preferred the three-volume format because it meant they could charge three times the fee they got for a one-volume novel. As Dickens became both more popular and more savvy, he would of course fashion contracts that awarded him a far greater return from such ancillary republications of his work.

As for *Pickwick,* it is doubtful that anyone could have anticipated the variety of offshoots that developed in its wake. A veritable cottage industry arose around the book's success, including the production of china figurines representing the book's characters, as well as Pickwick song books, hats, joke books, and cigars. There was even an unauthorized stage adaptation mounted at the Strand Theater (*Sam Weller, or The Pickwickians),* a bit of theft that roused Dickens to one of his first intemperate outbursts against those who were profiting off the glimmer trailing in his wake.

As Dickens wrote to Forster in September of 1837, several weeks after the show opened, "If the *Pickwick* has been the means of putting a few shillings in the vermin-eaten pockets of so miserable a creature [playwright William George Thomas Moncrieff], and has saved him from a workhouse or a jail, let him empty out his little pot of filth and welcome. I am quite content to have been the means of releasing him."

Part of Dickens's proclaimed equanimity likely stemmed from the fact that he had many other matters taking up his attention. In addition to producing installments of *The Pickwick Papers*, he had in November of 1836 agreed to serve as editor for a new magazine for publisher Richard Bentley, titled *Bentley's Miscellany*. The lucrative contract he signed with Bentley allowed him to free himself from what had become a distracting obligation to the *Morning Chronicle*, a position he resigned at once.

Along with his new editorship and the production of *The Pickwick Papers*, Dickens had also committed to write new material for a second edition of *Sketches by Boz*. And if that were not enough, he had signed a contract in May of 1836 with John Macrone, publisher of the *Sketches*, for the production of a novel in three volumes titled *Gabriel Vardon, the Locksmith of London*, which was to be delivered by November 30. (And then there was also the matter of the St. James Theater production of a comic operetta, *The Village Coquettes*, for which he had written the libretto.)

On top of all this, Dickens had also signed a contract with Bentley in August of 1836, agreeing to publish two more three-volume novels. Given that Bentley—with the Pickwick-related rise in Dickens's reputation—was offering £500 per book and Macrone had only promised £200, Dickens withdrew from the earlier agreement, which lifted some pressure from him. He wrote a stand-alone tale for the first issue of *Bentley's*, which appeared on the first day of the new year of 1837, and five days later, his first child, Charley, was born. Soon thereafter, Dickens announced to Bentley that he would be meeting his own commitment to write for the magazine by submitting installments of the adventures of a young hero by the name of Oliver Twist.

That was fine with Bentley, but when the publisher saw that Dickens was sometimes short of the sixteen pages he had promised for each issue, he began to dock the writer's pay accordingly. Dickens was already distraught over the sudden death in May 1837 of his sister-in-law Mary Hogarth (to whom some commentators suspect Dickens was more attracted than to his wife), and by Catherine's subsequent miscarriage of what would have been their second child. When the writer discovered what Bentley was doing, he countered by insisting that Bentley accept *Oliver Twist* as one of the novels he had promised.

Bentley objected in turn that Dickens was essentially asking to be paid twice for the same material, but Dickens responded that his value to Bentley had increased vastly in the year since they made their agreement regarding the novels. It was not until Dickens threatened to resign his editorship of the *Miscellany* that Bentley backed down. Dickens was thus able to wrap up the last of the *Pickwick Papers* in November 1837, and happily turn his attention back to *Oliver Twist*.

Though there is some question as to the originality of the project (George Cruickshank, the book's illustrator, claimed later that he had approached Dickens with the idea for a destitute child's misadventures among thieves), Dickens would work steadily on the book until the last installment appeared, in April of 1839. It was Dickens's second novel, and certainly—with its memorable scene of Oliver, gruel bowl in hand, innocently asking the workhouse master for "more"—the tale of Oliver's escape from the workhouse and into the clutches of the criminal mastermind Fagin has become one of his best known works.

Peter Ackroyd, author of the definitive modern biography of Dickens, contends that the novel was the first ever to employ a child as a protagonist, and even if the choice was the unconscious gesture of a writer summoning up his own dismal childhood memories or a response to the suggestion of an illustrator, the final outcome was no less powerful. In what has also been called the first Victorian novel (given that the queen had taken the throne in June of 1837), Dickens used the voice of a guileless and victimized Oliver to underscore the damning social criticism that the writer would proffer in one form or another all his life.

This natural inclination toward dramatizing injustice is at the heart of Dickens's most enduring work. There have been more elegant stylists and perhaps more subtle thinkers employed in the novelist's trade, and Dickens would improve in these regards as his career continued. Certainly his early plots are sometimes labored, some of his characters are one-dimensional, and he can be justly faulted for a tendency toward melodrama. But still, Dickens's innate sensitivity to society's essential flaws, along with the ability to portray elemental forces of good and evil locked in conflict in a form that few readers can turn from, constitute undeniable strengths, even in his early work. These are characteristics on prominent display in *Oliver Twist*.

There is no question that Dickens drew on his own experiences as a twelve-year-old working in Warren's blacking factory and living alone in a rooming house while his father and the rest of his family were ensconced in the Marshalsea debtors' prison. His descriptions of the lair of Fagin, the master thief, have clear parallels to his own recollections of the rat-infested factory, and even that miscreant's name is taken from Bob Fagin, one of young Dickens's coworkers at Warren's.

Dickens was profoundly ashamed of his childhood poverty and kept the details of his family's misfortune and his experience at Warren's a secret from everyone but his wife and Forster, who did not make them public until his publication of the *Life of Charles Dickens* following the writer's death. And while passages in *David Copperfield* and *Little Dorrit* would draw even more directly upon these memories, in *Oliver Twist,* readers saw for the first time the power of what many critics consider the most profound influence on Dickens's adult life and art.

Interpreting a work of art based upon knowledge of its author's life has its limitations. Such an approach can lead to psychobabble at its worst and even at its best can end by placing more value upon the biographical facts than upon the power and pleasure of the work itself. As observers debate the reason for the Mona Lisa's smile, the beauty of the smile itself seems to recede in direct proportion. But in reading a book such as *Oliver Twist,* it is surely impossible to watch Oliver's humiliation holding up his bowl for "more" without thinking of Dickens's own words regarding his experiences tying off blacking pots at Warren's while passersby gawked: "I know how all these things have worked together to make me what I am, but I never afterwards forgot, I never shall forget, I never can forget." And thank heavens, readers might respond—if he had forgotten, then Oliver Twist might never have come to life.

The novel was read widely, and everyone had an opinion on its social agenda, from the humble man on the street to the most prominent citizens of England. Queen Victoria found *Oliver Twist* "excessively interesting," even without any knowledge of Dickens's life. Prime Minister Lord Melbourne complained, however, "It's all among Workhouses, and Coffin Makers, and Pickpockets . . . I don't *like* these things; I wish to avoid them; I don't like them in *reality,* and therefore I don't wish them represented." Thackeray went so far as to accuse Dickens of romanticizing crime, and lumped the novel in with lurid pulp fiction of the day.

But perhaps the most telling evidence of the broad appeal of Dickens's second novel is the fact that six separate stage plays based on the book were put into production during 1838. Most were pale imitations of the language that Dickens had got onto the page, unfortunately, and though the author himself was sometimes lured to these unauthorized performances, they could be trying. During one, Dickens confessed later, he had to lie down on the floor of his box from the middle of the first act until the play had ended.

2.

In 1838, even before he had completed the final install-ments of *Oliver Twist* (its last issue appeared in April 1839), Dickens began work on his third novel, *Nicholas Nickleby,* published in twenty installments between March of 1838 and September of 1839. The story of a penniless young man who escapes from a cruel Yorkshire boarding school to fashion a better life for himself in London proved even more popular with audiences than did *Oliver Twist,* with its first number selling 50,000 copies.

It was *The Old Curiosity Shop,* however, that propelled Dickens into the literary stratosphere. The book, which featured the travails of the misbegotten waif Nell Trent, began its publication in weekly installments in April 1840 and was completed in February 1841, selling more than 100,000 copies per issue. Though the pure and pious Nell perishes midway through the proceedings, and critics were divided concerning whether Dickens had delivered the summa of all morality plays or a trifling melodramatic tract, readers flocked to the book, and Dickens himself declared, "I think I shall always like it better than anything I have done or may do."

It is worth noting here, that in attracting 100,000 readers to issues of *The Old Curiosity Shop,* Dickens was reaching an unprecedented portion of his country's audience. While no formal records of literacy rates were kept at the time, Francis Jeffrey (Lord Jeffrey), the eminent jurist and founder of the *Edinburgh Review,* wrote in an 1844 issue of that magazine that there might be 300,000 readers among the middle class in England (out of a total population of about 2 million), with perhaps another 30,000 in the upper classes. And even if the total readership was 500,000, as some commentators have suggested, Dickens was still selling his work to somewhere between one-fifth and one-quarter of the literate public of a nation. Compare those figures with modern-day America, where 200 million or so working, literate adults constitute the potential "book-buying public," and where a sale of 75,000 to 100,000 copies—one-twentieth of one percent—is often enough to put an author high up on the list of *New York Times* bestsellers.

Given that copies of each installment were often passed from hand to hand, and large audiences gathered regularly in pubs and coffeehouses to hear them read, the impact of Dickens's work upon the world around him was even more profound, and far beyond anything that had come before. If publishers had been longing for a second coming of Sir Walter Scott, then with regular sales of novels exceeding five and ten times those of *Ivanhoe,* Dickens had more than filled the bill. His success led to a complete remaking of the expectations of the book trade, commentators have pointed out, as well as "a new, unheard of scale of remuneration for popular writers."

And yet for all his success, Dickens was not infallible in

his judgments. While he was still wrapping up installments of *The Old Curiosity Shop*, Dickens began work on a fifth novel, *Barnaby Rudge*, a historical tale built around the Gordon Riots of 1780, during which hundreds of anti-Papist protesters were shot in the London streets by government troops. Dickens had toyed with the story for several years, though he had never been able to make much headway. In 1838 he wrote to Forster of his frustration with the piece, calling it "a hideous nightmare," which he could neither finish nor forget.

As it turned out, the latter course might have given him more peace. Though he finally threw himself into the project, publishing it between January and late November of 1841, the public's response to *Barnaby Rudge* was dramatically disappointing. Sales plunged from 100,000 for issues of *The Old Curiosity Shop* to 70,000 for the initial issues of its successor, and to 30,000 by the end.

Though Dickens staunchly defended his work, telling Forster he was confident that "it comes out strong to the last word," this downturn soon had him seriously considering an invitation issued by the American author Washington Irving. Irving, an ardent fan of Dickens's work, had suggested that his British colleague undertake an American tour, insisting that the visit would be "such a triumph from one end of the States to the other, as was never known by any Nation."

Dickens, a foe of conservative government and a champion of individual liberty, was well aware that the Gordon Riots had taken place during the same period as the Ameri-

can Revolution. Perhaps the anti-Tory sentiments of Barnaby
Rudge might be better appreciated in the United States than
they had been in his own country. Surely, Dickens thought,
he would be well received in a country where crowds were
said to have awaited the arrival of British packet ships bearing the latest installment of *The Old Curiosity Shop,* calling
out to crew members, "Is Little Nell still alive?"

Furthermore, as a child of poverty, Dickens felt a great
affinity for the underdog colonies and their great experiment
in democracy. And besides, personal accounts by British authors touring the States had become something of a phenomenon in publishing, and he might be able to earn some extra
income.

With such thoughts in mind, Dickens approached his
publishers, Chapman and Hall, hoping to persuade them to
advance the necessary funds for the trip. Not only would the
publicity help sell the books he had already published, Dickens argued, but the experience would become the stuff of a
forthcoming travel memoir of his own.

The publishers agreed, and on January 2, 1842, Dickens and his wife, Catherine, set sail aboard the 115-passen-
ger Britannia, leaving behind their four children—including
their youngest, only seven months old—in the care of Dickens's brother Fred. Though Catherine dreaded the prospect
of a risky and arduous North Atlantic journey of nearly three
weeks (the first steamship crossing had taken place only four
years previously), and though Dickens himself was taken
aback by the quality of the shipboard accommodations (pil-
lows "no thicker than crumpets" and a mattress that he said

was beaten as flat as a muffin), they arrived in Boston on January 22, where there began an assault by reporters, editors, admirers, and curiosity seekers that would not abate for the four and a half months of their visit.

The initial crush in Boston was so great that Dickens was forced to hire a secretary and arrange a formal daily reception at which the British consul would introduce him. In New York City, more than 3,000 turned out at the Park Theater for the Boz Ball on February 14, where a huge portrait of Dickens crowned by an eagle gazed down upon a series of staged tableaux representing various scenes and characters from his works.

During his stay, Dickens met essentially all of the new nation's most esteemed writers and thinkers, including his staunch admirer Washington Irving, Harriet Beecher Stowe, Edgar Allan Poe, William Cullen Bryant, Henry Wadsworth Longfellow, Oliver Wendell Holmes, John Greely, Henry Clay, James Russell Lowell, and Daniel Webster. In Washington, D.C., President John Tyler received him at the White House.

And yet, despite this unprecedented level of attention and acclaim, all did not go smoothly for Dickens in America. For one thing, some Americans found Dickens in person somewhat less impressive than the earth-bounding titan his success might have suggested. While accounts from his days as a junior law clerk describe a young man with a glowing pink complexion, "a fine forehead," and "beautiful expressive eyes full of animation," the American author Richard Henry Dana wrote to Bryant that the first sight of Dickens "may not wholly please you." Others commented that although he stood five feet nine inches (well above average for a man of his time), he nonetheless came across as short and stout, with ears a bit too big, and unkempt hair that he fussed with a bit too much in public and over dinner.

There was also Dickens's penchant for speaking in low, hurried tones, his accented speech somewhat thick and difficult for the American ear to apprehend. He also had a propensity for dressing in a way that trended beyond the artistic to the ostentatious, with too much jewelry on his fingers, wrists, and tie-keeps, and his colorful vests a bit too bright for local tastes. Thackeray had once described the couple at a society ball: "How splendid Mrs. Dickens was in pink satin and Mr. Dickens in geranium and ringlets." One can only imagine how his appearance struck a rawboned American audience.

"Foppish," one U.S. reporter described him, "of the flash order."

All that might have been accepted as artistic eccentricity, were it not for Dickens's inability to hold his tongue regarding a particular economic issue that pained him mightily. From his first public appearances in the United States onward, and though he was predictably complimentary regarding America's public institutions and philosophies, he invariably brought his speeches around to the matter that seemed to consume him: he painted a vivid picture of Sir Walter Scott lying penniless on his deathbed, the victim of international publishers who had pirated the great author's work without payment of any royalty. From that plaintive starting point, Dickens went on to call for a worldwide copyright agreement that would protect all authors' rights—his own of course included.

Given that literary piracy was common business practice in the former colonies (as it remains today in some countries in Eastern Europe and the Far East where copyright is not recognized), it was not long before newspapers with ties to or empathy for American publishers were attacking Dickens in print, alleging that his tour was undertaken as a veiled campaign for an international copyright agreement. Dickens was outraged, and wrote to an American friend, Jonathan Chapman, "I have never in my life been so shocked and disgusted, or made so sick and sore at heart as I have been by the treatment I have received in reference to the International Copyright question. I merely say that I hope the day will come when Writers will be justly treated; and straightway there fall upon me scores of your newspapers . . . attacking me in such terms of vagabond scurrility as they would denounce no murderer with."

The popular response to the copyright issue was not the only matter that diminished Dickens's original idealization of the United States. Following stops in Boston, New York, and Washington, D.C., he planned a tour of the American South, including a stay in Charleston, South Carolina, but got no farther than Richmond, Virginia.

As Dickens explained later in *American Notes*, he had already begun to realize that his long-held fantasies concerning the United States were at considerable odds with the reality he was experiencing. "When I came to consider the length of time which this journey would occupy, and the premature heat of the season, which even at Washington had been often very trying; and weighed, moreover, in my own mind, the pain of living in the constant contemplation of slavery . . . stripped of the disguises in which it would certainly be dressed," he wrote, he decided to cancel his trip to the deep South.

Dickens had also been dismayed by what he considered an appalling lack of personal hygiene among his American brethren, and while some newsmen had expressed surprise at the "common" manner of the great visiting writer, Dickens for his part found Americans to be rubes, lacking in the most basic civilities.

British diplomats had remarked from the beginning upon the lack of formality in the American White House; Thomas Jefferson had been known to greet visiting heads of state while wearing slippers. During his own visit, Dickens was flabbergasted to find President Tyler's reception room filled with lobbyists and congressmen jawing, smoking, and spitting as if they were idlers at a bar. Of the anteroom where he was taken while his arrival was announced, Dickens said it was "as unpromising and tiresome as any waiting-room in one of our public establishments, or any physician's dining-room during his hours of consultation at home."

There were fifteen or twenty others with him in the chamber, including a wiry old man from the West with a giant umbrella between his legs, "frowning steadily at the carpet, and twitching the hard lines about his mouth, as if he had made up his mind to fix the President on what he had to say, and wouldn't bate him a grain." Dickens ended this descriptive rhapsody with a portrait of another man who "did nothing but spit." Of this pervasive habit he noted that "indeed, all these gentlemen were so very persevering and energetic in this latter particular, and bestowed their favours so abundantly upon the carpet, that I take it for granted the Presidential housemaids have high wages."

Added to such disillusionments was the ever-mounting exhaustion both he and Catherine experienced at being constantly "on stage," their appearance, their dress, their every gesture and chance remark subject to scrutiny and, often, vilification. In the end, Dickens would write to his actor friend and sometime business partner William Macready, "I am disappointed. This is not the Republic I came to see. This is not the Republic of my imagination." On June 7, 1842, and following a month's respite in Canada, Dickens and Catherine debarked for their homeland, grateful to be leaving the shores where the writer had once dreamed of finding "cities growing up, like palaces in fairy tales, among the wilds and forests of the west."

3.

During his generally disappointing visit to the United States, Dickens wrote a number of lengthy letters to Macready and others, always intending them as the core of the book of "impressions" he planned to publish with Chapman and Hall upon his return. He quickly completed work on *American Notes for General Circulation* by October 1842, a volume that rather predictably focused on the national shortcomings he discovered there.

While his criticism of American table manners, its prison system ("rigid, strict, and hopeless . . . I believe it in its effects, to be cruel and wrong"), the institution of slavery, the rigors of travel both at sea and on the American frontier, and the hypocrisy, venality, and arrogance he found rampant might have been expected from Dickens, the indifference of his British readership to all this came as something of a surprise to him. Reviewers found little new in Dickens's observations, the gist of which had found its way into print in many previous editions from British writers eager to share the rough-hewn "American experience."

In contrast, the book sold rather well in the United States, though any pleasure that its author might have taken was tempered by the fact that it appeared there primarily in pirated versions and that the critical response was vituperative.

The most heartening response to the book came from American abolitionists, who welcomed Dickens's sentiments on the practice of slavery in their country.

Soon after the appearance of *American Notes,* Dickens began the publication of his sixth novel, *The Life and Adventures of Martin Chuzzlewit,* in January 1843. In 1842 Dickens had obtained an advance of £2,000 from Chapman and Hall, to see him through his travels in the United States and a corresponding furlough from writing, in return for a new novel to be published in monthly installments. The terms of his contract also specified that in addition to his advance, he would also receive three-quarters of the net profits from sales of the new novel. But, quite possibly owing to the disappointing sales of *Barnaby Rudge* and the fact that Dickens was already £3,000 in debt to the house, the publishers had insisted on a clause that would allow them to deduct £50 from his monthly payment of £200 should sales of *Martin Chuzzlewit* fail to reach numbers necessary to pay down his debt.

Insertion of such a clause was a first for Dickens and surely less than a stirring vote of confidence, but if Dickens thought much of it at the time, he said nothing to Chapman and Hall. Indeed, he seemed supremely confident as he went about the writing of his new book, the subject of which he announced as "English life and manners," and which centered on the machinations of a family assembled in a country house and jockeying for the fortune of Martin Chuzzlewit Sr.

Early on, Dickens wrote glowingly to John Forster, his friend and literary adviser, of his pleasure in seeing how his characters had "opened out." The publishers were plagued by falling sales, but he was particularly happy with his decision to send his young protagonist, Chuzzlewit junior, off to tour America by the time he was writing the twelfth episode of the book. Though some critics saw this turn as a desperate attempt to revive the sluggish sales, Dickens took great pleasure in the opportunity to unleash one more salvo against the nation that had so disappointed him. "Martin has made them all stark raving mad across the water," he crowed to Forster in August of 1843.

Among the things that rankled Americans (and cost him the friendship of his former booster Washington Irving) were observations like those of Martin's friend Mark Tapley, who explains how he might draw the likeness of a much-exalted American symbol. Says Tapley to Martin, as they stand at the bow of their ship, watching the shore of the States disappear behind them:

> "Why, I was a-thinking, sir . . . that if I was a painter and was called upon to paint the American Eagle, how should I do it?"
>
> "Paint it as like an Eagle as you could, I suppose."
>
> "No," said Mark. "That wouldn't do for me, sir. I should want to draw it like a Bat, for its shortsightedness; like a Bantam, for its bragging; like a Magpie, for its honesty; like a Peacock, for its vanity, like a Ostrich, for its putting its head in the mud, and thinking nobody sees it."

Still, if Dickens thought a fiction-based campaign against the United States would win him an increased readership in his homeland, he had once again miscalculated. Sales rose slightly for the later installments of the book, from 20,000 copies to 23,000, but that remained a far cry from the 50,000 per issue for *Nicholas Nickleby* and 100,000 for *The Old Curiosity Shop*. When publisher William Hall reminded Dickens of the clause in their contract allowing for a reduction in his salary based on slow sales, an already agitated Dickens exploded. He dashed off a letter to Forster in which he vowed never again to write for Chapman and Hall, and stated his intentions of striking an agreement with the firm of Bradbury and Evans, the printers of his books, who had demonstrated their generosity and loyalty—in the author's mind, at least—by sending him a turkey each Christmas.

From the outside, Dickens's response might seem petulant. There are few writers to this day even in countries with populations far larger than Victorian England who would not be thrilled with the prospect of 23,000 copies of anything they had written flying out the doors of bookshops over the course of a week or a month, and most of them would be willing to put up with the barbs of a few critics and the enmity of a public that lay an ocean away.

But the truth is—just as the bar is never lowered in the course of a vaulting competition—few writers drop their expectations from book to book. A diminution of sales, interest, and public gestures of approval is tantamount to a lowering of self-worth. And certainly, for anyone who had ascended to the heights of literary Olympus, as Dickens had, the prospect of banishment to the foothills would be unbearable.

As his friend Forster often bristled when reminded of his origins as the son of a butcher, Dickens would never forget whence he had come. He was no child of privilege. There was no trust fund backing his endeavors. There was no family estate to which he might retire. He was, as is often said, only as good as his next book.

He might have passed off the disappointing response to *Barnaby Rudge* as his own fault, a miscalculation born of exhaustion. His sense that he needed a bit of time away from the grind of writing to gather his perspective was one reason he had conceived of his tour to the United States, after all. And perhaps he could attribute the failure of *American Notes* to the glut of similar books—however inferior—already in print. But, given the relative indifference to *Martin Chuzzlewit,* how could he help doubting his own judgment? Which is to say, his literary talent. Which is to say, his very sense of self.

4.

When Charles Dickens made his way to Manchester to make his appearance before the Athenaeum, it is safe to say that he was wearing a sign of his cares on his brow. A French journalist who interviewed him during this time described him as having "long, brown, rather untidy hair . . . over the forehead of an unhealthy pallor." However, the reporter also noted, "The bright, restless eyes testify to an unusual sagacity and quick intelligence."

While a willingness to put a shoulder to the wheel to help improve the Athenaeum's fortunes was in keeping with Dickens's nature, he had come to Manchester (a place that Sir Charles Napier had described as "the entrance to Hell realized") primarily at the urging of his sister Frances, eighteen months his senior. Fanny, as she was known to her brother, had married a pious Evangelical named Henry Burnett, and the couple had lived in the Manchester suburb of Ardwick for some time. Dickens and Fanny had always been close, though given his distrust of organized religion in general and of restrictive, small-minded sects in particular, he was not so sure about her choice of a husband. Still, Dickens, weary of the ceaseless crush caused by his celebrity, had chosen to stay with his sister and her husband instead of taking a room at a local hotel.

It is highly unlikely that he would even have considered the invitation to Manchester if it had not been for his sister's involvement in the city's welfare. In recent months the writer had more than done his part for the greater good.

As biographer Peter Ackroyd notes, Dickens had delivered speeches at the Printers' Pension Society in London, the Hospital for Consumption and Diseases of the Chest, the Charitable Society for the Deaf and Dumb, the Literary Fund, and for the Sanitorium. He had also agreed to arrange a testimonial dinner for his friend Macready—who was leaving a post at the Drury Lane Theater—to head up the formation of a Guild of Authors, to chair a committee formed to act on behalf of international copyright for authors, and to direct the relief effort for the surviving children of an actor named Edward Elton, who had recently drowned.

Given such a full slate, it is little surprise that Dickens had tired a bit of the endless round of parties and social occasions to which he was called (including the ball at which Thackeray had conceived his sniping portrait of Dickens and his wife, Catherine). Proof of Dickens's deteriorating mood in this regard is evident in his notes on a dinner on behalf of the Charterhouse Square Infirmary, where he characterizes his fellow guests as "sleek, slobbering, bow-paunched, over-fed, apoplectic, snorting cattle."

Then, too, there had come news from Catherine that she was again pregnant, with their fifth child in only seven years. Biographers have generally surmised that Dickens settled for Catherine Hogarth when he married her in 1833, after the love of his young life, Maria Beadnell, a banker's daughter, had rejected him. But the relationship of Dickens and Catherine, if not passionate, had always been a fond and respectful one. The fact, then, that he called her "a Donkey" after she divulged to him that she was once more with child, suggests that Dickens was teetering on the edge of a very steep precipice indeed.

He had even gone so far as to suggest that they might think of moving their family, including Catherine's sister Georgina, who was now living with them, to some new home on the Continent, where they might live more frugally and Dickens could more easily supplement his income by writing travel pieces. Perhaps he was simply overexposed, Dickens theorized. Perhaps once he had stopped writing and was out of the public eye, readers and critics would come to appreciate what they had lost. But, meanwhile, he had come to Manchester, and the show there would have to go on.

A ccording to the memoirs of Sir E. W. Watkin, one of his Manchester hosts, there was no hint that the Dickens who arrived in Manchester was in any way out of sorts. To Watkin, whose recollections admittedly have the ring of enthusiasm, if not outright awe, for his subject, Dickens was the picture of affability and beneficence.

"We were indebted for the presence of Charles Dickens to the kind influence of his elder sister—Mrs. Burnett—a self-denying saint, if ever one existed," Watkin writes. The evening before Dickens's appearance at the Athenaeum,

Watkin and a few companions visited Dickens at the Bur-
netts' home.

Inside, the group found Dickens standing by the
fireplace, ready with a decanter of wine. "In passing the decanter, [he] upset his own glass," Watkin recalls, "and del-
uged a very pretty book lying on the table."

The mishap did not seem to bother Dickens, though,
who was quick to press the delegation for details of the next
day's program and to inquire of Watkin who they thought to
seat him beside. When Watkin suggested the author might
be most comfortable with his sister and brother-in-law at
hand, Dickens shook his head.

"No, I should not wish that," he told Watkin, "not by
any means. You must look upon your object in choosing my
supporters," he explained.

In that case, Watkin replied, how about Mr. Cobden on
one side of Dickens, and Mayor Kershaw of Manchester on
the other? And Dickens agreed that would do very well.

From there, the talk moved along to Dickens's hopes for
a decent crowd ("You had ten thousand in at the Education
meeting, had you not?" he asked one of Watkin's group).
And then, somewhat to Watkin's surprise, Dickens himself
launched into a fulsome and well-informed elucidation of the
Athenaeum's value, history, and current state of want.

"In all this Dickens appeared to take great interest,"
Watkin wrote appreciatively. When one of the group remarked upon the traditional opposition of conservatives to
such grassroots educational undertakings as the Athenaeum,
Dickens responded with vigor.

"If a certain party choose to oppose the education of the masses," he said, "we cannot help it. We must go on in spite of them."

Someone else wished to thank Dickens for his great generosity in lending his celebrity to their cause. An author of his accomplishment speaking on their behalf stood much more effectively than a mere politician, the Manchester man said, beaming.

"He modestly disclaimed the merit we wished to attach to his visit," Watkin reports. Dickens simply waved away such praise and reiterated that he was there because he supported the Athenaeum's position: there was "a too general desire to get the utmost possible amount of work out of men instead of a generous wish to give the utmost possible opportunity of improvement."

"I shall enforce the necessity and usefulness of education," Dickens told the group. "I must give it to them strong."

When talk turned finally to matters of pounds and shillings and pence, Dickens suggested that it would be a mistake to paint too dire a picture of the organization's circumstances during his address, as donors might be more likely to support a cause on its way up than to toss money at one sinking surely toward the bottom. "I may say that the debts of the institution are in rapid course of liquidation, eh?" he told them. "That will be the way."

The group agreed with that tack, and also agreed that it would be a mistake for Dickens to ask outright for money. "Too much like making a commodity of him," Watkin chimed in.

Dickens nodded. "I will try to excite their liberality in another and equally or more useful way," he assured the party.

They should remember that more was at stake than their own institution, Dickens went on to say. "The Manchester Athenaeum is not the sole thing depending upon your efforts. It is the principle of athenaeums that you are really struggling for." And with that, their meeting was closed.

5.

During a pre-performance tour of the Athenaeum the next afternoon, Dickens was introduced to Richard Cobden, the fiery orator, and the two exchanged compliments and ideas as they wound their way through the institution, and, according to Watkin, "diving into its cellars and mounting to its top, amid sundry jokes" about politics and politicians, including those at the expense of James Crossley, a rather stoutly built local who opposed Cobden fiercely.

One of the chief topics of discussion was Cobden's involvement in the national Anti–Corn Law League. Cobden, who had in 1839 spearheaded a similar local organization in Manchester, had been successful in organizing a national committee to unite all interests who sought to put an end to the tariffs protecting Britain's landed gentry. A former member of the Manchester Chamber of Commerce and one of the city's first aldermen, Cobden was elected to Parliament in 1841, and he quickly became one of the principal spokesmen against the vested interests propping up British grain prices and keeping the price of bread artificially high.

The severe depression of 1840–42, combined with a series of bad harvests, led to shortages and high prices that increased support among the general British population for

Cobden's position. The group also picked up the backing of manufacturers, who feared that the duties that kept corn prices inflated would ultimately lead to stoppages by workmen seeking higher wages. Cobden crisscrossed the whole of England, speaking to increasingly growing audiences, and had become a national workingman's hero by the time he and Dickens met in Manchester.

Disraeli, who would join them on stage—and though a Tory and a conservative at heart—had endeared himself to liberals for his demands that the landed interests were obligated to protect the rights and livelihood of the poor. Thus, the popular trio—politician, novelist, and novelist-cum-politician—made the perfect cast for the Athenaeum's playbill. Cobden and Disraeli were perhaps more experienced as public speakers. (Taunted once by William Gladstone that he would probably die "by hanging or of some vile disease," Disraeli retorted, "That would depend, sir, on whether I embraced your principles or your mistress.") But despite his recent setbacks, Dickens's long-standing celebrity made him the undisputed star of the show.

It would have been difficult for Dickens to throw himself into his savior's role in Manchester that night in 1843—his marriage was troubled, his career tottering, his finances ready to collapse. With all that on his mind, could he truly put it aside and rally an audience on behalf of workingmen's access to ideas, and arts, and education? But these principles formed the very heart and soul of Dickens's own best work, and furthermore, he had once been one of those men on whose behalf he spoke.

At thirty-one, he was still developing as an artist, to be sure, but with the publication of *Sketches by Boz* (diffuse, but displaying the wide array of his social interests), *The Pickwick Papers* (episodic, but rich in character and comedy), and *Oliver Twist* (at times melodramatic, but nonetheless unified in power of theme), he had demonstrated the range and depth and dramatic facility that would build on the accomplishments of those who had come before him (Fielding, Defoe, Smollett, Richardson, and Scott), and which would make him, in the eyes of most present-day commentators, the first truly modern novelist, as well as the chief spokesman for his age.

In the latter regard, Dickens was well aware of the authority he had achieved as a spokesman and an artist. It may be difficult to appreciate such a status today, when celebrities are excoriated for expressing their political views during an awards ceremony—or during a phase of twentieth-century criticism proclaiming that novels are the subjective fancies of their respective authors and bear no practical relation to reality (if there even is such a thing as "reality"). "Art cannot rescue anybody from anything," rings the last line of a well-known story by Gilbert Sorrentino.

But in Dickens's time, the notion of a narrator-author standing in the wings of a fictitious story, always ready to step forward and explain the actions and motives of a character or to deliver an exegesis on the nature of the world surrounding him, was completely acceptable. For one thing, in an age when education was less than universal and where relatively few attended university, it only stood to reason that an informed author who was at all serious about his craft might have something instructive to pass along about the workings of human nature and the laws that governed commerce. In Dickens's day, the novel was viewed not only as a source of entertainment but also very much as a potential source of information and enlightenment.

Furthermore, there existed in those times nothing like the network of governmental social services that a modern age takes for granted. Charitable enterprises for the poor and unfortunates of all types were run by churches and private organizations, many of which were guided by questionable motives and methods. Particularly galling to Dickens, who would "never, ever forget" his ignominious childhood, were the puritanical at heart, who demanded obeisance to their belief systems in return for a bowl of gruel. To Dickens, true charity was a matter of openhearted benevolence; to use the relief of poverty as a cudgel to beat a recipient into piousness was repellent and evil.

Dickens was no radical, and the theories of Marx and Engels (the latter's family owned a cotton mill in Manchester at the time of Dickens's appearance before the Athenaeum) went much too far for him. Dickens believed that a reasonable capitalistic society could be made to recognize its responsibility to all its citizens, and that it was the duty of those most fortunate to share a portion of their gain with those whose grasp had slipped while pulling at their bootstraps.

He opposed violent confrontation to achieve these

means, of course; but he well understood why desperate men would be driven to crime and violence. And he was severely critical of individuals and moneyed interests who sought to shirk their responsibilities to the poor. Legislation that oppressed the unfortunate (such as the Corn Laws and the imprisonment of debtors and the failure to properly regulate labor practices) were particular targets of his wrath—as were bureaucratic incompetency, the scarcity of public works and sanitation, and personal greed, gluttony, and indifference.

But Dickens was not a humorless reformer. The end he sought in all his zeal was a society in which the pleasures of life could be enjoyed by everyone: culture, entertainment, good food and drink, convivial fellowship, and a happy family. Were he alive to hear a man named Rodney King call out, "Why can't we all just get along?" the comment would have surely brought an approving nod and the Cockney-inflected phrase that Dickens was found of using: "Oh, law, yes."

Thus, though it may be true that Dickens had accepted his invitation to the Manchester Athenaeum because his sister Fanny had prevailed upon him to, everything in his philosophical makeup predisposed him to make that two-hundred-mile journey by rail from London. If England was at the world's forefront of industrial revolution—with the consolidation of small farms into large, and the mechanization of agriculture and steel production and textiles leading the way—then coal-fired Manchester was leading the charge.

From a population of 6,000 in 1685, the town—with its ready access to the shipping port of Liverpool and its proximity to coal deposits and rapidly flowing rivers providing power—had become the world's first modern industrial city, growing to 300,000 by 1830, and to more than 400,000 by the time that Dickens arrived. There were about 16 million residents in all of England at the time, and about 2 million living in London—a striking contrast to the United States, which had a comparable 17 million, but only 312,000 in its largest metropolis, New York City.

Prosperity for factory and mill and transportation interests had not come without cost, however. Owners lived like potentates, and a growing number of managerial workers were beginning to enjoy the relative ease of a middle class. But most of those who made the factories run were laborers, and they and their families lived in squalor.

In Manchester, Tocqueville wrote, "humanity attains its most complete development and its most brutish; here civilization works its miracles, and civilized man is turned back almost into a savage." Most of the city's streets were unpaved, and its laborers' districts were "untraversed by common sewers," leaving piles of excrement and trash for pedestrians to dodge. Many homes had dirt floors, lacked for windows and doors, and were described as "ill ventilated" and "unprovided with privies." As a result, wrote the social activist James Kay in 1832, "the streets which are narrow, unpaved and worn into deep ruts, become the common receptacles of mud, refuse, and disgusting ordure."

A decade later, just prior to Dickens's visit, Joseph

Adshead's *Distress in Manchester* pointed out that things had only become worse: "[D]estitution in its most rigorous form prevails to an appalling extent in Manchester," wrote Adshead, quoting a local doctor who said that "no inconsiderable portion of our fellow-creatures is living on food and in dwellings scarcely fit for brutes."

Friedrich Engels, who, at the time of Dickens's visit, was gathering steam for the economic analysis upon which Karl Marx would base the 1848 publication of the *Manifesto of the Communist Party,* wrote a treatise that decried the cycles of boom and bust that only exacerbated such conditions, and turned laborers from whole human beings into "hands," of which many were needed when demand for goods was high, and which would be discarded when business turned slow. Mechanization had turned men into one more statistical element in an equation of production, Marx and Engels would argue, putting an end to all paternal relationships between owners and workers left over from the feudal days, to leave "no other nexus between man and man than naked self-interest, than callous 'cash payment.'"

Conditions were so bad in Manchester, more than one modern labor economist has surmised, that had Engels come of age in some far more pleasant surroundings such as London, *The Communist Manifesto* might not have been written the way it was. Says analyst David McLellan, had Engels spent more time in that capital, "where manufacture was still dominated by artisans, he would have got a different picture." Of course, Dickens, who had spent some time in the so-called patriarchal employ of a London "artisan," might have begged to differ, but there is little disagreement with the fact that the Manchester of 1843 was a hellhole.

One out of every thirty-one people living in that city died each year, compared with a rate of one in forty-five for the country as a whole. Fifty-seven percent of children born to working-class parents died before they reached the age of five.

And the effects of the great depression of 1841–42 were still lingering, with as many as 3,000 people per day lining up at soup kitchens. A number of the city's 130 smoke- and gas-spewing mills had gone into bankruptcy with the down-turn in business, and in late 1842 Engels wrote of "crowds of unemployed working men at every street corner, and many mills . . . still standing idle."

The development of the power loom made earning a liv-ing particularly difficult on hand-weavers, whose wages—when they could still find work—had dropped by 60 percent between 1820 and 1840. As there were still about 100,000 of such craftsmen living and seeking work in the Manches-ter area, their desperation, according to one labor historian, "cast a pall over the entire period and over all the working classes." (Interestingly, the desperation of the times led to the emigration of one such unemployed Scottish hand-weaver named Carnegie to the United States, where his son Andrew would become the chief industrialist of all time.)

The city to which Dickens had come was in many ways the apotheosis, then, of all that he abhorred. He had made a brief visit in 1838, while he was beginning work on *Nicholas Nickleby*—"his purpose to see the interior of a cotton mill, I fancy with reference to some of his publications," wrote fellow novelist Harrison Ainsworth in a letter of introduction for Dickens. And what Dickens found in those factories had an indelible effect: "What I have seen [in Manchester] has disgusted and astonished me beyond all measure."

Still, he felt a great affinity for those who struggled on behalf of the downtrodden, and he had developed a number of friends among the locals in Manchester, including his first schoolmaster at Chatam, the Reverend William Giles. For that reason, he contended that despite conditions in the city, "I never came to Manchester without expecting pleasure, and I never left it without taking pleasure away," though one might wonder if he expected to take any away on this night.

Disraeli up there at the podium, the rising star, while he sat contemplating fortunes on the wane. His sales a fifth of what they had once been. His publishers ready to dock his salary. The critics turned shortsighted and vicious.

And this audience before him, expecting what? Wisdom? Comfort? Salvation? Good Lord, it seemed he could not keep himself afloat. What had he to offer all them?

But Disraeli had finished, and now it was Dickens's time.

After a hearty introduction and welcome that would surely have done something to boost his spirits, Dickens began his speech with a reminder of his faith in the power of reason, praising the occasion of their gathering in a venue "where we have no more knowledge of party difficulties, or public animosities between side and side . . . than if we were a public meeting in the commonwealth of Utopia." And he followed by reiterating the credo that would guide him in his art and in his public life: "I take it, that it is not of greater importance to all of us than it is to every man who has learned to know that he has an interest in the moral and social elevation, the harmless relaxation, the peace, happiness, and improvement, of the community at large."

Of Manchester and the Athenaeum on behalf of which he spoke, Dickens said, "It well becomes . . . this little world of labour, that . . . she should have a splendid temple sacred to the education and improvement of a large class of those who, in their various useful stations, assist in the production of our wealth."

And he went on to add a bit of the poet's touch in service of his point, with a gesture to the grand hall about them, "I think it is grand to know, that, while her factories re-echo with the clanking of stupendous engines, and the whirl and rattle of machinery, the immortal mechanism of God's own hand, the mind, is not forgotten in the din and uproar, but is lodged and tended in a palace of its own."

He then turned to the circumstances that had brought him to the city. He reminded his audience that "the Athenaeum was projected at a time when commerce was in a vigorous and flourishing condition, and when those classes of society to which it particularly addresses itself were fully employed, and in the receipt of regular incomes."

He was speaking, however, at a time when unemployment in the mills hovered between 15 and 20 percent, and wages had dropped a similar percentage over the past ten years. "A season of depression almost without a parallel ensued," he told his audience, "and large numbers of young men . . . suddenly found their occupation gone and themselves reduced to very straitened and penurious circumstances."

The downturn had led the Athenaeum—with its library of 6,000 volumes; classes for the study of languages, elocution, and music; exercise facilities; and regular programs of lectures and debate—to accumulate a debt of more than 3,000 pounds, Dickens told the audience; but the number of citizens willing to contribute a mere sixpence weekly for all the benefits had more than doubled in recent months, he said, and if more in the audience were willing to join, the amount of even that modest subscription would be reduced.

With that behind him, he launched into the meat of his address. There were a few "dead-and-gone" objections that had traditionally been raised against the formation of such institutions as the Athenaeum, he said, and their philosophy could be summed up in one short sentence: "How often have we heard from a large class of men wise in their generation, who would really seem to be born and bred for no other purpose than to pass into currency counterfeit and mischievous scraps of wisdom . . . that 'a little learning is a dangerous thing.'"

Dickens paused for emphasis, then went on. "Why, a little hanging was considered a very dangerous thing, according to the same authorities, with this difference, that, because a little hanging was dangerous, we had a great deal of it; and, because a little learning was dangerous, we were to have none at all."

We can imagine the roar of approval that those words brought from his audience. The lines carry the same pungency that had elevated the *Sketches,* and the observations of *Pickwick*'s Sam Weller, and the bite that kept *Oliver Twist* from collapsing under the weight of its convictions.

Warming to his theme, Dickens continued, "I should be glad to hear such people's estimate of the comparative danger of 'a little learning' and a vast amount of ignorance; I should be glad to know which they consider the most prolific parent of misery and crime." At this point he turned personal. "I should be glad to assist them in their calculations," he said of those who found learning a luxury, foreshadowing one of the plot devices of a certain novel-to-come, "by carrying them into certain gaols and nightly refuges I know of, where my own heart dies within me, when I see thousands of immortal creatures condemned . . . by years of this most wicked axiom."

He proclaimed his belief that with the pursuit and accumulation of knowledge, man had the capacity to change himself and his lot in life. With learning, said Dickens, a man "acquires for himself that property of soul which has in all times upheld struggling men of every degree." The more a man learns, Dickens said, "the better, gentler, kinder man he must become. When he knows how much great minds have suffered for the truth in every age and time . . . he will become more tolerant of other men's belief in all matters, and will incline more leniently to their sentiments when they chance to differ from his own."

He closed with the assertion to his Athenaeum audience that "long after your institution, and others of the same nature, have crumbled into dust, the noble harvest of the seed sown in them will shine out brightly in the wisdom, the mercy, and the forbearance of another race." It was a speech that would have taken no more than ten or twelve minutes to deliver in its entirety, and yet in it, Dickens conveyed the essence of his most passionate beliefs: championing education, decrying ignorance and those who sought to perpetuate it, and thereby affirming a belief in the possibility of an individual's capability for self-determination that fuels debate among social theorists to this day.

Dickens had lifted himself up from penniless wretch to become the leading literary practitioner of his day; Andrew Carnegie would carry a version of the by-one's-own-bootstraps gospel to America, remaking himself from bobbin boy into steel titan and richest man on earth—then building 3,000 free libraries so that others could presumably follow in his path. In this view, and with the application of his knowledge, reason, and innate decency, mankind had everything needed to make a just and happy world.

6.

If it is true that Dickens never left Manchester without bearing pleasure away, he could not have conceived of the gift that this 1843 visit to what had been called "the chimney of the world" would provide him. Yet it was in the hours after his speech at the Athenaeum, as he walked alone through the city's darkened streets with his mind churning, that the idea came upon him for a new work, one that would one day be called the best-known work of fiction in the language.

Dickens obviously had practical reasons for seeking inspiration: there was the matter of his debt to Chapman and Hall, and his marked decline in sales. But he also felt a deep desire to prove his critics wrong and an equal urgency to prove to himself as well as his public that he had not lost his touch.

There were more positive factors at work as well. He assured his audience at the close of his speech that night that he would long carry with him the pleasure of seeing the response that his remarks had brought—all those bright eyes and beaming faces looking up at him. And he also acknowledged that his audience was counting on him: he would not "easily forget this scene, the pleasing tasks your favour has devolved on me."

As his letters to his friend Forster record, he also carried other memories with him as he walked the streets that night. Shortly before the trip to Manchester, he had taken a tour of a so-called ragged school in London, in the company of Baroness Angela Burdett Coutts, philanthropist and heiress to a banking fortune. He had gone to the Field Lane School in Saffron Hill, perhaps the sorriest neighborhood in London, as research for *Martin Chuzzlewit,* hoping the visit would help him in efforts to shine a light on the wretched conditions of the country's workers and also strengthen his resolve to bring a "Sledge-hammer" down upon the rampant abuses of child labor. But *Chuzzlewit* was no longer looking like an effective vehicle with which to bring widespread attention to anything.

However, his visit to the Field Lane School—one of a number of free public schools for poor children—brought him face to face with a collection of young boys and girls who were the embodiment, in Dickens's words, of "profound ignorance and perfect barbarism." Most of these "students" were illiterate, all were filthy and shabbily dressed (thus the epithet "ragged"), and many resorted to thievery or prostitution in order to live.

Dickens, who entered the school in a gleaming pair of white trousers and brightly shined boots, was met by howls of derision, and a companion, Clarkson Stanfield, was so overwhelmed by the stench of the place that he fled the scene at once. But despite what he described as "a sickening atmosphere, in the midst of taint and dirt and pestilence: with all the deadly sins let loose, howling and shrieking at the doors,"

Dickens remained, doggedly asking question after question until the children finally began to sense compassion in this alien creature and actually began to talk with him.

What he beheld at the Saffron Hill school was bad enough—he told Miss Burdett Coutts that "in all the strange and dreadful things I have seen in London and elsewhere," seldom had he witnessed "anything so shocking as the dire neglect of soul and body exhibited in these children." But the truth is that in the England of Dickens's day, barely one child in three in the entire population attended school, and in London there were estimated to be as many as 100,000 poor children—5 percent of the city's population—who had not so much as darkened the door of any school, "ragged" or otherwise.

His shock and dismay led Miss Burdett Coutts to pledge funds on the spot for washrooms at the Field Lane School, and also for the rental of more-commodious, well-ventilated classrooms. But Dickens well knew that they were trying to douse an inferno with a teacup. "Side by side with Crime, Disease, and Misery in England," he would write disconsolately, "Ignorance is always brooding, and is always certain to be found."

With such thoughts, and the vision of his rapt Manchester audience, crowding his mind, Dickens strode about the drizzling streets of Manchester, debating the proper course of action. Indeed, a lesser individual might have packed it all in and fled to blessed anonymity on the

Continent, where he would have found sufficient work writing travel pieces to keep a cottage heated and bread on the table while he wrote books that would be "good for" an ungrateful public, whether they liked them or not. He would not have been the first artist, or the last, to suspect that he deserved a better audience.

But Dickens was not just good at what he did; he was the very best of his time, a man whose powers had at one point delighted 100,000 of his countrymen each week. Was he really going to walk away from all that at the age of thirty-one?

What actually happened that night was extraordinary. As his letters to Forster would make clear, Dickens began to take stock of himself in a way that any accomplished and acclaimed writer would find extremely difficult, much less the most famous writer of his time. And yet he forced himself to confront hard truths. Perhaps it was not "them"—the jealous critics and the fickle readers—in whom the fault lay. Perhaps he had let his disappointment with America in particular and with human nature in general overwhelm his powers of storytelling and characterization in his recent work—perhaps he had simply taken it for granted that an adoring public would sit still for whatever he offered it.

Perhaps he could still get a point across and write a book of which he could be rightfully proud. Most important, perhaps there was a way to do so without browbeating or scolding, or mounting a soapbox. Perhaps he could get them without their knowing they were got. If he could only find the way.

And so, as he walked the streets that night, a new story began to form. His nightly walks continued, even after his return from Manchester to London, his mind still whirling . . .

. . . until bit by bit his tale took shape, and, as his friend Forster put it, with "a strange mastery it seized him." He wept over it, laughed, and then wept again, as bits and pieces swam up before him, including the vision of two children named Ignorance and Want, those "wretched, abject, frightful, hideous, miserable" creatures who would, with Tiny Tim and Bob Cratchit and Scrooge and Marley and all the rest, stamp themselves on Dickens's imagination, and that of the world, forever.

Part Two

LET NOTHING
YE DISMAY

7.

As Dickens told his friend Cornelius Felton, a professor of Greek at Harvard University, through much of October he walked "about the black streets of London, fifteen and twenty miles, many a night when all the sober folks had gone to bed," working out in his head the story that would become *A Christmas Carol*. He had excited himself "in a most extraordinary manner in the composition," he told Felton, even though he was also struggling to complete the ill-starred *Martin Chuzzlewit* at the same time. (Monthly installments of the latter would continue through the twentieth and final section in July of 1844.)

To his attorney Thomas Mitton he described his work schedule as "pretty tight," but the clearer the concept of his little tale became, the more convinced Dickens became. He was so certain of the rightness of the idea, he told Mitton, that he could foresee "the immense effect I could produce" with future, full-length works centered around the same themes.

One of the chief forces driving Dickens was the press of time. Though he had long been accustomed to writing under deadline, Dickens had an added consideration in this case. Given its subject, *A Christmas Carol* would not only have to be completed within a few short weeks, but it would also have to be edited, illustrated, typeset, printed, bound, advertised, and distributed to the shops several days before the twenty-fifth of December, or the whole endeavor would have to be put on hold for an entire year.

Furthermore, Dickens found himself in quite an unusual position regarding the publication of *A Christmas Carol*. In the case of his previous books, all he had to do was write them. He often took part in the choice of illustrations and opined about the nature of the design and printing itself, but in essence, the *production* of the book, and its subsequent marketing and distribution, were the province of the publisher, which not only paid Dickens for his writings but also risked all the costs involved in readying them for sale.

When he went to Chapman and Hall full of fervor regarding his brilliant new idea, however, the publishers were depressingly unenthused. "*Chuzzlewit* had fallen short of all the expectations formed of it in regard to sale," noted Dickens's old friend Forster, and though the novel was, in his first biographer's eyes, "the most masterly of his writings" to that point, "the public had rallied to it in far less number than to any of its predecessors." Forster attributed some of the drop-off in sales to the fact that his previous two novels had been published in weekly (as opposed to monthly) installments, "for into everything in this world mere habit enters more largely than we are apt to suppose." Nor did Forster think that Dickens's decision to stop writing for six months while he traipsed off across an ocean had been a good idea.

"This is also to be added," Forster pointed out, "that the excitement by which a popular reputation is kept up to the highest selling mark will always be subject to lulls too capricious for explanation." In other words, the public could simply be fickle, without regard to any diminution of a writer's talents. But, whatever the case, as Forster pointed out, the decline was "present, and to be dealt with accordingly."

One way of dealing with it, as Dickens had already suggested to Hall, was to quit Chapman and Hall altogether. This Forster did not think a good idea, for he had been the one to bring Dickens into an association with Chapman and Hall to begin with. He had guided the author through his resignation as the editor of *Bentley's Miscellany* back in 1839, and had also assisted in Chapman and Hall's assumption of copyright of *Oliver Twist* and that book's remaining unsold copies from Bentley. Forster believed that the consolidation of Dickens's interests with one reputable publishing house (Chapman and Hall had also purchased the rights to *Sketches by Boz* and *The Pickwick Papers*) would allow Dickens to focus his attention more easily on his work alone.

And indeed the association between Dickens and Chapman and Hall proved a mutually beneficial one. Installments of *Pickwick* and *The Adventures of Nicholas Nickleby* (March 1838–September 1839), the follow-up to Oliver Twist that Dickens delivered to Chapman and Hall, rose as high as 50,000 per issue. The story of Little Nell in *The Old Curiosity Shop* pushed Dickens's numbers into the stratosphere, beyond 100,000. And even *Barnaby Rudge* had issues that managed to top the 60,000 and 70,000 marks. But then had come *American Notes* and *Chuzzlewit,* and suddenly Chapman and Hall were watching sales hover near

20,000 and wondering what Dickens had accomplished for them lately.

But Dickens had been infuriated by the prospect previously mentioned by Hall that they might indeed reduce Dickens's draw by the fifty pounds stipulated in his contract for *Chuzzlewit*. "I am so irritated," Dickens had told Forster when it happened, "so rubbed in the tenderest part of my eyelids with bay-salt, that I don't think I *can* write."

Though Hall never acted on his suggestion that the clause *might* be enforced, the threat had festered in Dickens and prompted him to write to Forster that he dreamed of severing his ties with Chapman and Hall and simply disappearing to the Continent: "If I had money," he told Forster, "I should unquestionably fade away from the public eye for a year, and enlarge my stock of description and observation by seeing countries new to me; which it is most necessary that I should see."

Forster had already seen one form of that plan carried out in the disastrous furlough to America, however—and look what had come of that. Far better, he thought, to stick it out with Chapman and Hall: carry on with *Martin Chuzzlewit*, and see what they thought of *A Christmas Carol*.

Alas, Chapman and Hall did not think much of the project that had inflamed their author's vision. As Forster put it, "The communication [Dickens] had desired me to make to his printers had taken them too much by surprise to enable them to form a clear judgment respecting it."

Uninterested in the prospect of some Christmas book dashed off on the quick, Forster reported back, Chapman and Hall "enlarged upon the great results that would follow a re-issue of his [previous] writings in a cheap form" (analogous to a paperback release of a book originally published in hardcover today). In addition, the publishers told Forster, they would "invest to any desired amount in the establishment of a magazine or other periodical to be edited by him."

All of this, said Forster, brought home an inescapable truth: "that publishers are bitter bad judges of an author, and are seldom safe persons to consult in regard to the fate or fortunes that may probably await him." Certainly, no more forceful proof exists than what ensued between Dickens and Chapman and Hall.

Informed of his publishers' response, Dickens was resolute. "Don't be startled by the novelty and extent of my project," he wrote back to Forster. "Both startled me at first; but I am well assured of its wisdom and necessity."

"Look upon my project as a *settled thing*," he told his friend, dismissing the notion of launching a new magazine as an enormous drain on his energy. And he believed that publication of a cheap edition of his work would devalue what they already had achieved: "it would damage me and damage the property, *enormously*."

In the end, Dickens did a remarkable thing for a writer of his stature. Bowing to Forster's advice, he stopped short of breaking off with his publishers altogether, but he was not about to abandon an idea on which he had now irrevocably settled.

If Chapman and Hall would not agree to publish *A Christmas Carol* under normal terms, then he would entrust it to them "for publication on his own account." He would be responsible for the costs of the book's production, which would be deducted from its sales. He would also oversee the book's design, hire its illustrator, and consult on its advertising. In essence, his publishers—which would receive a fixed commission tied to sales—had become merely his printer. In contemporary terms, then, *A Christmas Carol* was to be an exercise in vanity publishing.

It was the turning point of Dickens's career, Forster says, "and the issue, though not immediately, ultimately justified him." Meanwhile, "Let disappointments or annoyances beset him as they might, once heartily in his work and all was forgotten." Thoughts of moving to a "cheap and delightful climate, in Normandy or Brittany" were set aside. Dickens had six weeks in which to write and produce *A Christmas Carol* (and there were at least two installments of *Martin Chuzzlewit* due as well).

"I was most horribly put out for a little while," Dickens wrote to Forster, "but having eased my mind by that note to you, and taken a turn or two up and down the room, I went at it again, and soon got so interested that I blazed away till late last night; only stopping ten minutes for dinner."

8.

Of course, as he was writing, Dickens—especially given his recent experience—could not be certain of the reception for his new project. He could only follow his instincts and hope that he was right.

So he pressed on with the writing of it, though he was sometimes resentful of his other obligations, including that ill-received novel he was committed to. On November 10, he wrote to Forster, "I have been all day in *Chuzzlewit* agonies—conceiving only. I hope to bring forth tomorrow." But from there he went on to the object closer to his heart: "Will you come here at six? I want to say a word or two about the cover of the *Carol* and the advertising, and to consult you on a nice point in the tale. It will come wonderfully I think."

It might be helpful to interject a note here on typical publishing practice of the day. Although publishers, including Chapman and Hall, certainly made the decisions about what they were and were not interested in publishing (and indeed often approached authors rather than the other way around), once an agreement was struck, relatively little editing of a submitted manuscript went on inside the publishing house. That chore was left largely to the writer, though sometimes an "adviser" or unofficial editor such as Forster might take a hand in the process.

As a glance at the substantially marked-up original manuscript of *A Christmas Carol* in the Pierpont Morgan Library in New York bears out, Dickens was careful and demanding of himself. And once such a manuscript was submitted to the publisher, it would become a poor printer's task to decipher the ink-blotted annotations of the author and create page proofs.

In Dickens's case, both he and Forster would receive copies of the proofs for final review. Forster's emendations were usually limited to minor matters of grammar and punctuation, though he occasionally gave more substantive advice. He wrote, in fact, that he had been the one to suggest one of the most powerful developments in *The Old Curiosity Shop*. Of Little Nell, Forster explained, Dickens "had not thought of killing her."

In any case, Forster, for his part, was glad to see Dickens so galvanized over his new project. "My reluctance to any present change in his publishing arrangements," his adviser says in *The Life*, "was connected with the little story, which amid all his troubles and 'Chuzzlewit agonies,' he was steadily carrying to its close; and which remains a splendid proof of the consciousness of power felt by him, and of his confidence that it had never been greater than when his readers were thus falling off from him."

With such dogged certainty guiding him, Dickens plunged ahead on what he was calling *A Christmas Carol in Prose: Being a Ghost Story of Christmas*. And as he wrote, he also planned for what would become of all that writing.

For an illustrator, Dickens sought out John Leech,

a popular cartoonist for *Punch,* whom Dickens had met shortly after the suicide of Seymour, his original collaborator on *The Pickwick Papers.* Leech, only nineteen at the time, was one of a number of illustrators who sought to replace Seymour, but Dickens wrote back to Leech that while the sample of work that he had submitted was "extremely well received, and executed," unfortunately Chapman and Hall had already chosen another artist.

In the meantime, however, Leech had begun to make a name for himself. In 1840 he placed a series of etchings in *Bentley's Miscellany* (his mother was a relative of Richard Bentley), and in 1841 he began to publish his work in *Punch.* The magazine, which began publication in July of that year, with Mark Lemon its editor, Douglas Jerrold its most acerbic writer, and Leech its principal graphic artist, was the *Harvard Lampoon* or *Onion* of its day, attracting Dickens's favor for its irreverent and often radical stance on social issues.

As Ackroyd notes, the stance adopted by the creators of *Punch,* as well as by Dickens himself, was a curious blend of conservatism and liberalism. Though they supported such causes as relief for the poor and an end to restrictive tariffs that favored the vested interests, Dickens and others like him had no use for revolt or violence as suggested by supporters of Marx and Engels. Even those who had turned to crime as a way out of their unfortunate circumstances did not get much sympathy from Dickens, who once said of a "model prison" movement in England that, sadly, imprisoned criminals looked to be gaining a "manifest advantage" in their living conditions over those who were simply poor and ended up in harsh workhouses.

When Leech, who had recently won a contract to illustrate a novel for the popular writer Robert Smith Surtees, approached Dickens in late 1842 to be considered as the illustrator for *Martin Chuzzlewit,* Dickens wrote back an encouraging letter: "If it can possibly be arranged, consistently with that regard that I feel bound to pay to Mr. Browne [who assumed that Chapman and Hall would continue to use him on the monthly publications as they had for *The Old Curiosity Shop* and *Barnaby Rudge*], I shall be truly happy to avail myself of your genius in my forthcoming Monthly Work."

Chapman and Hall, however, prevailed in their preference for Browne (or "Phiz," as he often signed his work), and once again Dickens had to turn Leech down, but he did so in a most considerate way.

"I have never forgotten having seen you some years ago or ceased to watch your progress with much interest and satisfaction," Dickens wrote. "I congratulate you heartily on your success and myself on having had my eye upon the means by which you have obtained it."

Less than a year later, and aware that Leech had been awarded the design of a Christmas novel titled *The Wassail Bowl,* by his friend Albert Smith, Dickens decided that the time had come. Dickens wanted four woodcuts and four hand-colored etchings to be included in *A Christmas Carol,* and Leech would be the man to do them.

As for the design of the book, Dickens decided that it should be bound in red cloth, with the title stamped in gold on the cover, and the edges of the book papers trimmed in gold as well. In addition, he fixed the price at five shillings, a relative bargain at a time when a modestly packaged three-volume novel might sell for thirty-one shillings (a pound and a half). As a further guide, one might consider that monthly issues of a Dickens novel sold for a single shilling—though the whole would come to twenty shillings in the end, at least it was being purchased on the installment plan. By contrast, *Carol* character Bob Cratchit's weekly salary (typical of the time) was fifteen shillings a week, with which he managed to support a wife and six children. Even at five shillings, then, it was not as if an average workingman could snatch up a copy of the new Dickens work without a second thought.

Still, Dickens placed faith not only in his concept but in the knowledge that there was nothing on the publishing scene quite equivalent to his book. In his book *The Annotated Christmas Carol,* Michael Patrick Hearn points out that most of the Yule-themed publishing of the time consisted of richly decorated volumes that celebrated such verities as love and goodwill, lacking any direct reference to the holiday itself.

In Dickens's mind he had all that was necessary for a grand success, then—one that, as he confided to friends, might earn him as much as a quick £1,000, not an insignificant sum for a man who had been making £200 a month for installments of *Martin Chuzzlewit.* "I plunged headlong into a little scheme," he told Macvey Napier, editor of the *Edinburgh Review,* and after setting "an artist at work upon it," put everything else out of his mind, "For carrying out the notion I speak of, and being punctual with *Chuzzlewit,* will occupy every moment of my working time, up to the Christmas Holidays."

For all his calculations regarding the undertaking, Dickens was apparently consumed by the emotional power of his own creation. "I was very much affected by the little Book myself," he told the journalist and songwriter Charles Mackay. "In various ways, as I wrote it; and had an interest in the idea, which made me reluctant to lay it aside for a moment."

His zeal led him to decline social outings with friends such as the illustrator George Cruickshank, to whom he wrote on November 25, "I am afraid I may not be in the way tomorrow; and therefore write to you. For I am finishing a little Book for Christmas, and contemplate a Bolt, to do so in peace. As soon as I have done, I will let you know, and then I hope we shall take a glass of Grog together: for I have not seen you since I was grey."

Likewise he put off a late-November meeting with his lawyer Thomas Mitton, promising, "On Monday Evening I will come to you. Your note found me in the full passion of a roaring Christmas scene." (He perhaps meant the Cratchit family feast, though the most "roaring" of the scenes in the book describes Fezziwigs' Christmas party early on, where "There were more dances, and there were forfeits, and more dances, and there was cake, and was negus [wine punch], and there was a great piece of Cold Roast, and there was a great piece of Cold Boiled, and there were mince-pies, and plenty of beer." And there was also Mrs. Fezziwig being twirled around and around in dance by Mr. Fezziwig, whose stockinged calves "shone in every part of the dance like moons.")

On November 25, he also wrote to his friend Marion Ely, offering similar apologies for his conduct as a correspondent: "Forgive my not having answered your kind note; but I have been working from morning until night upon my little Christmas Book; and have really had no time to think of anything but that." To his fellow novelist Edward Bulwer-Lytton (whose novel *Paul Clifford* started with the now-famous line "It was a dark and stormy night") he would confide, "I was so closely occupied with my little *Carol* (the idea of which had just occurred to me), that I never left home before the owls went out; and led quite a solitary life."

Driven by such singlemindedness, Dickens completed work on the manuscript in late November, scarcely six weeks after he had begun. And though it was a demanding stretch, *A Christmas Carol* did not total a quarter of the word count of his earlier, twenty-installment works. Furthermore, Dickens had enjoyed the luxury of completing a project as a whole for the first time. There were no installments, no intrusions by the critics as he went along, and—for all his cares and pressures—far fewer interruptions by outsiders (the "persons from Porlock," as Coleridge termed the unwanted intruders upon an artist's den).

Dickens made a few last, judicious edits, including those in the first sentence of the last succinct paragraph, where he transformed a weak "He never had any further intercourse with spirits," into the authoritative prose that marks the whole, saying of Scrooge, "He had no further intercourse with spirits." And with that work done, Dickens scrawled an emphatic "The End" and added three pairs of double underscores for emphasis.

Then he went to work on actually producing the book itself. He sat with Leech, examining preliminary drawings of each of the illustrations, and noting at one point that Leech had erroneously colored the robes of the Ghost of Christmas Present red. Dickens tactfully asked that the artist change them to green, as was clearly stated in the text.

When Leech, himself a painstaking worker, worried that the craftsmen who had colored in the etchings had been a bit too exuberant, Dickens, who was well pleased by what his illustrator had accomplished, tried to put him at ease. "You unconsciously exaggerate the evil done by the colourers," Dickens told Leech. "You can't think how much better they will look in a neat book, than you suppose."

However supportive he was of his somewhat high-strung illustrator, Dickens himself was fretting over the details of his project to the last minute. In addition to Leech's color plates and woodcuts, he had called for title pages printed with bright red and green, and hand-colored endpapers of a green to match. When in early December he examined a few pre-publication copies run off by Chapman and Hall, however, he was greatly disappointed. The green titles seemed drab to his eyes, and the hand coloring on the endpapers had rubbed off and smudged. In addition, he noted that Chapman and Hall, perhaps seeking to extend the shelf life of the book, had noted its year of publication as 1844.

Dickens immediately reverted the date to 1843—what on earth could they have been *thinking*?—and ordered the color of the endpapers switched to yellow, which would not require any hand work. He also changed the colors of the title page to red and blue, and the half-title page to blue. Though it was a lot to get done in a short time (resulting in the production of a few rare copies that jumbled some of Dickens's instructions), the printers managed to complete their work by December 17. And on December 19, Dickens had 6,000 copies of his "little Carol"—its cover a bit more russet than bright red—finally ready for sale.

9.

The concept for *A Christmas Carol*—the simple story of a miser named Ebenezer Scrooge, haunted on Christmas Eve by his dead partner and the Ghosts of Christmas Past, Present, and Future—did not come to its author out of nowhere, for Dickens had always been greatly enamored of the holiday: "I have always thought of Christmas time as . . . the only time I know of, in the long calendar of the year," says Scrooge's nephew Fred as the story opens, "when men and women seem by one consent to open their shut-up hearts freely, and to think of people below them as if they really were fellow-passengers to the grave, and not another race of creatures bound on other journeys." The holiday "has done me good," he continued, "and will do me good; and I say, God bless it."

While the words are attributed to a character in a novel, there is little doubt that the sentiments are those of the author. Dickens had in fact expressed similar feelings about the season in previous works, including one sketch describing a happy Christmas family gathering during which a number of simmering feuds and resentments are laid to rest. Titled "Christmas Festivities," it was originally published in *Bell's Life in London* in December 1835, and later it was included in *Sketches by Boz* as "A Christmas Dinner."

"That man must be a misanthrope indeed, in whose breast something like a jovial feeling is not roused—in whose mind some pleasant associations are not awakened—by the recurrence of Christmas," the piece begins. And if the mention of such a misanthrope conjures up images of a Scrooge-to-be, later in the sketch there also comes a reference to an innocent child who dies:

"Look on the merry faces of your children (if you have any) as they sit round the fire. One little seat may be empty; one slight form that gladdened the father's heart, and roused the mother's pride to look upon, may not be there.

"Dwell not upon the past; think not that one short year ago, the fair child now resolving into dust, sat before you, with the bloom of health upon its cheek, and the gaiety of infancy in its joyous eye. Reflect upon your present blessings . . . not upon your past misfortunes. . . . Fill your glass again, with a merry face and contented heart . . . your Christmas shall be merry, and your new year a happy one!"

For the Christmas issue of *The Pickwick Papers* in 1836, Dickens had also written "The Story of the Goblins Who Stole a Sexton," a short fiction about a gravedigger who is redeemed by the intervention of a pack of goblins. Grub is described as "an ill-conditioned, cross-grained, surly fellow—a morose and lonely man, who consorted with nobody but himself, and an old wicker bottle which fitted into his large deep waistcoat pocket." He is the sort of fellow who raps a carol-singing urchin's head with his knuckles, and who delights to find a coffin arrived at his graveyard on the holiday: "A coffin at Christmas! A Christmas Box. Ho! Ho! Ho!"

Yet after Grub is mystically spirited away by the goblins and treated to a series of glimpses of the lives of the unfortunate, including one family's grief as the "fairest and youngest child lay dying," he comes to understand the error of his ways. "He saw that men who worked hard, and earned their scanty bread with lives of labour, were cheerful and happy. . . . Above all, he saw that men like himself, who snarled at the mirth and cheerfulness of others, were the foulest weeds on the fair surface of the earth [and] he came to the conclusion that it was a very decent and respectable sort of world after all."

This little fable, while a pale shadow of what a more mature Dickens would create some seven years later, is proof that the basic elements of *A Christmas Carol* had been incubating for some time. There are also some hints of the delightfully mordant humor that would leaven Scrooge's miserliness. It is difficult not to appreciate a grump who can chortle over a coffin as a "Christmas box."

In such touches, we see hints of what would flower in *A Christmas Carol*, with its misanthrope so riled by goodwill that he declares a curse on holiday revelers: "If I could work my will," says Ebenezer Scrooge to his nephew, "every idiot who goes about with 'Merry Christmas' on his lips, should be boiled with his own pudding, and buried with a stake of holly through his heart. He should!" Or, that immortal reply to poor Fred's wish that he have a Merry Christmas: "Bah! Humbug!"

And while it may seem superfluous to summarize such a well-known tale (one commentator has said of it that "if every copy were destroyed to-day, it could be rewritten tomorrow, so many know the story by heart"), still, a brief recounting of what grew bit by bit in Dickens's mind as he strode about the dark London streets seems in order.

After being accosted in his offices at the accounting firm of Scrooge and Marley by his far-too-merry nephew Fred, our aging bachelor protagonist, Ebenezer Scrooge, is next approached by a do-gooder seeking donations for the poor:

"Many thousands are in want of common necessaries," this portly gentleman informs Scrooge, "hundreds of thousands are in want of common comforts, sir."

"Are there no prisons?" Scrooge asks the man. "And the Union workhouses? Are they still in operation?"

Having dismissed this emissary, Scrooge tidies his desk and makes his way home through the bustling Christmas Eve streets unmolested, though he is somewhat disconcerted to find that his doorknocker seems briefly to take the shape of the face of his years-dead partner Jacob Marley—a vision with "a dismal light about it, like a bad lobster in a dark cellar."

The moment passes, however, and Scrooge goes on inside, where, as he takes his evening gruel, the ghost of Marley appears before him in whole form. Marley explains to a disbelieving Scrooge that for his own sins of avarice he has been condemned to wander in a kind of purgatory all the seven years since his death, and he further announces that three ghosts will follow on his heels to Scrooge's chambers.

"Without their visits," Marley tells Scrooge, "you cannot hope to shun the path I tread." The first, he says, will arrive by one o'clock in the morning, and though Scrooge asks—in the spirit of efficiency, of course—if it mightn't be easier if all three came at once, Marley disappears.

While Scrooge wonders if that visit of Marley's is nothing more than a bad dream occasioned by an undigested bit of beef or a fragment of an underdone potato, he is indeed roused at the appointed hour. A spirit who seems by turns youthful and greatly aged carries Scrooge on a tour of his past, where he is reminded of a friendless childhood, and one evening in particular, abandoned in a dismal schoolhouse with only the characters in books for company.

Following a brief appearance of his beloved and long since departed younger sister, the dream-tour shifts to the warehouse offices of Scrooge's first employer Fezziwig, where business is quickly pushed aside for a Christmas Eve party of epic proportions. Hardly has Scrooge recovered from this display of Fezziwig's huge spirit, than the Ghost carries him along to a memory of his one and only sweetheart as she breaks off their engagement: she knows that a rival has displaced her in his eyes, and when young Scrooge demands to know whom, she tells him simply, "Gain."

The tour of Christmas Past ends with a quick glimpse of what might have been—his former fiancée now married, with a brood of children tearing about a festive house on Christmas Eve, and a good-humored husband arrived home to let her know that he has chanced to see her former friend

Scrooge this day, alone and pitiful in his countinghouse as his partner Marley lies dying.

The memories are almost more than Scrooge can bear, and he falls upon the Ghost in a fury—"Leave me. Take me back. Haunt me no longer"—and finds himself abruptly returned to his bed.

The ordeal so exhausts Scrooge that he apparently sleeps through Christmas day, awakening again the next morning at the stroke of one, and this time ready for anything. Given what has already taken place, "nothing between a baby and a rhinoceros would have astonished him very much."

Thus, when a voice calls from his living room, Scrooge climbs down from his bed without hesitation. When he opens the door to his living room, he finds those spartan chambers transformed into a veritable Yule forest bedecked for the holidays, a fire raging in his normally meager hearth, and a jolly Christmas Viking-Ghost seated atop a thronelike assemblage of roasted game and turkeys, geese and sucklings, puddings, pies, and cakes.

The bewreathed Ghost of Christmas Present, clad in fur-trimmed robes of green, takes Scrooge on a tour of the holiday-thronged streets of London that ends with a visit to the home of Bob Cratchit, Scrooge's clerk, where a poor but grateful family—including the crippled Tiny Tim and his several siblings—enjoy a feast of goose and applesauce and mashed potatoes and gravy, and, finally, a pudding "like a speckled cannonball . . . bedight with Christmas holly stuck into the top."

Scrooge is struck by the affection that passes between

Cratchit and his afflicted son and even asks of the Ghost if Tiny Tim will live, but the miser is equally touched by Cratchit's gentle reproach of his wife when she refers to Scrooge as "an odious, hard, unfeeling, stingy man," this despite the fact that we have seen the clerk unable to pry as much as an extra lump of coal from his boss to stoke the office fire.

These characters who fascinate Scrooge so are not a handsome family, we are told, and their clothes are worn and scanty. "But they were happy, grateful, pleased with one another, and contented with the time." And even as the vision fades away, Scrooge holds "his eye upon them, and especially on Tiny Tim, until the last."

There is one more stop with Christmas Present, this at an evening dinner party to which Scrooge's nephew had invited his uncle during their encounter of the day before, and where this time it is the nephew who defends Scrooge and his fabled hardheartedness against the slurs and catcalls of the others of the group. Yes, it is a shame that his uncle cannot appreciate the spirit of the holidays, his nephew Fred admits, but adds quickly, "I am sorry for him. . . . Who suffers by his ill whims? Himself, always."

The tour of Christmas Present might have ended on that vaguely generous note, if Scrooge had not then noticed what seemed to be a claw poking from beneath the Ghost's robes. Seeing his surprise, the Ghost pulls back the robes to reveal the wretched sight of a boy and girl huddled there: "Yellow, meager, ragged, scowling, wolfish. . . . Where angels might have sat enthroned, devils lurked, and glared out menacing."

In response to Scrooge's stunned wonderment as to

where these two have come from, the Spirit tells him, "They are Man's. . . . This boy is Ignorance. This girl is Want. Beware them both, and all of their degree."

Scrooge stares back at these children of the Saffron Hill school incarnate. "Have they no refuge or resource?" he murmurs.

"Are there no prisons?" comes the Spirit's mocking answer. "Are there no workhouses?" And before Scrooge can answer, the clock strikes midnight, and Christmas Present is gone.

The final Spirit, that of Christmas Yet To Come, is much more threatening than his predecessors, a sepulchral creature that glides toward Scrooge "like a mist," its face hooded and using only a spectral hand to communicate. This ominous creature guides Scrooge through the London streets, first to a knot of men who discuss in callous tones the death of an unnamed associate and their disinclination to so much as attend the funeral, unless, of course, "a lunch is provided."

From there, the hooded Spirit conveys Scrooge to a dismal boneyard, where a charwoman brings a heap of bedclothes taken from her former employer's house to pawn: "Ha, ha!" the woman laughs as the boneyard master pays her for her troubles. "This is the end of it, you see! He frightened every one away from him when he was alive, to profit us when he was dead! Ha, ha, ha!"

Though it dawns on Scrooge that "the case of this unhappy man might be my own," even a visit to a deserted bedchamber where a corpse lies wrapped in sheeting cannot entirely lift the fog of his obliviousness. When he begs the Spirit for a glimpse of anyone in all London who might mourn this dead man's passing, Scrooge is permitted to watch one couple lament that their creditor has died before the husband could beg him to relieve their debt.

The culmination of the final Spirit's visit comes with a visit to the Cratchit home, where Bob Cratchit has just returned from a visit to Tiny Tim's grave. As he tries to keep himself together, the clerk admonishes his family to remember Tim's mild example. "We shall never quarrel among ourselves, and forget poor Tiny Tim in doing it," Cratchit says, and his remaining children assure him that they will not.

By now the entire family is in tears, with Cratchit doing his best to hold up. "I am very happy," he says, "I am very happy!" And the whole group comes to embrace their wretched father.

With that, the Ghost of Christmas Yet To Come snatches Scrooge away, conveying him quickly past his closed-up office and to a churchyard, and thence to a tombstone in it, where the mystery, if it has not yet sunk in, is finally revealed. Our miser stands reading the chiseled name of EBENEZER SCROOGE upon the stone in shock, then—enlightened at last—turns to beg his guide for one more chance to mend his ways.

"Oh, tell me I may sponge away the writing on this stone," cries Scrooge. He lunges for the spectral hand of the phantom, holding tightly to it in supplication . . . and wakens then to find himself clutching the wooden post of his own bed, daylight flooding the room, and the bedclothes he had seen pawned in a boneyard back in their rightful place.

A breathless Scrooge runs to his window to thrust his head out and call to a shop boy in the streets below. It is but Christmas Day, the boy assures him, and Scrooge marvels that the Spirits have done their work in the space of a single night after all. Overjoyed to find himself still alive, he sends the shop boy off to the poulterer's for a turkey—"Not the little prize Turkey: the big one," and sends the thing—"twice the size of Tiny Tim"—off to the Cratchits'.

As quickly as he can manage it, he is shaved and dressed and out into the streets, where he meets the do-gooder whom he rebuffed the day before. When he whispers an unspecified amount into the gentleman's ear, it leaves his beneficiary gaping in astonishment.

From that encounter he is off to his nephew Fred's, for dinner, and after that delightful time, returns home for a good night's rest. The next morning he is quickly off to his office morning to await the arrival of Bob Cratchit, who enters in a nervous sweat, a "full eighteen minutes and a half behind his time."

"I am not going to stand this sort of thing any longer," Scrooge tells the frightened Cratchit—then claps his clerk jovially on the back. "I'll raise your salary, and endeavour to assist your struggling family, and we will discuss your affairs this very afternoon, over a Christmas bowl of smoking bishop, Bob! Make up the fires, and buy another coal-scuttle before you dot another i, Bob Cratchit!"

Ever afterward, we are told, it was always said of Scrooge

that he knew how to keep Christmas well, "if any man alive possessed the knowledge. May that be truly said of us, and all of us! And so, as Tiny Tim observed, God bless Us, Every One!"

In summary, *A Christmas Carol* is a bald-faced parable that underscores Dickens's enduring themes: the deleterious effects of ignorance and want, the necessity for charity, the benefits of goodwill, family unity, and the need for celebration of the life force, including the pleasures of good food and drink, and good company. And, admittedly, Dickens is in some ways repeating concepts that he had put in print before.

But that aside, the accomplishment of this slender story, which more than one critic has termed Dickens's "most perfect" work, is to be found in the details of its rendering. In *A Christmas Carol*, a contemptible gravedigger is replaced by the much more estimable figure of a wealthy businessman. Ebenezer Scrooge is no castoff drunk, but the very emblem of economic achievement. And in place of specious advice to parents who might well want to grieve a lost child at Christmastime, he offers but a chilling vision of the Cratchit family's life without Tiny Tim, then hurries to bring that crippled child back to life again.

Furthermore, the ghosts who assail him are not vaguely drawn creatures from familiar myths. The tripartite Spirits of Christmas, preceded by the shade of Scrooge's dead partner, are as originally conceived as they are powerful in their detailed, quasi-human form. Marley appears looking very nearly as he had in life, save for the fact that "His body was transparent; so that Scrooge, observing him, and looking through his waistcoat, could see the two buttons on his coat behind. . . . [Scrooge] felt the chilling influence of its death-cold eyes; and marked the very texture of the folded kerchief bound about its head and chin, which wrapper he had not observed before."

Lest all this frightfulness open the artist to the charge of melodrama, however, Dickens slips in a typically caustic aside: "Scrooge had often heard it said that Marley had no bowels, but he had never believed it until now."

It is the sort of wit that creeps in throughout, allowing the cynical reader to proceed contentedly through the story alongside the sentimentalist. (It is not surprising, then, that one of the more enjoyable modern interpretations of the tale was performed by the comedian Jonathan Winters, master of the cutting jibe.)

And while only the hardest hearts fail to be moved along with Scrooge by the plight of the Cratchit family and the stiff-upper-lippedness of Tiny Tim, there are also moments in the text when Dickens's powers distinguish him as much as a stylist as he is a master dramatist.

Of the vast, echoing staircase in Scrooge's dimly lit town home, the narrator says, "You may talk vaguely about driving a coach-and-six up a good old flight of stairs, or through a bad young Act of Parliament; but I mean to say you might have got a hearse up that staircase, and taken it broadwise, with the splinter-bar toward the wall and the door toward the ballustrades: and done it easy. There was plenty of width for that, and room to spare; which is perhaps the reason why Scrooge thought he saw a locomotive hearse going on before him in the gloom."

The cadences, the detail, the wry humor, and the ease with which the narrator shifts from what is real to what is not—these are elements that are sometimes unrevealed to modern audiences who know *A Christmas Carol* only from dramatic adaptations, where the author's descriptive voice is replaced by a camera or by a set designer's vision. But this quality of writing contributes as much to the book's ability to work its magic upon readers as do any number of fine and noble sentiments. In such details lie the reasons why Ebenezer Scrooge and his preposterous self-centeredness would live on through history, and why Gabriel Grub, cut from the same thematic bolt of cloth, would not.

10.

For all the strengths that are evident to the modern eye in *A Christmas Carol*, and despite his own confidence in the power of his tale, Dickens had at least two good reasons to be apprehensive as publication day for his story approached. One had to do with the nature of the holiday itself, and the other with the dire financial straits he found himself in.

As for the first, Christmas in 1843 was not at all the premier occasion that it is today, when Christmas stories and their Grinches and elves and Santas abound, when "Christmas stores" purvey Yule decorations the four seasons round, and a marketing effort that begins sometime in mid-October is said to determine the fate of an entire year for retailers.

There were no Christmas cards in 1843 England, no Christmas trees at royal residences or White Houses, no Christmas turkeys, no department-store Santa or his million clones, no outpouring of "Yuletide greetings," no weeklong cessation of business affairs through the New Year, no overblown gift-giving, no ubiquitous public display of nativity scenes (or court fights regarding them), no holiday lighting extravaganzas, and no plethora of midnight services celebrating the birth of a savior. In fact, despite all of Dickens's enthusiasms, the holiday was a relatively minor affair that ranked far below Easter, causing little more stir than Memorial Day or St. George's Day does today. In the eyes of the relatively enlightened Anglican Church, moreover, the entire enterprise of celebrating Christmas smacked vaguely of paganism, and were there Puritans still around, acknowledging the holiday might have landed one in the stocks.

In fact, for much of the first two centuries of settlement in New England, Christmas was scarcely celebrated. As Yule scholar Stephen Nissenbaum points out, from 1659 to 1681 there was actually a law on the books in the Massachusetts Colony that forbade the practice and levied a fine of five shillings upon anyone caught in the act. Sitting down with their new native friends for a Thanksgiving feast might have been perfectly acceptable, but when Governor William Bradford discovered a few of his fellow Pilgrims trying to celebrate Christmas the year after their arrival, he broke up the ceremonies and ordered everyone back to their jobs.

Part of the reason that Puritans found the holiday such anathema lies in the holiday's roots in pagan celebrations that date back to Roman times. There is in fact no reference in the Christian gospels to the birth of Jesus taking place on the twenty-fifth of December, or in any specific month at all. When Luke says, "For unto you is born this day in the city of David a Savior," there is not the slightest indication of what day that might have been. Moreover, as climatologists have pointed out, the typical weather patterns in the high desert region, then as now, make it difficult to believe that shepherds would have been out tending their flocks during frigid, late-December nights, when nighttime lows often dipped below freezing.

For the first several hundred years of Christianity's practice, and while the death and rebirth of Jesus were venerated upon the highest holy day of Easter, the birth of the savior was not celebrated. It was Pope Julius I who, during the fourth century, designated December 25 as the official date for the birth of Jesus, and scholars believe that he chose the date so that Christianity might attract new members by co-opting the lingering sentiments for the ancient festival of Saturnalia, held annually by Romans in honor of their god of agriculture. Beginning the week before the winter solstice (which occurs between December 20 and 23 each year) and for an entire month, Romans turned their ordinary world topsy-turvy and embarked upon an orgy of drinking and feasting, during which businesses and schools were closed, the government of the city was turned over to the peasants, and slaves were relieved of their masters.

The decision to create Christmas (the term derives from the original "dismissal" or "festival," i.e., "Mass of Christ"), officially celebrating the birth of Jesus for the first time, brought mixed blessings to the Church. Indeed, many pagans found the new religion that embraced their old customs inviting, and the membership rolls grew. On the other hand, Church leaders found that their new Christmas celebrations often got out of hand. As soon as services were over for the day, churchgoers in early modern Europe found it perfectly acceptable to transition directly to a drunken bacchanal, especially if they were part of the disenfranchised class.

One young man of no special standing would be chosen as the "lord of misrule," and was often provided with a "wife" for the day. The revelers would eagerly make themselves available to carry out his whimsical orders, especially if they involved some mischief at the expense of their true masters. Throngs of the needy and less fortunate would present themselves at the gates of the wealthy, demanding food and drink.

In time, elements of these practices were modified into the custom of Boxing Day in England, during which members of the upper classes would package up some of their castoff goods and clothing as year-end gifts for their servants. And, Nissenbaum points out, even to this day, officers of the British Army are compelled to wait upon their enlisted men at Christmas meals. On this side of the Atlantic, Halloween has become the day when anyone has the right to bang on any door and demand a gift from those inside, and the December issues of popular magazines print "tipping guides" for those who wish to stay in the good graces of their paperboys, manicurists, and barbers for the ensuing year.

By the early 1600s, however, the excesses of "Christmas-keepers" in England had only increased, when such practices as "mumming" had become common. Among other things, mumming men and women were wont to exercise their passion for the season by exchanging their clothing and going from one neighbor's house to the next, engaging in the sorts of behavior that one might expect when undressing and cross-dressing were involved. Such carnality distressed Anglicans such as the Reverend Henry Bourne of Newcastle most grievously; in his eyes, Christmas was "a pretense for Drunkenness, and Rioting, and Wantonness." His Puritan counterpart in America, Cotton Mather of Boston, whose outrage would carry over to the Salem witch trials, chimed in: "Christ's Nativity is spent in Reveling, Dicing, Carding, Masking and in all Licentious Liberty."

There might have been practical reasons for men less fortunate or upright to blow off some steam from time to time, but that was of little concern to such church leaders as Bourne and Mather. They may well have understood that the beginning of the winter season was the time when wine and beer were finally fermented and ready to drink, and when meat and game could finally be slaughtered without the fear of spoilage. And of course, who could fail to understand a common man's wish for a bit of bounty and the chance for some fooling around when he spent most of his year grubbing just to stay alive?

But in the eyes of Bourne and Mather and those with similar views of the practice of Christianity, things had simply gotten out of hand. Father Christmas, an elderly folk figure that had developed as an avuncular emblem of the celebration, was now painted as a blasphemous icon, and these libidinous urges of his fellow-travelers, natural as they might have been, were no different from the natural inclinations of the beasts. If not controlled, they would lead man to his moral and spiritual ruin. Christmas, then—characterized "by mad Mirth, by long Eating, by hard Drinking, by lewd Gaming, by rude Reveling"—must be brought under control.

When Oliver Cromwell and his Puritan adherents took over the government of England in the mid-1600s, they did so with a vow to cleanse the country of its wickedness and excess. Ornate cathedrals, for instance, were no longer seen as testaments to God's power and magnificence, but as temples to human pretention. The lengthy seasonal celebrations leading up to major holidays only encouraged intervening lapses of piety and would have to be eliminated. More effective in reminding man of his proper relationship to his creator would be the steady, day-by-day and week-by-week focus on one's behavior and responsibilities, a practice that would be punctuated every Sabbath day by stern leaders like Mather, conducted in utilitarian "meeting houses" where distractions could be held to a minimum.

As for Christmas, which had been given over utterly to "carnall and sensual delights," Parliament put it into law in 1644 that December 25 was from then on to be a day of fasting and repentance. Such legislation led to discontent and even rioting in rural corners of the land, but the ban on Christmas would stay in place until Charles II returned in 1660 and the monarchy was restored.

Things might have been bad for Christmas in England in the mid-seventeenth century, but in the United States, conditions were even worse. Puritans had gone so far as to expunge the names of days of the week like Thursday (Thor's Day) and Saturday (Saturn's Day) from their calendars (replacing them with simple numbers) because of their pagan associations. Though Massachusetts was the only colony that had made the observation of Christmas illegal, there was no formalized celebration of the holiday by church or state throughout New England.

In all colonial records, according to Nissenbaum, there appears only one instance of scofflaws flaunting the Massachusetts decree. In 1679, four young men from Salem village were spurned by orchard owner John Rowden when they came caroling, seeking a cup of a fine pear wine that he produced. When they had finished their singing, one of the men called out to Rowden, "How do you like this, father? Is this not worth a cup of perry?"

"I do not like it so well," Rowden answered, and added, "Pray begone."

His suggestion led to a riot in which his assailants "threw stones, bones, and other things" at him and his house, keeping up their assault for an hour and a half, during which they "beat down much of the daubing in several places," stole several bushels of apples from a storage bin, and broke down a considerable length of fence. A "wassail gone bad," Nissenbaum terms the incident.

If the case was a rare one to reach the courts, the anti-Christmas laws soon came to be honored more in the breach than in the observance, and over time, both in the colonies and in England, it became obvious that an outright ban was a tool of limited reach. In 1684 the Puritan-dominated charter of Massachusetts was revoked by the mother country and a government headed by Edmund Andros, an Anglican, was put in its place. One of Andros's first actions was to permit the celebration of a number of seasonal festivals, including Christmas, by anyone or any group wishing to do so.

But in England as well as the colonies, the new watchword for such celebration was "moderation." Even Mather and his followers might have been more inclined to suffer the celebration of Christmas—despite the fact that it had not been divinely ordained—if it were not for the "Abominable Things" that were done in its name. By the mid-eighteenth century, almanac makers such as Nathanael Ames and Benjamin Franklin were speaking out in favor of seasonal celebrations like Christmas, so long as they were enjoyed without excess. At this same time, the traditional Bay Psalm Book, a rendition of the Old Testament psalms used by most New England congregations and containing no reference to the birth of Christ, was being replaced by two new versions containing Christmas hymns.

In England, despite the return of Charles II to the throne, the ferocious opposition of Cromwell and his Roundheads to the holiday had sapped something of its vitality. Also, the advances of Enlightenment thinking had weakened adherence to all subjective belief systems, traditional religions and pagan practices included. Doubt had begun to enter the modern mind, and if the hold of the Puritans had begun to slip, the power of Zeus and his Titans and Father Christmas had been reduced to just about nothing at all.

"Enlightened" men were reasonable men, not sentimental ones, and they were not to excuse themselves to a month or so of drinking and licentiousness for the sake of a pagan custom. As the diaries of Samuel Pepys attest, while Christmas had made something of a comeback in the years following the restoration of the monarchy in 1660, the season was no longer the excuse for a monthlong binge. Pepys writes of working late on Christmas Eve, and even on Christmas Day as well, though he did attend church services in the morning and evening. He also partook of the custom of a hearty Christmas meal, including such dishes as roasted pullet, "a mess of brave plum pudding," a shoulder of mutton, and mince pie.

Though the best-known entries in Pepys's diaries record his observations on the Great Plague of 1665 and the London Fire of 1666, his recollections of everyday life of the times are one of history's most valuable guides to the period. Quite an earthy character, who was willing to speak candidly of his carnal escapades with serving girls, Pepys nevertheless does not attribute such behavior to any license of the Christmas season. He does, however, speak of his participation in a pale vestige of the Christmas ritual of misrule that had persisted into the Restoration period—a parlor game (Bean & Pea) during which guests would draw lots and "become" one or another member of the royal court and play their chosen role for the evening.

Related to such amateur theatricals were mummers' plays, vestiges of the practice of mumming, often staged impromptu in public houses, on the streets, and in private homes. Presentations by "guisers," or groups of performers in costume, went on the year-round, but they were particularly popular at the Christmas season, when the storylines, such as they were, tended to feature Father Christmas. Though no manuscripts of such plays survive, this recreation by a modern scholar, Roderick Marshall, provides a sense of what they might have been like. "In comes I, Old Hind before, I comes fust to open your door. . . . Welcome or welcome not, I hope old Father Christmas will never be forgot," go the opening lines, as the familiar folk-figure laments his fallen fortunes and reminds his audience that "Christmas comes but once a year, And when it comes, it brings good cheer, Roast beef, plum pudding, strong ale, and mince pie, who likes that better than I?"

In *Dickens's Christmas*, the noted British actor Simon Callow describes the character of Father Christmas in mummers' plays as the prototype of the modern Santa: typically fat, with his backside and belly stuffed with straw, and, though old and bearded, nonetheless vigorous. He distinguishes himself from his current counterpart by carrying a sword and dragging a tail, attributes that suggest the roots of the character in the Devil figure in medieval morality plays, and to the Devil's own predecessor, Pan, the libidinous font of vitality in pagan myth.

Still, if a few remnants of the pre-Puritan celebration of Christmas had survived, by the late 1700s the holiday had become a pale shadow of its former self, cloaked in piousness, sometimes celebrated in public, but rarely at home, shorn of domestic application almost entirely. Traces of the "old" tradition survived, but in tiny villages and distant corners of the English countryside, where enlightenment had not found its way, and among common folk who were not all that anxious to shed every vestige of faith and superstition.

And yet there were also a few literary figures who thought

that such traditions deserved reexamination by a modern world, a world that—in its pursuit of progress and the almighty pound—was becoming increasingly sterile, mechanized, and soulless. With the publication of such historical romances as *Waverly* (1814), *Rob Roy* (1818), and *Ivanhoe* (1819), Scotland's Sir Walter Scott had done yeoman's work in resurrecting an appreciation for his country's legendary past and its heroes. The books may seem clumsy and overly earnest to modern readers, but they were enormously popular in their day, and Scott's death in 1832 left a void in the public consciousness that was waiting for someone like Dickens to fill.

Working this sentimental vein at more or less the same time as Scott was the American-born author Washington Irving, who had moved to England to help salvage his family's business fortunes after the War of 1812 was settled. Irving proved a far better writer than a businessman. He stayed in Europe from 1815 to 1832, touring the nooks and crannies of the Continent and producing a series of stories, observations, and sketches that transformed local customs, legend, and folktales into literary gold. He had similar success with material illustrating traditional folkways in the United States. *The Sketch Book of Geoffrey Crayon*, published in 1819–20, contained the stories "Rip Van Winkle" and "The Legend of Sleepy Hollow" and proved enormously popular.

One of Irving's major subjects in *Geoffrey Crayon* is Christmas, and he begins one chapter with the declaration, "Nothing in England exercises a more delightful spell over my imagination, than the lingerings of the holiday customs and rural games of former times." Those vestiges of a bygone era, Irving continues, "recall the pictures my fancy used to draw in the May morning of life, when as yet I only knew the world through books, and believed it to be all that poets had painted it; and they bring with them the flavor of those honest days of yore, in which, perhaps, with equal fallacy, I am apt to think the world was more homebred, social, and joyous than at present."

Irving posits that it is a false progress indeed that robs mankind of its deeper sources of contentment: "Many of the games and ceremonials of Christmas have entirely disappeared, and, like the sherris sack of old Falstaff, are become matters of speculation and dispute among commentators," he says. "They flourished in times full of spirit and lustihood, when men enjoyed life roughly, but heartily and vigorously; times wild and picturesque, which have furnished poetry with its richest materials, and the drama with its most attractive variety of characters and manners."

It is a damnable place his contemporaries found themselves in, Irving suggests: "The world has become more worldly. There is more of dissipation, and less of enjoyment." And yet there is hope to be found in the celebration of Christmas, with its emphasis on family love, gift-giving, and festivity: "The preparations making on every side for the social board that is again to unite friends and kindred; the presents of good cheer passing and repassing, those tokens of regard, and quickeners of kind feelings; the evergreens distributed about houses and churches, emblems of peace and gladness; all these have the most pleasing effect in producing fond associations, and kindling benevolent sympathies."

In Irving's works, excited descriptions of Christmas Eve parties and Christmas dinners abound, most of them in comfortable rural settings where there are still hints of the libidinous tomfoolery that was said to swell the birthrate of every September in England until the Puritans toppled the throne and put their collective foot down: "The mistletoe is still hung up in farmhouses and kitchens at Christmas; and the young men have the privilege of kissing the girls under it, plucking each time a berry from the bush. When the berries are all plucked, the privilege ceases."

Irving's sentiments regarding the joy and fellow-feeling brought about by Christmas could not have fallen on any ears more predisposed to hear them than those of Charles Dickens. In an essay, Dickens once wrote of how the sight of one of those "new German toys," i.e., a Christmas tree— freshly popularized by Queen Victoria's Bavarian husband, Prince Albert—surrounded by a crowd of excited children aroused in him the veritable reexperience of his own child-hood celebrations of the season. "I begin to consider," Dickens says, "what do we all remember best upon the branches of the Christmas Tree of our own young Christmas days, by which we climbed to real life."

And what he remembers of his own early days is not always pleasurable. Though there were toys enough scat-tered throughout his earliest recollections, some of them had a demonic effect on the imagination of the youthful Dickens, including a jack-in-the-box that particularly troubled him:

"[an] infernal snuff-box, out of which there sprang a demo-niacal Counsellor in a black gown, with an obnoxious head of hair, and a red cloth mouth, wide open, who was not to be endured on any terms, but could not be put away either; for he used suddenly, in a highly magnified state, to fly out of Mammoth Snuff-boxes in dreams, when least expected."

But in the main, Christmas for the young Dickens was a time that encouraged his imagination to soar, when, as he puts it, the most significant of the "decorations" of the holidays of his youth were the books and legends that he came to read and hear at that time. At Christmas, it seemed to him, "Oh, now all common things become uncommon and enchanted to me. All lamps are wonderful; all rings are talismans."

Judging from his recollections, the Christmas season itself accounts in large part for his development as an artist. At this time of year, he says, "Any iron ring let into stone is the entrance to a cave which only waits for the magician, and the little fire, and the necromancy, that will make the earth shake."

For Dickens it was a time when the mundane world could be put aside, "school-books shut up; Ovid and Virgil silenced; the Rule of Three, with its cool impertinent inquiries, long disposed of; Terence and Plautus acted no more."

This cessation of serious endeavor was necessary, Dickens said, defending his abiding interest in the holiday: "And I do come home at Christmas. We all do, or we all should. We all come home, or ought to come home, for a short holiday—the longer, the better—from the great boarding-school, where we are for ever working at our arithmetical slates, to take, and give a rest."

Much of Dickens's enthusiasm for the season transcended religiosity. He was appreciative of the benevolence associated with the example of the Christian savior and embodied in the star atop the tree: "In every cheerful image and suggestion that the season brings, may the bright star that rested above the poor roof, be the star of all the Christian World." But it was the tree that enraptured him: "Encircled by the social thoughts of Christmas-time, still let the benignant figure of my childhood stand unchanged!"

Dickens was surely banking that in *A Christmas Carol* he could convey his own enthusiasm for the Christmas holidays to his readers; but, oddly enough, the pleasure that he found in the season as an adult may well have derived from the terrible upset that he suffered when his family's fortunes collapsed. Given what that experience had done to his childhood, it is possible to see his glowing portrait of an idealized, Edenic Christmas as an attempt to compensate for all that he had lost.

Dickens may have been distressed enough by his father's imprisonment, but perhaps as devastating was his mother's suggestion to him when the family was finally released from the poorhouse: in fact, it might be a good thing if he kept up his employment there at Warren's despite the fact that the rest of them were free, she told young Charles, for the family still needed the money.

And he did remain there for many months after his family had been released, standing near a window as he worked "for the sake of the light," and feeling "inexpressible grief and humiliation" when pedestrians gathered to watch. Imagine the day, in fact, when young Dickens glanced out to see his own father—free and easy on a London street corner—staring up along with the other gawkers as he worked.

In time, Dickens's perspective on the chief misfortune of his childhood would change. The twelve-year-old boy who might have gone to work for Jonathan Warren in resignation, to help his father struggle out of debt, became the adult who looked back with bitterness upon a kind of betrayal.

An older Dickens began to ask himself how his father could have ended up in such a position, anyway. Naval pay clerks were not paid like princes, of course, but the fact is that John Dickens was making about £350 in 1820, far more than the £40 or so that a poor wretch like Cratchit made, and certainly enough to live comfortably on. In time, Dickens became aware that his father and mother were poor managers of their money all their adult lives, and, along with his shame at what he had been forced to do, he came to feel resentment toward his parents as well.

At the time of the writing of *A Christmas Carol*, in fact, as Forster points out, Dickens was not only having trouble meeting his own financial obligations: "Beyond his own domestic expenses necessarily increasing, there were many, never-satisfied, constantly-recurring claims from family quarters, not the more easily avoidable because unreasonable and unjust."

Dickens had, in essence, been paying his parents' expenses for a number of years, with his father's stay in the Marshalsea debtors' prison—if the most distressing—only the first in a string of financial embarrassments. John Dickens had been released from Marshalsea, in fact, only after declaring himself bankrupt, giving up any item in his possession worth more than £20, and agreeing to discharge his debts—which totaled £700—as soon as he was able.

As it turned out, he inherited £450 from his mother, who died only a few days after his release, but even with this windfall, and the annual pension of £146 granted him upon his subsequent discharge from service to the navy, it was more than two years before his debts were finally cleared.

Despite this, John Dickens was buoyed by his release from prison, and soon embarked upon a second career as a journalist for the *British Press*. He was able to remove Charles from Warren's Blacking and send him back to school, and to enroll Charles's sister Fanny in the Royal Academy of Music. For a time it seemed that the family's fortunes were on the upswing.

Disaster struck again, however, when the *British Press* failed in 1827, and the loss of income forced the family's eviction from their rented house. Once again, Charles—now fifteen—was removed from school, and Fanny was forced to give up her studies at the academy. Charles would end up in his law clerkship, and Fanny would teach music to a series of her own pupils, helping to keep the family afloat.

John Dickens continued an erstwhile career as a journalist, squeaking by on that spotty income, the contributions of his children, and his pension from the Admiralty, though the fact that he was sued for debt in 1831, 1834, and 1835 testifies to the difficulties he faced all his adult life.

In 1834 Charles—then twenty-two, and beginning to establish himself in his own right—moved out of the family home. Not long thereafter his earnings grew to the point where he could, and did, assume chief responsibility for his parents' support. John Dickens, however, proved able to spend his son's money as easily as he spent his own, and in 1839 the frustrated Charles hit upon a solution. He rented a cottage for his parents in Devon, far from the London shops and pubs that seemed to siphon off so much money, and John and his wife, Elizabeth, lived there until 1842. The fact that his parents had no ostensible vices—no gambling, no shoddy investment practices, no particular fondness for jewels—was likely to account for the extraordinary patience that Charles displayed in providing for them. They simply were and always had been the sort of people who earned seven pounds a week and spent eight.

But by 1842, things were beginning to deteriorate once again. John Dickens had taken to selling scraps of manuscript he'd pilfered from his son's dustbin, and was offering up the odd document containing Charles's signature as well. He even wrote Dickens's publishers and friends, complaining of one financial embarrassment and another, and seeking loans to set himself right. "Contemporaneous events of this nature place me in a difficulty," went such a letter to Miss Burdett Coutts, "[one] from which, without some anticipatory pecuniary effort, I cannot extricate myself." If only he could avail himself of twenty-five pounds, he told her, things might be set aright.

His father's actions led Dickens to place advertisements in the London papers declaring himself unaccountable for the debts of anyone other than himself. In April of 1842, he wrote to his lawyer, Thomas Mitton, of his exasperation with his father's irresponsible behavior, saying that he had decided to bring his parents back from Devon so that he might keep a better eye on them.

Despite that move, the troubles continued. "The thought of him besets me, night and day," Dickens wrote early in 1843, "and I really do not know what is to be done with him." By September of that year, with his own outlook bleak, he was reaching the end of his rope. His father had gone so far as to write to Chapman and Hall, asking if the publishers might provide him with a ticket for passage on the Thames riverboat so that he could visit the British Museum. Otherwise, "I must doze away the future," John Dickens complained, "in my armchair in re-reading the works of Boz."

Charles was more than embarrassed by such petty, bald-faced begging. "He, and all of them," he wrote, "look upon me as something to be plucked and torn to pieces for their advantage." Such intrusions were one more thing that led the beleaguered author to consider a flight to France or Italy. "My soul sickens at the thought of them," he wrote. "I am amazed and confounded by the audacity of his ingratitude. Nothing makes me so wretched."

Indeed, the ability to immerse himself in the writing of *A Christmas Carol* had provided a much-needed respite for

Dickens's psyche. It was as if, in writing the book, he could will into existence a world of universal charity, empathy, and family harmony that he had not experienced in his life. The writing had been a tonic to his spirits, all right. Now if only its reception could offer a similar remedy to his pocketbook, he might just stay sane yet.

11.

"You fear the world too much," Ebenezer Scrooge's fiancée tells him when she breaks off their engagement. "All your other hopes have merged into the hope of being beyond the chance of its sordid reproach."

More than one commentator has suggested that in this fictional exchange Dickens is also speaking obliquely of himself and his own fears and doubts. Though an outside observer might have thought that a person of Dickens's accomplishments would have left behind such feelings forever, he was clearly still burdened with quite ordinary concerns. Given his current uncertainties—both artistic and economic—*A Christmas Carol* could easily be read as an allegory for his own life: a once-successful man receives a final opportunity to redeem himself.

Certainly, Dickens was well aware of how the deprivations of a childhood, monetary or otherwise, could have profound effects later in life. While the works of William James and Sigmund Freud were still a half-century away, Wordsworth's lines had been around since 1802:

> *So was it when my life began;*
> *So is it now I am a man;*

So be it when I shall grow old . . .
The Child is father of the Man. . . .

Though Dickens was not himself a miserly person, his correspondence makes it clear that he was more than a little preoccupied with his own monetary affairs and with the desire to earn as much money as possible. He had once asserted to one of his brothers, regarding his potential for greed, that "there is not a successful man in the world who attaches less importance to the possession of money," but as he was laying out his publication plan for *A Christmas Carol*, he was also capable of writing, "I hope to get a great deal of money out of the idea."

Certainly, one of the principal themes of *A Christmas Carol* is avarice, and Scrooge's only hope of salvation is to learn the concept of charity. But if Scrooge's arc of development from miser to benevolent merrymaker can be viewed as a theoretical reminder from the author to himself, Dickens also had practical concerns on the line. He was placing his hopes for a resuscitation of his own finances upon a cautionary tale that he had written about money.

If asked, Dickens would likely have shrugged it off. He had never been a rich man, he once wrote, "and never was, and never shall be," but he had a wife and four children, with a fifth on the way, and on the morning of December 19, he was not thinking so much about getting rich—as he wrote to Thomas Mitton, he was simply hoping to keep his personal enterprise afloat:

"For on looking into the matter this morning, for the first time these 6 weeks, I find (to my horror) that I have already overdrawn my account. This month's money I have paid [out]. Next month's is bespoke. And therefore I must anticipate the Christmas Book, by the sum I mention, which will enable me to keep comfortable."

In that same letter, he begged Mitton for a loan of £200 to put off some of his creditors, closing with the gloomy observation that Chapman and Hall were not doing their part to help the book's prospects: "Can you believe that with the exception of Blackwood, the *Carol is not advertized in One of the Magazines?*"

It was a bit of an exaggeration on the author's part. In truth, *A Christmas Carol* had been advertised in the November 18 issue of the weekly literary review the *Examiner,* as well as in the November 25 editions of several other weekly papers, and it was also featured by Chapman and Hall, who—foreshadowing the practice of placing similar advertisements for forthcoming works in an author's current paperback editions—folded into the December installment of *Martin Chuzzlewit* a full-page announcement:

A New Christmas Book
by Mr. Dickens.
In December will be published ... with
Four Coloured Etchings and Woodcuts by Leech
A CHRISTMAS CAROL In Prose.
Being a Ghost Story of Christmas.

The ads in the weeklies and in *Blackwood's Monthly,* and the announcement in *Chuzzlewit* would have been welcome, of course, but Dickens was rightly concerned that the book would not be given wide placement in the holiday issues of the monthly magazines. Still, Chapman and Hall might be forgiven for holding back on advertising a book that was not fully their enterprise. While they would receive a commission on sales, this was Dickens's project, after all.

William Bradbury, who printed Dickens's works for Chapman and Hall, had told Dickens that he, for one, could not believe this omission. "And he [Bradbury] says that nothing but a tremendous push can possibly atone for such fatal negligence," an anxious Dickens wrote to Mitton.

Mitton, who had already received a copy of the proofs of *A Christmas Carol,* came through with the loan and wrote back to buck up the spirits of his friend and client, assuring Dickens that it was excellent work indeed. Dickens responded graciously, "I am extremely glad you *feel* the Carol," he told him. "For I knew I meant a good thing." Still, there was a hint of desperation in the postscript of this letter to his solicitor: "Bradbury predicts Heaven knows what. I am sure it will do me a great deal of good; and I hope it will sell, well."

Along with the proofs to Mitton, Dickens is known to have presented pre-publication copies of *A Christmas Carol* to at least eleven others, including Miss Burdett Coutts, Thomas Carlyle, Forster, Walter Savage Landor, and William Makepeace Thackeray, whose copy is inscribed, "To W. M. Thackeray from Charles Dickens (Whom he made very happy once, a long way from home)." While the source of the sentiment of this inscription is uncertain, and while Thackeray was known to be somewhat patronizing even when approving of Dickens's work, the reference is probably to a scathing review Thackeray wrote the year before for *Fraser's Magazine,* a condemnation of a bastardized French stage production of *Nicholas Nickleby.* ("Of the worthy Boz," Thackeray said, "he has no more connection with the geniuses who invested this drama than a peg has with a gold-laced hat.") Dickens also sent off a presentation copy to the poet Samuel Rogers. "If you should ever have inclination and patience to read the accompanying little book," he told Rogers, who was then in his eighties, "I hope you will like the slight fancy it embodies."

While Forster, Mitton, and others had written encouraging replies to Dickens regarding *A Christmas Carol,* it is fortunate for the author that he didn't know what Rogers thought of it. Rogers's nephew wrote to an acquaintance that when Dickens's new book was mentioned, his uncle "said he had been looking at it the night before; the first half hour was so dull it sent him to sleep, and the next hour was so painful that he should be obliged to finish it to get rid of the impression. He blamed Dickens's style very much, and said there was no wit in putting bad grammar into the mouths of all his characters, and showing their vulgar pronunciation by spelling 'are' 'air', a horse without an h: none of our best writers do that."

What Dickens did hear in the form of the first public pronouncement upon his book came in the *Morning Chronicle* on December 19. Charles Mackay began his review in that paper by declaring, "Mr. Dickens here has produced a most appropriate Christmas offering and one which, if properly made use of, may yet we hope, lead to some more valuable result . . . than mere amusement."

Mackay, a subeditor at the paper, went on to say, "It is impossible to read this little volume through, however hastily, without perceiving that its composition was prompted by a spirit of wide and wholesome philanthropy—a spirit to which selfishness in enjoyment is an inconceivable idea—a spirit that knows where happiness can exist, and ought to exist, and will not be happy itself till it has done something toward promoting its growth here. If such spirits could be multiplied, as the copies of this little book we doubt not will be . . . what a happy Christmas indeed should we yet have this 1843!" Mackay closed his review by assuring readers, "We heartily recommend this little volume as an amusing companion, and a wholesome monitor, to all who would enjoy in truth and in spirit 'A merry Christmas and a happy New Year.'"

On the twenty-second, the reviewer for the *Sun* urged the book upon its readers, and added, "[D]o not suppose because it is a ghost-story that it is a mere frivolous exercise of the fancy." And the *Atlas* cautioned its readers not to mistake the book for some trivial piece of seasonal fluff. Anyone "who perhaps took it up in the expectation of finding some careless trifle thrown off for the occasion . . . like the contribution to an annual, will find himself agreeably mistaken. A glance at the first page or two will convince him that only Boz in his happier vein could have penned it."

On December 23 the *Athenaeum* pronounced that *A Christmas Carol* was "[a] tale to make the reader laugh and cry—open his hands, and open his heart to charity even towards the uncharitable—wrought up with a thousand minute and tender touches of the true 'Boz' workmanship—is indeed—a dainty dish to set before a King." The reviewer describes the story as "capitally *caroled* in prose by Mr. Dickens and will call out, we hope a chorus of 'Amens' . . . from the Land's End to John o'Groat's house."

Fellow essayist and friend Leigh Hunt opined on that same day in the *Examiner* that the slender volume would soon be in "everyone's hands," praising its vivid and hearty style and predicting that "thousands on thousands of readers" would find it the excuse to raise a chorus of praise to Christmas.

Meanwhile, along with such glowing reports, what Dickens heard principally over those first halcyon days of his "little project" was the jingling of coins into booksellers' tills. In four short days, every one of the 6,000 copies that Dickens had printed was sold.

Such an unqualified commercial and critical reception of the book was enough to send its author into a paroxysm of joy and a celebration of the season unlike any before: As he wrote his American friend Felton, "Such dinings, such dancings, such conjurings, such blind man's huffings, such theatre-goings, such kissings-out of old years and kissings-in of new ones, never took place in these parts before." In the space of only hours, many of the cares that had oppressed him for nearly two years seemed to evaporate.

Jane Carlyle, wife of the noted satirist and herself among the most attractive and lively members of the London literary set, wrote a letter to a friend the day after she attended a children's Christmas party where the rejuvenated Dickens was also a guest, suggesting something of the effect his success had produced in him:

"It was the very most agreeable party that ever I was at in London," she gushed. "Dickens and Forster above all exerted themselves till the perspiration was pouring down and they seemed *drunk* with their efforts. Only think of that Dickens playing the *conjuror* for one whole hour—the best conjuror I ever saw."

Mrs. Carlyle described how Dickens, with Forster serving as his assistant, boiled a plum pudding in someone's top hat, transformed ladies' handkerchiefs into candies, and a boxful of bran into a squealing guinea pig. It was all done quite professionally, Mrs. Carlyle thought, enough so that Dickens might think of taking up that line of endeavor should the book trade ever let him down.

"Dickens did all but go down on his knees to make *me*—waltz with *him*," she added, "but I thought I did my part well enough in talking the maddest nonsense with him, Forster, Thackeray and Maclise—without attempting the Impossible."

Mrs. Carlyle's account suggests that what had begun as a children's party ended by approaching the level of a Roman Saturnalia: "In fact the thing was rising into something not unlike the rape of the Sabines!" she said, "when somebody looked [at] her watch and exclaimed 'twelve o'clock!'

Whereupon we all rushed to the cloak-room—and there and in the lobby and up to the last moment the mirth raged on—Dickens took home Thackeray and Forster with him and his wife 'to finish the night there' and a royal night they would have of it I fancy!"

Indeed, Dickens now seemed to embody the very spirit of generosity he had written about in *A Christmas Carol*. He wrote at once to Mackay at the *Morning Chronicle* to express his gratitude for that first glowing review, saying, "Believe me that your pleasure in the Carol, so earnestly and spontaneously expressed, gives me real gratification of heart. It has delighted me very much . . . your praise is manly and generous; and well worth having. Thank you heartily."

With every copy of *A Christmas Carol* sold, his doubts about his ability diminished; and the same critics who had dismissed him for his recent dreary stories were now stumbling over themselves to praise his uplifting message. If Dickens had ever believed the old maxim that he was only as good as his next book, then suddenly he was very good indeed. Chapman and Hall rushed through a second printing, and then, before the passing of the New Year, ordered up a third.

Inevitably, not all the reviews were entirely favorable. While the *Dublin Review* grumbled that the book might have strayed a bit too far from the holy antecedents that gave the season its true meaning, nonetheless, the editors admitted, "It is long since we read prose or poetry which pleased us more." The *Morning Post* weighed in with certain reservations as well, noting that the book "has all Mr. Dickens's mannerisms, and is so far (to us) displeasing and absurd; but it has touches of genius too, mixed up with its huge extravagance, and a few of those little happy strokes of simple pathos," attributes that, the editors rather astutely noted, were also those that accounted for "his great popularity."

But for the most part, the reviews were glowing enough to fulfill any writer's most ardent fantasies. *Bell's Weekly Messenger* said that Dickens had, in *A Christmas Carol,* "converted an incredible fiction into one of the strongest exhibitions of religious and moral truth, and into one of the most picturesque poetical allegories which we possess in our language."

The *Magazine of Domestic Economy and Family Review* chimed in, declaring, "If ever a writer deserved public honours for the service he has rendered to his kind, that man is Charles Dickens and the *Christmas Carol* should be read and reverenced in all to come as a glorious manual of Christian duties."

The *Sunday Times* proclaimed the book "an exquisite gem in its way. . . . Generally the tone of the story is sweet and subdued, but occasionally it soars, and becomes altogether sublime." And even the presumptuous Thackeray had to throw up his hands when searching for something negative to say. "I do not mean that the *Christmas Carol* is quite as brilliant or self-evident as the sun at noonday," he began, "but it is so spread over England by this time that no skeptic, no *Frasers's Magazine* [where his review was being run]—no, not even the gold-like and ancient *Quarterly* itself . . . could review it down."

Thackeray gave it his all in trying to find something negative to say about the book, but clearly Dickens, "even if he had little Latin and less Greek," had put him to the test this time out. "I am not sure the allegory is a very complete one," he muttered, "and [I] protest, with the classics, against the use of blank verse in prose; but here all objections stop."

By the end, this university-educated blue-blood, who had always begrudged the self-taught Dickens's success and popular appeal, simply bowed his head before the book's power: "The last two people I heard speak of it were women; neither knew the other, or the author, and both said, by way of criticism, 'God bless him!'" For once, Thackeray was willing to be magnanimous. "What a feeling this is for a writer to be able to inspire, and what a reward to reap!"

12.

Dickens wrote a simple preface to the original edition of his *Carol,* in which he expressed relatively modest hopes: "I have endeavored in this Ghostly little book," he said, "to raise the Ghost of an idea, which shall not put my readers out of humor with themselves, with each other, with the season, or with me. May it haunt their houses pleasantly, and no one wish to lay it!"

As it happened, few did choose to turn away from *A Christmas Carol.* Dickens also wrote enthusiastically to Miss Burdett Coutts on December 27: "You will be glad to hear, I know, that my *Carol* is a prodigious success." Forster would say, "Never had little book an outset so full of brilliancy of promise. It was hailed on every side with enthusiastic greeting. The first edition of six thousand copies was sold the first day [sic], and on 3 January, he wrote to me that 'two thousand of the three printed for second and third editions are already taken by the trade.'"

Shortly after the New Year, Dickens wrote to his American friend Cornelius Felton, including his own version of the party where he so dazzled Mrs. Carlyle: "If you could have seen me at a children's party at Macreadys the other night, going down a country dance (something longer than the Library at Cambridge) with Mrs M. you would have thought I was a country Gentleman of independent property, residing on a tip-top farm, with the wind blowing straight in my face every day."

And in that same missive he used a favorite device, discussing himself in the third person to describe the triumph of his new book: "By every post, all manner of strangers write all manner of letters to him about their homes and hearths, and how this same Carol is read aloud there and kept on a very little shelf by itself. Indeed it is the greatest success as I am told, that this ruffian and rascal has ever achieved."

Heady times indeed for a ruffian and rascal. But being a novelist as well, Dickens might have begun to wonder if any circumstance that appeared so bright might not have some dark underside about to surface. Sure enough, scarcely had Dickens begun to exult in his good fortune than there appeared equal cause to lament.

For one thing, the great swell of approval in England for the book suggested that the American public, which had clamored for news of Little Nell, would be equally receptive to *A Christmas Carol*. And though this proved to be the case, not all of those clamoring would act in Dickens's best interests. The first shipment of books arrived in Boston on January 21, and as Michael Patrick Hearn puts it, "the pirates must have been waiting at the dock."

The American press was by and large favorably impressed by this offering from a Brit who had savaged their country in *American Notes* and *Chuzzlewit*. "It is one of those stories, the reading of which makes every one better, more contented with life, more resigned to misfortune, more hopeful, more charitable," declared the *New World*.

But once Dickens's authorized edition arrived on American shelves, little time passed before the familiar depredations began. Almost immediately the New York firm of Harper and Brothers was advertising in the newspapers that their own edition of *A Christmas Carol* would hit the stands on January 24. This blatant act of expropriation appeared in the form of a pale imitation of Dickens's lavish book, with two columns of text crowded on a page, lacking illustrations, bound in cheap blue paper, and selling at six cents a copy.

Given that a pound exchanged for about five American dollars at the time, the price was quite a bargain compared to the $1.25 that buyers forked over for an authorized copy. At that discount, the absence of gilt edging and a few colored engravings could probably be forgiven by many of Dickens's U.S. fans. Dickens, however, would see not as much as a ha'penny from Harper and Brothers or any of the several other American pirates who gleefully reprinted his new work.

It was not that Americans were altogether heedless of the concept of copyright. Indeed, one of the earliest accomplishments of the U.S. Congress was the passage of the Copyright Act of 1790, which was established to "promote the progress of science and the useful arts," and to protect the rights of authors and publishers . . . so long as they were American citizens, that is. Anything published by anyone living elsewhere was simply fair game for reprinting in the United States.

And while Dickens and other writers in England and elsewhere were outraged by the equanimity with which

American publishers went about their thievery, a number of American authors, Washington Irving among them, were just as upset with their own treatment by publishers across the pond. England had acknowledged the concept of copyright since the establishment of the Statute of Queen Anne in 1710, which introduced the then-revolutionary concept of an artist retaining a stake in his own creation. Though the legislation was enacted primarily to put an end to the formation of monopolies by publishers that traditionally paid only a flat fee to "own" a literary work, much as a collector of statuary might buy a chiseled rendering of a general on a rearing horse outright, the practical effect of it was to allow writers an ongoing financial interest in their own works.

By 1844, however, England had not yet gotten around to establishing a reciprocal agreement regarding intellectual property rights with the United States, a situation that was exacerbated by the fact that politically powerful publishers on both sides were making significant sums through piracy. Thus, just as Dickens suffered in America, when a British publisher released an edition of "The Masque of the Red Death" or "The Fall of the House of Usher," Edgar Allan Poe saw not a penny from it. It was a situation that lingered until the 1870s, when price wars reached a critical point in American publishing. Instead of undercutting one another on competing editions of identical material, publishers began to understand the competitive advantage in securing exclusive rights to an author's work. As a result they were more willing to enter into agreements with writers from England and the Continent as well. This in turn led to the establishment of more-orderly copyright relations with England and the Continent.

For Dickens, however, there would be no immediate remedy in America. The six-cent version of *A Christmas Carol* put out by Harper and Brothers was followed in short order by editions in the New York paper *True Sun,* which first serialized it in five episodes, then reprinted the whole in an edition that it sold for only three cents. Shortly thereafter, the well-known literary magazine the *New World* blithely serialized the story as well, though it did not neglect to add insult to injury by scolding Dickens for his negative portrayals of the United States in *American Notes* and *Chuzzlewit.*

Dickens probably expected such treatment from the U.S. market, and in any case there was little he could do about it there. But when he discovered the outrage that Lee and Haddock, a London publisher, had perpetrated, he dropped his long-standing practice of ignoring domestic poachers and went directly to chancellor's court.

What he sought there was an injunction to restrain Richard Egan Lee and his partners from selling an issue of a periodical titled *Parley's Illuminated Library* and dated January 6, 1844. The item, which sold for two pennies, contained something called "A Christmas Ghost Story, re-originated from the original by Charles Dickens, and analytically condensed expressly for this work." In this case, "re-originating" apparently meant writing two or three lines of introduction and then reprinting the complete text of Dickens's book with minor alterations.

Dickens, as might be imagined, was beside himself, but

it was not as if this were his first brush with domestic piracy and plagiarism. Though his literal texts were protected by British copyright law, his immense popularity had encouraged any number of hacks and fly-by-night publishers to profit from the most blatant imitations of his work. One of the earliest of these was *The Posthumous Notes of the Pickwick Club,* by "Bos," a miserably executed lift from the original, which sold for a penny (one-twelfth of the going rate for the real thing). It was followed by other such efforts as *Pickwick in America, Oliver Twiss, Nickelas Nicklebery, Barnaby Budge,* and more by Bos, Buz, Poz, and others.

Though the penny imitations were truly dreadful, and read primarily by the poor and semi-illiterate who would have been hard-pressed to appreciate the difference from the actual Boz, there were also imitations aimed at the same middle-class audience who loved Dickens and who simply could not get enough of their favorite author. A journalist and editor by the name of G.W.M. Reynolds began a cottage industry of his own by aping Dickens in the pages of *Monthly Magazine.* Reynolds defended his serialization of something he titled "Pickwick Abroad" by saying that while he might have appropriated Dickens's characters, the stories and the writing were his alone. If Dickens had been too shortsighted to continue Pickwick's run on his own, "it is not my fault," said Reynolds.

Dickens was not particularly happy about any of these shenanigans, and had in days past inquired halfheartedly of his solicitors what might be done, but he had never taken the trouble to pursue any actions in court. In the case of *A*

Christmas Carol, however, he was not only the writer but the publisher as well, and so was particularly vulnerable to such thievery. Furthermore, his circumstances were far more dire than they had been. As they would learn, Lee and Haddock were trifling with a desperate man.

"I have not the least doubt that these Vagabonds can be stopped, they must be," Dickens wrote to Mitton the day after the abominable issue of *Parley's Illuminated* had appeared. "Let us go to work in such terrible earnest that everything tumble down before it. . . . Let us be *sledge-hammer* in this, or I shall be beset by hundreds of the same crew, when I come out with a long story."

If Dickens had invoked the term *sledge-hammer,* then Mitton well knew that this was an undertaking that truly mattered to his client. Accordingly, the attorney filed a bill of complaint on January 9, in which Dickens, as the orator, or plaintiff, stated that while he had invented and written *A Christmas Carol,* the defendants had nevertheless on the sixth of that month published a "colourable imitation" of one half of his book in the sixteenth issue of a periodical known as *Parley's Illuminated Library.* Therefore, Dickens was asking for an injunction to restrain the defendants from "printing, publishing, selling, or otherwise disposing of said publication, or any continuation thereof."

In his affidavit, Dickens pointed out that "the subject, characters, personages, and incidents" were identical to those in his own novel, "except that the name 'Fezziwig' has been altered to 'Fuzziwig.'" By "colourable," he continued, he meant that while much of the original language of his own had been altered, it was only to conceal the fact of the theft. In total, Dickens sought injunctions against five separate parties, including a number of booksellers who had planned to sell what Lee and Haddock had published.

Injunctions against all five were granted immediately by the judge with whom the complaint was filed, and four of the parties agreed to destroy or deliver up their stocks of the offending magazines. Only publisher Lee countered (Haddock seems to have disappeared), asking that the injunction be dissolved, and going so far as to argue that "A Christmas Ghost Story," as written by its author, Henry Hewitt, contained a number of "very considerable improvements and large original additions."

In Dickens's book, Lee pointed out, "Tiny Tim is merely described as having sung a song," whereas Mr. Hewitt had "written a song of sixty lines, such song being admirably adapted to the occasion and replete with pathos and poetry." Furthermore, Lee, in what might seem an excess of zeal, called attention to the fact that Hewitt had "re-originated" several of Dickens's works before, including *The Old Curiosity Shop* and *Barnaby Rudge,* and there had been no complaint. In fact, Lee suggested, Dickens had probably found his inspiration for *A Christmas Carol* in Hewitt's writings, rather than the other way around.

And if Dickens's jaw might have dropped in astonishment at such a preposterous claim, Hewitt in his own affidavit gives some clue to what his publisher might have meant. Since he had "re-originated" the works of a number of well-known authors for his employers, and had even sent gift copies of these versions—as well as his abridgements of *The Old Curiosity Shop* and *Barnaby Rudge*—to Dickens for his enjoyment, it is quite likely that Dickens was introduced to the books of Washington Irving through Hewitt's work, including Irving's books celebrating Christmas.

Dickens, Hewitt proposed, was complaining about the theft of material that Dickens had himself stolen from Washington Irving, albeit from versions of Irving "re-originated" by Hewitt. Thus, Hewitt had the gall to say, he "verily believes Dickens to be more indebted to Washington Irving for the materials of his *Christmas Carol* than the deponent [Hewitt] is to Dickens as regards the Christmas Ghost Story." Furthermore, Hewitt said, in the tones of a humble fellow just trying to eke out a living (he was probably paid about ten shillings to "pot down" *A Christmas Carol*), that he was actually doing a great favor for the "humbler classes" who had neither the time nor the money to spend on "larger, or high-priced works." There is no record describing Dickens's expression as he read these depositions, but one can well imagine it.

Still, as Mitton would have explained to his client, there were certain things in the statements of Lee and Hewitt that would have to be responded to, outlandish as they might seem. As Supreme Court solicitor E. T. Jaques explained in a turn-of-the-century monograph, *Charles Dickens in Chancery,* Lee and Hewitt's allegation of "laches and acquiescence" on Dickens's part was a perfectly acceptable issue to raise in a court of claims. If indeed Dickens had been aware of the previous "re-originations" and had done nothing to stop them, then the court might legitimately find that he had in fact condoned their piracy through inaction.

Thus Dickens was reduced to making a counterclaim in which he denied having received any inscribed volumes of *Parley's Illustrated Library,* including Hewitt's "re-originations" of Washington Irving, his own work, or that of anyone else. And, furthermore, if any such items had been deposited on his doorstep, he had certainly never read them. It was to be clearly understood, Dickens said, "that he has never sanctioned, or knowingly permitted, anyone to copy or imitate the *Carol, The Old Curiosity Shop,* or *Barnaby Rudge,* or any of them."

The motion by Lee and the absent Haddock to dissolve the injunction against them was heard before Judge Knight Bruce on January 18. If we go by Dickens's account to Forster, the lead attorney for the petitioners had a difficult time of it: "He [Judge Bruce] had interrupted Anderton [actually Thomas Oliver Anderson] constantly by asking him to produce a passage which was not an expanded or contracted idea from my book. And at every successive passage he cried out: 'That is Mr. Dickens's case. Find another!'"

When Anderson and his subcounsel had finally run down, and as Thomas Noon Talfourd, hired by Dickens to argue his side of the matter, was scraping back his chair to begin, Judge Bruce motioned him to stay still. According to Dickens, the judge's subsequent words warmed the cockles of his heart: "He said that there was not a shadow of doubt upon the matter," he reported gleefully to Forster. "That there was no authority which could bear a construction in their favour; the piracy going beyond all previous instances. They might mention it again in a week . . . if they liked, and might have an issue if they pleased, but they would probably consider it unnecessary after that strong expression of his opinion."

E. T. Jaques, a veteran combatant in the courts of chancery, adds a poignant postscript to his account of the court battle: "It adds a new interest to Westminster Hall when one thinks of the radiant party which turned out of Knight Bruce's court after judgment had been delivered: Dickens—the eager, beautiful young Dickens of Maclise's drawings [he was, for all his accomplishments and his travails, only thirty-one]—all aglow with his victory, and bubbling over with thanks to Talfourd and the rest . . . and Mitton, nearly as excited as the plaintiff himself."

In this regard, it might be noted that what Dickens saw vindicated that day was not simply his right to control the sale of his intellectual property (for it would be the rare author who regarded his writings solely as "property"). This battle was over far more than pounds and pennies. To the extent that his words—especially the words that were woven up into *A Christmas Carol*—were an inextricable expression of himself, then Judge Bruce's decree had also vindicated the core of Dickens's being. Absolutely, the author would have glowed.

"The pirates," Dickens wrote to Forster in the aftermath, "are beaten flat. They are bruised, bloody, battered, smashed, squelched, and utterly undone." Two days later he was ready to state that he might even profit from the whole affair. In a letter to Forster, Dickens suggested that he could actually steal something back from Lee and Hewitt and their cohorts, by simply copying the preposterous claims they had made in their various depositions: "The further affidavits put in by way of extenuation by the printing rascals are rather strong, and give one a pretty correct idea of what the men must be who hold on to the heels of literature." He told Forster that he was giving serious thought to printing these amazing depositions into his own fiction, "without a word of comment, and sewing them up with *Chuzzlewit*."

Furthermore, he was not through with Lee and Haddock, vowing that they would have to account personally for their slander against his good name. He told Forster, "I am determined that I will have an apology for their affidavits. The other men may pay their costs and get out of it, but I will stick to my friend the author."

He also playfully confessed to Forster his lingering guilt concerning his old friend Thomas Noon Talfourd, who had needlessly gone to so much trouble in the matter: "Oh! the agony of Talfourd at Knight Bruce's not hearing him! He had sat up till three in the morning, he says, preparing his speech; and would have done all kinds of things with the affidavits. It certainly was a splendid subject."

And while the petition of Lee and Haddock to have the injunction against them lifted had been dismissed, he pointed out that final disposition of his case against the pirates was still to come: "Talfourd is strongly disinclined to compromise with the printers on any terms. In which case it would be referred to the master to ascertain what profits had been made by the piracy, and to order the same to be paid to me. But wear and tear of law is my consideration."

To be sure, weathering the many irritations and costs of a civil suit was difficult enough. Given Dickens's early experience with the workings of the courts, however, it is hard to believe that he did not have some inkling of the blow that was coming next.

Despite Talfourd's feelings, and as court records show, Dickens made an effort to settle the matter with Lee and Haddock, stating that "the plaintiff entertained no vindictive feelings towards the defendants, and authorized them to offer that if the defendants would pay the costs and apologise, no further litigation would follow." However, Lee and Haddock were having none of that. "Mr. Anderson declined to enter into any arrangement," the record states. "The plaintiff must take his remedy at law."

In the end, however, the law could offer Dickens no remedy. Faced with Dickens's pending claim of £1,000 to cover lost sales and legal expenses and its almost certain adjudication in his favor, Lee and Haddock promptly declared bankruptcy. And because they listed no assets (beyond, one supposes, their unsold inventory of *A Christmas Ghost Story*), the plaintiff was responsible to the court for their costs as well.

Dickens, who was already deep in debt, could scarcely afford more. He wrote to Talfourd, "I have dropped— dropped!—the action and the Chancery Suit against the Bankrupt Pirates," for there was little hope of recovering anything, and he was not about to incur further expense.

As to the other four booksellers named as defendants, they "have come in and compounded, so that I lose nothing by them," he said. But, "by Lee and Haddock (the vagabonds) I do lose, of course, all my expenses, costs and charges in those suits."

He may have stopped the proceedings, but damage to Dickens's pocketbook was already done. E. T. Jaques estimates the cost of such a case as at least £700, and while Dickens had only had to pursue one suit of the five filed against the booksellers, even the costs of preparing and filing the others—which were necessary to flush out which parties had actually published the offending volume—would have been significant.

It was an illustration of what befalls a man who sues a beggar, but as Jaques points out, at least Dickens was in fact able to salvage some material for future books. From this misadventure almost certainly would spring that wonderful scene in the chancery court of *Bleak House,* wherein eighteen lawyers, "Eighteen of Mr. Tangle's learned friends, each armed with a little summary of eighteen hundred sheets, bob up like eighteen hammers in a pianoforte, make eighteen bows, and drop into their eighteen places of obscurity."

In the end, though, it seems to have been another bitter disappointment for Dickens. Two years later, when the possibility of a similar court action arose, he wrote to Forster: "My feeling . . . is the feeling common, I suppose, to three-fourths of the reflecting part of the community . . . and that is, that it is better to suffer a great wrong than to have recourse to the much greater wrong of the law. I shall not easily forget the expense, and anxiety, and horrible injustice of the *Carol* case, wherein, in asserting the plainest right on earth, I was really treated as if I were the robber instead of the robbed. Given such . . . I know of nothing that *could* come, even of a successful action, which would be worth the mental trouble and disturbance it would cost."

Glum words indeed. But when he was confronted with the first financial statement from his publishers regarding *A Christmas Carol,* Dickens probably wondered if any good would ever come from his little book.

13.

It is worth remembering that Dickens had hoped to earn as much as £1,000 from his "little Carol," and in the first heady days of its life, such dreams must have seemed not only attainable but positively modest. As Forster put it, "There poured upon its author daily, all through that Christmas time, letters from complete strangers to him which I remember reading with a wonder of pleasure; not literary at all, but of the simplest domestic kind; of which the general burden was to tell him, amid many confidences, about their homes, how the *Carol* had come to be read aloud there, and was to be kept upon a little shelf by itself, and was to do them no end of good. Anything more to be said of it will not add much to this."

And a pleasant story it would be if only good news flowed in the immediate wake of *A Christmas Carol*'s publication. The truth is, however, that along with all those delightful letters pouring in to thank Dickens for what he had created, there came a missive of an entirely different nature from Chapman and Hall.

"Such a night as I have passed," Dickens wrote to Forster on the Saturday morning of February 10, after he had scanned the contents of that packet from the publishers. "I really believed I should never get up again, until I had passed through all the horrors of a fever."

One can only imagine Forster's reaction to such an opening, of course. What ailment, what terrible misfortune could have befallen his friend?

Dickens had come home the evening before, he told his agent, to find the statement of accounts regarding *A Christmas Carol* waiting, and this was the cause of his great distress.

It is not difficult to imagine the author, sinking into the chair at his desk, hoping that his first quick glance at the bottom line had been askew, a vision, the result perhaps, as Scrooge might have put it, "of an undigested bit of beef" or a crumb of cheese.

He would have placed the account sheet on the desk before him, adjusted his lamp, perhaps rubbed his face just to get the blood running before he checked again: Calm down now, Dickens, take it as it comes, first things first:

Proceeds from sales, tops on the list. "6,000, less approximately 103 gift, library, and press copies, sold 26 as 25 in cloth for 3s. 6d. each." (The abbreviation for shillings is s., and the abbreviation for pence is d.) Yes, yes, he would have nodded, such gifts and discounts to booksellers were simply unavoidable, the cost of doing business . . . and thus the tally of gross proceeds, at £992 5s. *Not bad, not bad at all.*

There would have been a quick mental check of the math, of course, 6,000 at three and a half per, yes, a thousand pounds give or take. Though perhaps it had been a mistake to insist on that five-shilling cover price, after all.

On to the expenses next, possibly something there, some error, some explanation for the pounding of his heart, the bottomless feeling in his bowels:

"Printing, £74 2s." Yes, about right.

"Paper, £89 2s." Might have gotten away with less, but the look of the thing was all-important . . .

"Drawing and Engravings, £49 18s." *Laws, laws.* Mr. Stiff, the hack with the Dickensian name who had designed, illustrated, and engraved *A Christmas Ghost Story* for that pack of thieves at *Parley's,* might have been paid a pound for all his trouble. Then again, Leech's work was of the first quality, was it not?

There were also charges for two steel plates at £1 4s., the printing plates themselves at £15 17s., and paper for the plates at £7 12s. All in order, it appeared.

But then the charges for coloring—*Lord*—£120. And the binding of the books, at £180. . . . Though what a handsome volume it was.

Incidentals and Advertising, at £168 7s. 8d. Down to the penny with their bloody "incidentals" were Chapman and Hall.

And, lastly, "Commission to Publishers," 15 percent of receipts off the top, and totaling £148 16s.

All those expenses, then, and the total of them, £855 8d. And that final, dreadful, bottom line:

"Balance of account to Mr. Dickens's credit: £137 4s.

4d." *Egad*. No matter how long he stared at it, the number would not change.

Dickens was shattered, and said as much to his agent: "I had set my heart and soul upon a Thousand, clear. What a wonderful thing it is, that such a great success should occasion me such intolerable anxiety and disappointment."

Nor was Dickens satisfied with that down-to-the-pence accounting supplied by Chapman and Hall. He dashed off an angry note to Mitton, saying that he had not the least doubt that his publishers "have run the expense up, anyhow, purposely to bring me back and disgust me with charges. If you add up the different charges for the plates, you will find that they cost more than I get."

Still roiling in a bath of anger and disappointment—on the one hand this tremendous accomplishment, and on the other hand next to nothing to show for it—Dickens told Forster, "My year's bills, unpaid, are so terrific, that all the energy and determination I can possibly exert will be required to clear me."

He reiterated his determination to go abroad, no matter what his financial condition, "if next June come and find me alive," then lamented, "Good Heaven, if I had only taken heart a year ago!"

Of course, had he gone abroad the year before, there likely would have been no *Carol*, but Dickens skipped that point. "I was so utterly knocked down last night," he told Forster, but his resolve was now steel. "I will be off to some seaside place as soon as a tenant [for his house] offers. I am

143

not afraid, if I reduce my expenses; but if I do not, I shall be ruined past all mortal hope of redemption."

The largest part of those expenses went toward the upkeep of that house, a thirteen-room manse on Devonshire Terrace, where Dickens had moved his family in 1839 when the money was rolling in from *Pickwick* and the rest. Located opposite the York Gate entrance to Regents Park (just around the corner from another famed set of literary lodgings, the 221B Baker Street flat of Conan Doyle's Mr. Holmes), and including spacious gardens, the house had required an eleven-year lease of £800, plus an additional rent of £160 per year. Dickens had upgraded the doors of the home to mahogany, replaced its mantelpieces with Italian marble, and ordered the study soundproofed against the clamor of a household that, with the birth of his son Francis in January, now included five children.

Dickens described it as a house of "undeniable situation and excessive splendour," and given that he had written some of his most successful works there, including *The Old Curiosity Shop* and *A Christmas Carol,* it would surely have pained him to leave it. But, as he told Forster, his mind was made up.

There was a bit of impatience in those letters he dashed off to Forster and Mitton, certainly, for in fact sales continued strong for his Carol, well after the Christmas season had come and gone. The second and third printings ordered up in January would be succeeded by half a dozen more over the course of 1844, until by the end of the year nearly 15,000 copies would be sold. Only seventy copies would remain in

Chapman and Hall's warehouse at the close of business on December 31, and the bottom line of their closing statement records that "Amount of Profit on the Work" had climbed to £726.

However gratifying the continued enthusiasm for the book might have been, the amount was still well short of that "quick £1,000" that Dickens had hoped to gain. Furthermore, once his work on *Martin Chuzzlewit* was completed in June of 1844, his £200 monthly income from that source would disappear as well. Dickens stood resolute on his decision to leave Chapman and Hall, however, and Forster accordingly informed those men that once Dickens had completed his commitment to them for *Martin Chuzzlewit*, their association would be terminated.

On June 1, shortly before the publication of the final installment of *Chuzzlewit*, Dickens signed a publishing contract with William Bradbury and Frederick Evans, the two men who had been printing his books from the beginning. While Bradbury and Evans had little experience with the publishing side of the business—the editing, advertising, and retailing—Dickens trusted the pair and figured that their inexperience might be all the better, given his needs. In fact, "a printer is better than a bookseller," he said, sniping at the abilities of Chapman and Hall to market his books to the trade. And, in the belief that his advice to Bradbury and Evans would constitute all they really needed to know about purveying his books, he hammered out an unusual agreement with his new publishers. Instead of the author receiving a percentage of sales or profits, Dickens agreed to give

Bradbury and Evans a 25-percent share of the net proceeds from anything he might write over the next eight years.

Bradbury and Evans would have no say about what Dickens might write, though the parties did agree that if Dickens were to undertake the editing and publishing of a periodical during that period, then his share of any profits from such an enterprise would drop to 66 percent and theirs would rise accordingly. In return, Bradbury and Evans would advance Dickens £2,800, which was the amount he reckoned necessary to see him through a year abroad and another furlough from writing.

He might or might not attempt a book about his planned travels in Italy and elsewhere, Dickens allowed, but from now on he would be the one to decide the course of his career. There was only one small exception: it was understood by all parties at the time of the signing that he would have a follow-up book to *A Christmas Carol* ready for the Christmas season of 1844.

With that promise made and the contract signed, Dickens turned his thoughts from writing for a time, and set about making preparations for his move. Of course he continued to take pride in his *Carol*'s continued success, and would even describe himself in a letter the following year as "the author of *A Christmas Carol* in Prose and other works." And undoubtedly, he took the time to savor letters such as that from Lord Jeffrey: "Blessings on your kind heart . . . for you may be sure you have done more good by this little publication, fostered more kindly feelings, and prompted more positive acts of beneficence, than can be traced to all the pulpits and confessionals in Christendom since Christmas 1842."

But for all intents and purposes, with the publication of *A Christmas Carol* behind him, Dickens had closed the books on one part of his adult life, and was intent upon making the transition to another. Though only thirty-two, he had established himself as an author and as a person of renown, and, furthermore, he had survived the storm of blows and backlash that often follow in the wake of great success. Even though the public had been indifferent to his *Chuzzlewit*, Dickens wrote Forster following the completion of its final chapter that in his own heart rested the knowledge that the book had been a hundred times better than anything he had done before.

And in addition, at the nadir of his most gloomy days, he had in six feverish weeks produced a book based upon the very same themes—skewering pomposity, excoriating greed, championing charity for the unfortunate—but he had done it differently, pointing to the possibility of change, and in such a way that readers everywhere embraced his words and praised him for acknowledging their shortcomings and encouraging them to become more generous and loving. Truly, he had proven to himself that he was capable of writing books that needed to be written. So, out with the old, in with the new.

He packed up his family and headed off for Italy to see what might strike his writer's fancy, though he assured Forster of one certain thing: he was going to follow up the *Carol* with a Christmas book to "knock it out of the field."

Part Three

WHAT GIFT
IS THIS

14.

Dickens may well have intended to begin a new chapter in his career when he set out for the Continent, but the legacy of all that he had done by that time would trail his steps forever. And of everything that he had written to that point, nothing would prove more persistent and pervasive and powerful than *A Christmas Carol*.

In addition to the piracies and the imitations, soon after the publication of the novel there appeared on London stages the inevitable—and mostly unlicensed—dramatic adaptations of the kind that followed the publication of any moderately successful book. It was a backhanded form of acclaim that Dickens endured from the earliest days. And in those unauthorized imitations of his first novels, Dickens actually saw more reason to be flattered than aggrieved or threatened. For one thing, there was little money in the theater for a writer in those days. Even a licensed adaptation might bring an author a pound per act at most, and Dickens had come to view the productions more as free advertising and evidence of the broad appeal of his work than anything else.

Until 1843, in fact, the national licensing laws permitted only the Royal Theatres at Drury Lane and Covent Garden to present serious dramatic productions. While there was plenty of spectacle available elsewhere, in saloons, meetinghouses, and other public venues, these presentations generally took the form of vaudeville, including burlesques, sketches and scenes from popular sources interspersed with music, and various conglomerations of pantomime, soliloquy, magic acts, mesmerism, ventriloquism, and acrobatics, antedating the variety shows of the television age to come.

As a young man, Dickens had been fascinated with this shaggy form of theater, and he often took part in school and amateur productions. Only the onset of a terrible head cold had kept him from auditioning for a part in a Covent Garden production during his early days as a journalist, in retrospect a happy accident that may have forestalled quite a different career path. Though his success with *Sketches by Boz* may have displaced any serious aspirations as an actor, Dickens's interest in the theater never left him. In 1838 he penned a farce titled *The Strange Gentleman,* which was doing well enough to encourage him in further dramaturgical endeavors, until the landslide popularity of *The Pickwick Papers* swept him irreversibly in a different direction.

Still, Dickens remained a resolute theatergoer, and often an eager performer. During the Canadian segment of his American tour, he directed and appeared in a series of farces staged by the officers of the Royal Garrison in Montreal, giving the unpaid role his all. As he wrote Forster, "[T]he pain and perspiration I have expended during the last ten days exceed anything you can imagine."

In addition, he counted a number of playwrights and theater critics among his closest friends, including Forster, the multitalented Bulwer-Lytton, and lawyer-cum-playwright

Thomas Noon Talfourd, who represented him in the *Parley's Illuminated* case, and whose work had been produced at Covent Garden. And while involvement in the theater remained a vaguely disreputable enterprise well into the nineteenth century, the passage of the Theatres Act in 1843 changed things greatly. The act diminished the rather dictatorial powers of the Lord Chamberlain to restrict the licensing of theaters and limited him to the prohibition only of performances where he thought it "fitting for the preservation of good manners, decorum or of the public peace so to do."

While such ambiguous language would remain largely in effect until 1968, and prompt more than a bit of debate about what was offensive to twentieth-century manners, the Theatres Act was a boon to serious playwrights, extending the reach of their work into a wide range of venues and thus to middle-class England. Theaters thereby gained a heightened respectability and more secure economic footing. The boom in 1840s theater-building would result, in fact, in the creation of London's famed West End district.

Prior to 1843, however, theater in London was something of a mongrelized enterprise. The concept of copyright for a stage play was laughable—and besides, why would any director or producer pay an artiste serious money to concoct an original composition, when any number of hacks would be glad to "re-originate" the works of Defoe, Fielding, Richardson, or Smollett for a few shillings?

One of Dickens's early stories, "A Bloomsbury Christening," was co-opted in this way in 1834, and Dickens himself was happy to review the proceedings, where he noted good-naturedly that the characters were "old and particular friends." Dickens scholar Paul Schlicke estimates that by 1840 *The Pickwick Papers, Oliver Twist,* and *Nicholas Nickleby* had been staged at least sixty times, and the author had become somewhat resigned to the matter, though it did annoy him when the productions were poorly done, or his dialogue carelessly transcribed, or the conclusions to his stories given away before the final publication in book form.

Of everything Dickens had written up to that time, however, *A Christmas Carol,* with its brevity, tight-knit story line, vivid characters, and colorful dialogue, was a natural for the stage, and the adaptations (carefully cataloged by Dickens scholar H. Philip Bolton) began to appear almost immediately. On Monday, February 5, 1844, three productions opened simultaneously in London.

One, titled *A Christmas Carol: or, The Miser's Warning,* a drama in two acts, was penned by C. Z. Barnett and performed at the Surrey Theatre. Described by critics as "much grimmer" than the others, and lacking any songs, its run was brief. A second, *Scrooge, The Miser's Dream,* was penned by Charles Webb and opened at Sadler's Wells, where it lasted fifteen performances. The third was the only version actually sanctioned by Dickens (and thus the only version for which he would receive a share of the profits). *A Christmas Carol: or, Past, Present, and Future,* in three acts, by Edward Stirling, opened at the Adelphi, the theater with the best reputation at the time, and ran for more than forty nights.

Dickens attended a production of the last, and though a bit apprehensive before going in—"Oh, Heaven! If any forecast of this was ever in my mind!"—he seemed pleased by what he saw: "Better than usual," he dubbed the effort, adding that the actor playing Scrooge ("O. Smith," a scenery-chewing veteran who had starred in the lead of *Frankenstein,* as well as in a few adaptations of Dickens's work previously) "was drearily better than I expected. It is a great comfort to have that kind of meat underdone, and his face is quite perfect."

The production of Webb's version would close relatively quickly at Sadler's Wells, but it had already begun a simultaneous run at the Strand in London. Not only did it run at that theater well into March, but Webb's rendition was so popular that it was given at least five productions elsewhere during the season.

Before the year was out, there would be at least sixteen productions of the story to reach the stage in England, some of them taking great liberties with the original. In one, Scrooge was reunited with his long-lost fiancée, while one of the Webb versions culminated in a near-riot when the three Spirits of Christmas came back on stage to join such stalwarts as Puck, Punch, Pan, and Apollo in a veritable chorus-line grand finale.

Stirling's authorized version actually crossed the Atlantic, where it was performed at the Park Theater in New York City during the Christmas season of 1844. And revivals of both the Webb and Stirling versions were again mounted in London that season.

If the gratifying reviews in respected newspapers had restored Dickens's reputation in literary circles, the unprecedented number of dramatic productions spread his name to an exponentially wider audience, in the same way a successful film adaptation might for a popular novel today. And yet, while these days nearly every American has attended, acted in a school version, or at least seen the notices for *some* holiday production of *A Christmas Carol,* 1844 marked the high-water point for the number of theatrical adaptations of the story for more than half a century. Part of the drop-off after that year can be attributed to the fact that Dickens churned out four Christmas books in the five years following, and one of those, 1845's *The Cricket on the Hearth,* became by far the most dramatized of its brethren during the writer's lifetime. That story actually ranked third in frequency of Dickens adaptations during that period, after versions of *Nicholas Nickleby* and *Oliver Twist.* In addition, Dickens himself began offering live readings of *A Christmas Carol* in the 1850s, a practice that proved immensely popular, and which he continued to his death.

In total, the number of early productions of *A Christmas Carol* came to about half those of *Oliver Twist* and were about the same in number as the adaptations of *Martin Chuzzlewit,* though it should be noted that the *Carol* figures are quite respectable for a "one-installment" publication. Most of the other novels, appearing in twenty installments over many months, would have a much longer shelf life in the popular entertainment consciousness.

One other influence particular to Dickens's time is also worth considering. Even though the Theatre Act of 1843 weakened government influence over theatrical productions, the office of the Examiner of Plays still remained, wielding considerable influence over what appeared on stage, with subject matter that suggested the merest possibility of the profane receiving special scrutiny. Prayers, biblical quotations, and representations of established church figures were routinely excised by government censors. Thus, *A Christmas Carol,* secular though it is, may have been considered controversial by more staid—or more timid—production companies of the time.

Even years later, advertising copy for an 1885 production in Edinburgh went so far as to tout the "strictly moral" nature of the play. "The Very Rev. DEAN STANLEY," the producers wished to remind the public, "in his funeral Sermon preached at the Grave of CHARLES DICKENS in Westminster Abbey, pronounced the 'CHRISTMAS CAROL' to be the finest Charity Sermon in the English language."

Whether moral concerns played into it or not, the tally of productions of *A Christmas Carol* over the next fifty years was about half the number mounted in 1844 alone. In fact, it was not until the turn of the twentieth century that a significant uptick in adaptations of the story came, and that was a development that came with the advent of a brand new way of storytelling.

Novelist and Dickens admirer John Irving asserts that the particular strength of a Dickens novel is to make an audience feel more than think. And while it might be argued that in most fiction the aim is to entertain first and edify second, if ever there were a medium where the manipulation of an audience's emotion is paramount, then the motion picture form is it.

In *A Christmas Carol,* film producers were to discover the mother lode. The first motion picture version of the tale was a silent picture called *Scrooge, or Marley's Ghost,* produced in Great Britain in 1901. That was followed by half a dozen more silent films on both sides of the Atlantic, including one 1910 version by Thomas Edison. The first sound version, also called *Scrooge,* was made in 1928 in Great Britain.

In 1934 Lionel Barrymore starred in a U.S. radio-play adaptation titled *A Christmas Carol,* an event that proved so popular that the piece became a holiday tradition that lasted into the 1950s—his brother John Barrymore and Orson Welles successfully took over during two different seasons when Barrymore fell ill. It is Barrymore's series, in fact, that is generally credited with making Dickens's story the popular phenomenon it has become in the United States.

There was another filmed version, *Scrooge,* produced in Great Britain in 1935, and in 1938 came the first significant film production in the United States, titled *A Christmas Carol,* produced by Joseph Mankiewicz and starring Reginald Owen as Scrooge. *Variety* gave the film kudos—"Top production, inspired direction, superb acting"—and indeed the version holds up well to this day.

In the 1940s the new medium of television got into the act, with John Carradine and Vincent Price starring in different versions, and in 1949 Ronald Colman narrated the first commercial sound recording of the story.

It is the consensus of most critics that the very best film adaptation of Dickens's story came in 1951 with the British production of *Scrooge* (released in the United States as *A Christmas Carol*), with Alastair Sim as Scrooge and Mervyn Jones as Bob Cratchit. The film received favorable reviews in the United States, but, likely because of its rather downbeat portrayal of Scrooge, it did not become widely popular until the 1970s, when it began to receive regular television airings during the Christmas season.

Other notable adaptations include a musical version— *Scrooge*—produced in Great Britain in 1970, starring Albert Finney in the title role and Alec Guinness as Marley's Ghost. The film was nominated for several Oscars, and Finney won a Golden Globe for Best Actor in a Musical/Comedy. In 1984 Clive Donner, who had edited the Alastair Sim production of 1951, directed another well-received British version, *A Christmas Carol,* starring George C. Scott. The film was originally shown on the CBS television network in the United States, where it won Scott an Emmy nomination for Best Actor.

In all, the story has spawned at least twenty-eight film adaptations, including versions starring Bill Murray as a greedy U.S. television executive (*Scrooged,* 1988); a Disney version starring none other than Scrooge McDuck in the title role; and cartoon versions featuring the Flintstones, the Muppets, Alvin and the Chipmunks, and the Jetsons.

Nor is there any sign that the practice is at an end. In 2007 director Robert Zemeckis (*Back to the Future, Forrest Gump, The Polar Express*) announced plans for a major animated version of the story starring the voices of Jim Carrey, Christopher Lloyd, Bob Hoskins, Gary Oldman, and others. The story has also inspired at least two operatic versions in the twentieth century, including one by Thea Musgrave in 1978; a one-man Broadway show with Patrick Stewart in the 1990s; a widely performed Christian-themed version called *The Gospel According to Scrooge;* long-running adaptations at regional theaters (thirty-three seasons at the Raleigh, North Carolina, Theater in the Park, twenty-five at the Indiana Repertory Theater); numerous sound recordings; and parodies by the likes of Lord Buckley, Stan Freberg, and even Beavis and Butthead.

According to a count made in the late 1980s, at least 225 live stagings, films, radio dramas, and television plays based on Dickens's "little Carol" had been produced after 1950, and that number does not take into account the untold number of amateur and regional productions staged every year. Not only has *A Christmas Carol* become the most "adapted" of all the author's works, but it would be hard to name any other work of fiction that has thereby become so ubiquitous a part of Western popular culture.

Undoubtedly Dickens would have been chagrined that he never saw a penny from all this modern-day "re-originating," but surely the man who had vowed to deliver a "sledge-hammer blow" upon the consciousness of an insensitive public around him would also have been gratified to see how intertwined—indeed, how synonymous—his "little Carol" has become with the "season of giving." Celebrating Christmas without some reference to *A Christmas Carol* seems impossible, a remarkable fact given that the book was published more than 150 years ago. Indeed, the resonance of the story has remained so strong through the generations that commentators have referred to Dickens as the man who invented Christmas.

15.

Certainly, Dickens would not have made such a claim on his own behalf. As the record makes clear, he was well aware of the traditional celebration of the Christmas holiday, he enjoyed it, and he had written of it with enthusiasm on a number of occasions before he wrote *A Christmas Carol*. And the work of many of his illustrious predecessors demonstrates that Dickens did not singlehandedly dream up the concept of a yuletide season with its various accouterments.

As early as 1712, in his *Spectator* installment "Christmas with Sir Roger," Joseph Addison has his fictional narrator wax eloquent regarding the holiday, "when the poor People would suffer very much from their Poverty and Cold, if they had not good Cheer, had not good Cheer, warm Fires, and *Christmas* Gambols to support them. I love to rejoyce their poor Hearts at this Season, and to see the whole Village merry in my great Hall."

Nearly a century later, in 1808, Sir Walter Scott published his long poem *Marmion,* which begins its sixth canto with a vivid description of a Christmas feast: "The fire, with well-dried logs supplied / Went roaring up the chimney wide . . . The wassel round, in good brown bowls / Garnished with ribbons, blithely trowls / There the huge sirloin reck'd; hard by / Plum-porridge stood, and Christmas pie. / Nor failed old Scotland to produce / At such high tide, her savoury goose / Then came the merry maskers in / And carols roar'd with blithesome din."

Such celebration and sentiment was further glorified by Washington Irving, who begins the Christmas section of *The Sketchbook of Geoffrey Crayon* by noting that "The English . . . have always been fond of those festivals and holidays which agreeably interrupt the stillness of country life; and they were, in former days, particularly observant of the religious and social rites of Christmas."

Irving goes on to enumerate any number of the features that characterize what are now thought of as belonging to the "Victorian" or "Dickensian" Christmas, but were actually practices that Irving thought had been too long neglected in England, including "the complete abandonment to mirth and good fellowship, with which this festival was celebrated. It seemed to throw open every door, and unlock every heart. It brought the peasant and the peer together, and blended all ranks in one warm generous flow of joy and kindness. . . . Even the poorest cottage welcomed the festive season with green decorations of bay and holly—the cheerful fire glanced its rays through the lattice, inviting the passenger to raise the latch, and join the gossip knot huddled round the hearth, beguiling the long evening with legendary jokes, and oft told Christmas tales."

It is probably true that Irving and others who appreciated the ideals of Christmas and the rituals formerly associated with its practice had reason to complain. In those days, when December 25 rolled around in London—and given the assaults of Cromwell and the Puritans and the grind of an industrialized society's life—it must have seemed at times a bloodless, unromantic place. But though there had been this gloomily evocative writing by Addison and Scott and Irving and the industry of artists and scribes and publishers who had concocted Christmas annuals and seasonal periodical issues (including Dickens himself), never before December of 1843 had there appeared a piece of writing of the nature of *A Christmas Carol.*

One thing that sets Dickens apart is that unlike a wistful predecessor such as Washington Irving, who seemed content to lament the passing of those grand and glorious celebrations of yore and the general malaise of the society around him, Dickens was convinced that he had the tonic for what ailed his countrymen. His approach was to restore Christmas, not lament its passing.

Furthermore, Dickens's tale does not merely describe the season or its aspects as much as it embodies them in its characters and actions. And its form—that of a "ghost story," or fairy tale—is perfectly suited to transmit such concepts as good fellowship, compassion, and charity from the realm of the abstract into a tangible shape that can be experienced by an ordinary audience. At the same time, when the writer employs a ghost as a character, and introduces the supernatural into a narrative, he forms an implicit contract with the reader that while the proceedings are realistic, they are not real, and are not to be taken too seriously. Thus, a reader can journey into the "ghost story" safely, seeking his entertainment, and with no suspicion lurking that the writer is trying to convince him of anything.

Of course, most writers who use the form of the ghost story have absolutely no serious designs upon their readers. In escapist literature of the kind, the aim is simply to thrill and amaze, and indeed there is plenty of that in *A Christmas Carol*. But the real work of the volume, as Dickens made abundantly clear, was to deliver that "sledge-hammer blow" on behalf of the poor and unfortunate. The beauty of the book is, then, his use of a deceptively innocent form to do such serious work. Many other writers since have married the "ghost story" genre to serious intent, including Henry James (*The Turn of the Screw*) and Shirley Jackson (*The Haunting of Hill House*). But as history would have it, Dickens was the first to do it so adeptly, and he came to the rescue of a downtrodden holiday that a repressed Western world was fairly bursting to revive.

There may have been other factors to account for the widespread public embracing of Dickens's story, including Queen Victoria's marriage to a German husband, who brought with him an affinity for certain aspects of the season's symbology and practice, and popularized them among the English people, including the now-obligatory Christmas tree with its ornaments and its presents piled high, not to mention the great value Germans placed on family unity and communal celebration.

But one of the primary gifts that Dickens gave his contemporaries was a secular counterpart to the story of the Nativity—which is, after all, the basis for the celebration.

Dickens, though nominally an Anglican, was a vocal critic of organized religion, especially where he saw hypocritical divergences between the preaching and the practice of Christian charity. Many critics have suggested that in his little Christmas fable—whether consciously or unconsciously—he complemented the glorification of the nativity of Christ with a specific set of practices derived from Christ's example: charity and compassion in the form of educational opportunity, humane working conditions, and a decent life for all. Just as vital as the celebration of the birth of a holy savior into a human family was the glorification and defense of the family unit itself.

In *A Christmas Carol,* the chief focus of the reader's sympathy becomes the crippled Tiny Tim, rather than a Christ child. When Scrooge is treated to a vision of a world in which that child has died, readers instinctively understand that the most important question for the remainder of the narrative concerns just how an earthly child might be saved.

The portrayal of Tiny Tim—derived from Dickens's memories of his sickly younger brother, whom he called "Tiny Fred"—has proved "real" enough to prompt modern-day physicians to puzzle over the exact nature of the fictional child's affliction. One researcher suggests that Tiny Tim suffered from a kidney disease known today as renal tubular acidosis, a condition that can retard growth and weaken bones. In 1844, had the child been presented for care, doctors might not have used that name, but they would have recognized his symptoms and would have had effective dietary methods of treatment at hand.

More likely, however, Tiny Tim and Tiny Fred suffered from rickets, a common affliction of that time in cities where smog frequently blocked sunlight, the natural source of vitamin D. In the days before vitamin supplements, children were particularly susceptible to the disease, which leads to loss of bone density, muscle weakness, and osteoporosis. Such symptoms could have been reversed by an improvement in diet, which the Cratchit family would have enjoyed once Scrooge gave his clerk a raise.

Medical diagnosis aside, the sanctification of the family found in *A Christmas Carol* would become one of the chief tenets of Victorian thinking, and it is one reason for the virtual deification of Dickens by some intellectuals of the time. Inspired by the secular humanism he so admired in Dickens's work, the Jewish writer Benjamin Farjeon authored some sixty novels between 1866 and 1904, including a number of Christmas tales in a similar vein, and earning high praise from the British press that described him as "a preacher of the brotherhood of rich and poor, more powerful, graphic, and tender than any since Dickens." Today as well, there are Jewish families who, in the Farjeon manner of thinking and with no affinity whatsoever toward the Christian underpinnings of the holiday, might still put up a "Chanukah Bush" for a season devoted to togetherness and love.

At the same time that Dickens was writing *A Christmas Carol,* intellectual forces were gathering that would strike a series of mighty blows at traditional religious thought. The publication of Darwin's *On the Origin of Species* was only sixteen years away, and while the world would have to wait a bit to hear from Freud, it would not be long before the vision of man as an exalted creature, descended from a holy spark and only six days in the making, would be replaced by one of him as a dust mote in history's whirl, or slithered up from prehistoric ooze, possessing not an iota of the divine, his consciousness formed by the accident of stimulus and response, and his fate at the mercy of a universe indifferent to his presence.

Given the batterings of modern scientific thought on the ordinary psyche, Dickens's version of the Gospels offers something of a comforting compromise, and they did so not only for his contemporaries but for modern readers as well. There are no "holy" ghosts in *A Christmas Carol,* but the secular apparitions that appear offer a comforting counterpoint to the reader in need of some compass by which to set his moral bearings in an age of upheaval. If there is a deeper reason why Dickens's tale survives, beyond its obvious delights, then that honorable intention is as good as any.

Whatever the moral underpinnings of its appeal, Dickens's story has had a lasting practical impact on our culture well beyond the ubiquitous yearly dramatizations. The name of Scrooge has entered our vocabulary as one of the more colorful synonyms for "miser" (*scrooge* was a verb used in Dickens's day, meaning "to squeeze, or crush" and derived from the Old English *scruze*); and "Bah! Humbug!" has become a favorite rejoinder to any declaration that strikes a listener as ridiculous or overly sentimental. Furthermore, when Scrooge dispatched a street urchin to buy that prize turkey for the Cratchit family (the *big* prize turkey, not the little one, mind you), it had a profound impact upon the British economy, one that has trickled down to that of the United States as well:

"Go and buy it, and tell 'em to bring it here, that I may give them the direction where to take it. Come back with the man, and I'll give you a shilling. Come back with him in less than five minutes, and I'll give you half-a-crown."

The boy was off like a shot. He must have had a steady hand at a trigger who could have got a shot off half so fast.

"I'll send it to Bob Cratchit's!" whispered Scrooge, rubbing his hands, and splitting with a laugh. "He shan't know who sends it. It's twice the size of Tiny Tim. . . ."

The hand in which he wrote the address was not a steady one, but write it he did, somehow, and went down stairs to open the street door, ready for the coming of the poulterer's man. . . .

"—Here's the Turkey. Hallo. Whoop. How are you? Merry Christmas."

It was a Turkey! He never could have stood upon his legs, that bird. He would have snapped 'em short off in a minute, like sticks of sealing-wax.

"Why, it's impossible to carry that to Camden Town," said Scrooge. "You must have a cab."

The chuckle with which he said this, and the chuckle

with which he paid for the Turkey, and the chuckle with which he paid for the cab, and the chuckle with which he recompensed the boy, were only to be exceeded by the chuckle with which he sat down breathless in his chair again, and chuckled till he cried.

Prior to this small moment at the end of Dickens's tale, the traditional bird for the well-provisioned Christmas table in England was the goose, and the impact of *A Christmas Carol* was said to have sent the nation's goose-raising industry to near ruin. By 1868 the authoritative voice of Isabella Beeton, in *Mrs. Beeton's Every Day Cookery and Housekeeping Book,* was assuring readers,

> A noble dish is a turkey, roast or boiled. A Christmas dinner, with the middle-class of this empire, would scarcely be a Christmas dinner without its turkey; and we can hardly imagine an object of greater envy than that presented by a respected portly paterfamilias carving, at the season devoted to good cheer and genial charity, his own fat turkey, and carving it well.

In the United States, wild turkeys were always abundant, and the creatures found their way, along with geese, to early American holiday tables. Today, however, geese are generally left alone, while some 270 million turkeys annually are raised and carried to market, about one-quarter of them during the month between Thanksgiving and Christmas. Perhaps in the tradition of a reborn Scrooge, the bounty of an American host is often expressed in terms of the height of his Christmas tree and by the size of the bird trundled home from the local market.

Many of the decorative elements and amusements mentioned in *A Christmas Carol* at the Fezziwig party and elsewhere were not so much Dickens's inventions as traditional elements given a fresh gloss by their appearance in such splendid literary surroundings: blazing fireplaces, mince pies and wassail bowls, carol-singing, plum puddings, holly sprigs, mistletoe, fiddling and dancing, blind-man bluffings, and the parlor game of forfeits had been seen in holiday festivities previously, but the effect of Dickens's tale was to make the incorporation of such elements seem obligatory for anyone's proper Christmas.

And for those tempted to blame Dickens for the contemporary excess of gift-giving, it is worth noting that for all its emphasis on the concept of charity, few gaily wrapped presents appear in *A Christmas Carol*. Aside from that fabulous turkey carried to the Cratchits' at story's close and a brief toys-for-tots moment during Scrooge's first spirit tour, the most valuable gifts exchanged between its characters are those of love and goodwill.

There are other customs associated with Dickens and the Victorian Christmas. The first commercially printed Christmas card, for instance, appeared in that same holiday season in which *A Christmas Carol* was published, the work of Sir Henry Cole and John C. Horsely. It was not unusual for the aristocracy of the period to include season's greetings in personal correspondence or on calling cards. Queen

Victoria sent a letter to Lord Melbourne in 1841, its paper "adorned with many quaint and humorous Christmas devices," and, gentleman that he was, Melbourne wrote back at once to offer, "most sincerely and most fervently, the good wishes of the Season."

But as to the Christmas card itself, the story is generally told that in 1843, Cole, a noted civil servant and industrial designer credited with the design of the first postage stamp, found himself strapped for time as the holidays approached. To speed the task of sending out all those personal greetings, then, he employed his friend, the artist J. C. Horsley, to produce 1,000 lithographed images on cardboard stock.

The card depicts a family of distinctly Fezziwiggian mien, raising a toast above a banner wishing "A Merry Christmas and a Happy New Year" to the card's recipients. And while the image of adults and children alike tossing back goblets of wine drew some criticism from the nation's temperance leaders, Horsley also added side panels that depicted the charitable acts of feeding and clothing the unfortunate—in all a most *Carol*-like diorama.

Sir Henry's idea caught on quickly in England, though it would take more than thirty years for the practice to find its way to the United States. In 1875 a Boston printer, Louis Prang, a native of Germany, began publishing such cards, earning for himself the sobriquet of "father of the American Christmas card." Prang found the going difficult, though— his elaborate creations proved too pricey for the American market, and by the early 1890s he was bankrupt, forced out of business by competitors hawking their wares for a penny apiece. From that point, the industry caught fire, and today it is estimated that more than one billion Christmas cards are sold each year in Britain and the United States.

It is likewise difficult to imagine a true Victorian Christmas without a Christmas tree, though no such object appears in either the text or the illustrations of *A Christmas Carol*. Certainly Dickens was fond of the icon, however. In 1850 he would write a sketch celebrating his childhood memories of such trees, a piece that became one of his most popular. Prince Albert may have increased the English affection for the German custom (where mythology equated the fir tree with the tree of life from the Gospels, and transformed it into a symbol for the birth of Christ) when he married Queen Victoria, but, as Dickens's sketch makes clear, the practice of putting up a Christmas tree was established well before that 1840 royal wedding. Court historians describe the work of Charlotte, wife of George III, in decorating and lighting evergreen trees as part of Christmas festivities during the 1780s and 1790s. And Victoria herself wrote of fond childhood memories of a season in 1833, including "trees hung with lights and sugar ornaments."

Like Dickens, both Victoria and Albert were great boosters of the season, and their practice of erecting a tree at Windsor Castle each year following their 1840 marriage greatly popularized the practice. In 1848 the *Illustrated London News* printed an engraving of the royal family gathered around a decorated tree beneath which lay a number of presents. The tree itself was described in breathless terms by the rival *Times*: "On each branch are arranged a dozen wax tapers. Pendant from the branches are elegant trays, baskets, and bonbonniers, and other placements for sweetmeats of the most varied kind, and all forms, colours, and degree of beauty." By the following year, the *News* and other publications were running features and seasonal supplements advising readers on such topics as tree decoration, gift-wrapping, Christmas party planning, and the proper placement of mistletoe, holly, and ivy.

Copies of the *News* engraving, retouched somewhat to remove the queen's offending tiara, were reprinted in U.S. publications, including *Godey's Lady Book* in 1850, but the practice of putting up a tree was not unknown in the New World. Though some say German troops brought the Christmas tree to the United States (Washington supposedly was able to cross the Delaware in 1776 because the Hessians were preoccupied with their Christmas celebrations), it is an undocumented claim. The first recorded appearance of the Christmas tree was made by a visitor to the Pennsylvania Dutch country near Lancaster, Pennsylvania, in the early 1800s, and the practice picked up following the 1838 publication of a travel pamphlet describing the quaint custom being practiced on the Pennsylvania frontier.

The first commercially available Christmas trees appeared in Philadelphia markets in 1848, and by the mid-nineteenth century, as Dickens's rhapsodic essay on the subject made its way across the Atlantic, trees were being cut by the mountainside in the Catskills and trucked to busy lots in Manhattan. In 1856 the first Christmas tree went up at the White House, though it would not be until 1923 that the practice of the annual lighting of the National Christmas Tree began. Today there is a National Christmas Tree Association in the United States, an organization that claims some 21,000 registered tree growers, who provide the majority of the 35 million or so sold each year.

Mention might be made of one final major Christmas icon, a figure that is generally attributed to the work of American author and Columbia University professor Clement Clark Moore. In 1822 Moore published his legendary poem "A Visit from St. Nicholas," also known as "The Night Before Christmas," which featured a character from Dutch legend whom Washington Irving had discussed at some length in his Knickerbocker sketches. Moore, however, transformed St. Nicholas from a somewhat foreboding figure of judgment who might show up at almost any time of year to deliver gifts to good boys and girls and a spirited caning to their less obedient counterparts, into a jolly old elf whose appearance was scheduled each year for the night before Christmas, in houses where none stirred, "not even a mouse." Over time, *Sinterklaas,* the Dutch contraction for Sint (Saint) Nicholas, became Anglicized as Santa Claus.

Over time, "Santa" morphed from the gaunt-looking dwarf Moore had found in his sources into the jovial, red-robed rotund elf popularized by *Harper's Magazine* illustrator Thomas Nast in the 1860s, and finally into the familiar bearded and overweight department-store Santa that we know today. This latter image is attributable to an illustration done by Haddon H. Sundbloom in 1931 for the Coca-Cola Company's seasonal promotion. While modern Santas and feeble, his spirit eroded by the indifference of a forgetful public and the antipathy of zealous Puritans. It is interesting to note how, in their respective Christmas tales, both Moore and Dickens transformed a traditional character with complex moral baggage (being equally quick with the cane and the candy) into their figures of unmistakable power and beneficence. Britons, in fact, were as eager to fold Santa Claus into their own mythos of the season as Americans were to welcome Scrooge and Cratchit and Tiny Tim into theirs. Father Christmas and Santa Claus have become virtually synonymous in contemporary England, and it is difficult to watch a modern dramatic presentation of *A Christmas Carol* on either side of the Atlantic without thinking of jolly Santa when Scrooge encounters his second Christmas ghost.

No individual can claim credit for the creation of Christmas, of course—except, perhaps, the figure that the day is named for. But Charles Dickens, given his immense and lasting influence and his association with all things Victorian, played a major role in transforming a celebration dating back to pre-Christian times, revitalizing forgotten customs and introducing new ones that now define the holiday. Peter Ackroyd and other modern commentators have credited Dickens with having singlehandedly created the modern idea of Christmas, and if that is a grand claim, it is grounded in the facts. If Dickens did not invent Christmas, he certainly reinvented it.

Considered against the backdrop of an era when the British Empire expanded to its zenith and when advancement in science and industry suggested that Western man was truly the master of his own fate, the themes of *A Christmas Carol*, the real reasons for its vast appeal and influence, seem evident: with the support of a tight-knit family, with education and charity and the expenditure of goodwill from one to all—with time out for celebration not neglected—such problems as Ignorance and Want could be banished from the world.

Such notions could not only be applauded in an era that Dickens saw opening before him, but they could also be believed. And it is testament to the power of his vision that even to this day, when audiences experience his little Carol—his "sledge-hammer"—they dare to share in his dream.

Part Four

LANG SYNE

16.

The Dickens scholar Paul Davis points out that *A Christmas Carol* inverts the traditional folktale process. Instead of beginning as an oral story that is finally written down and formalized, Dickens's story has worked the other way. His story entered the world as a fully formed "perfect" work, says Davis, and in the century and a half since its arrival, its original self has exploded like a sun into a supernova. Its hundreds and thousands of adaptations and productions—all those retellings and "re-originations"—have transformed a work of literature into part of the DNA of Western culture. "Disguised as Lionel Barrymore or Mister Magoo," Davis says, "Scrooge has become common cultural property and is as deeply embedded in our consciousness as George Washington or Dick Whittington, Merlin or Moses."

It is probably the secret dream of many writers to produce a work with such enduring power, and it is one of the several conundrums of the writing life that one can never live to see how it all turns out. Dickens knew that he had produced something very good when he wrote *A Christmas Carol,* but he had no way of knowing it would become his most-loved book. In early November of 1844, he wrote to

Mitton from Genoa certain that he could surpass what he had achieved with *A Christmas Carol.*

He was already hard at work on a new holiday book for Bradbury and Evans, he explained. "The cause of my not having written to you, is too obvious to need any explanation. I have worn myself to Death, in the Month I have been at Work." He told his solicitor that he had not been able "to divest myself of the story—have suffered very much in my sleep, in consequence—and am so shaken by such work in this trying climate that I am nervous as a man who is dying of Drink: and as haggard as a Murderer."

To Forster he wrote of waking up for a cold bath at seven, and after a bit of breakfast, would "blaze away, wrathful and red-hot, until three o'clock or so." He was "fierce to finish," Dickens told his friend, "and to shame the cruel and the canting," referring to readers who would profit by its lessons. When he finally finished, a few weeks later, he wrote joyously to Mitton: "I believe I have written a tremendous Book; and knocked the Carol out of the field. It will make a great uproar, I have no doubt."

Though the contemporary reader probably will not recognize *The Chimes* as having achieved that goal, the follow-up volume to *A Christmas Carol* was not exactly a disappointment in Dickens's own time. The book appeared on December 16, 1844, and—because they were distributing the books for Bradbury and Evans—the title page listed Chapman and Hall as publishers. The book carried the subtitle *A Goblin Story of Some Bells that Rang an Old Year*

Out and a New Year In, and included illustrations by Leech as well as by Richard Doyle, scenarist Clarkson Stanfield, and Dickens's close friend Daniel Maclise (whose 1839 oil of Dickens hangs today at the National Portrait Gallery).

The book tells the story of a porter named Toby ("Trotty") Veck, who has come more and more to feel that his laborer's life is inconsequential and meaningless—even the arrival of his daughter Meg on New Year's Eve, announcing that she and her longtime fiancé Richard will be married on the next day, fails to rouse Trotty from his gloom. Later that night he wanders to the steps of the nearby church, and is drawn up the steps of the bell tower by an uncanny premonition. In the tower, he encounters the goblins who are the embodied spirits of the bells, creatures who promptly tell him that he has actually fallen from the tower to his death.

The spirits then carry him through a series of ever more dour visions of the future, culminating in a scene in which his daughter Meg, despairing over the ruin of her marriage to a now-alcoholic Richard, is about to drown herself and her child. Trotty had been certain that the poor and unfortunate were doomed by their own natures to their sad fates, but now realizes that what has happened to Meg and Richard is the result of the avarice and oppression of others, and not any inborn mark of weakness. All men and women have the capacity to succeed. As a distraught Trotty confesses to the goblins the error of his thinking and proclaims the innate virtue of all mankind, the vision ends. When he wakes, Trotty finds himself in his bed on New Year's morning, and, as a result of his encounter with the goblins, resolves to make merry at the wedding of his daughter later that day.

Dickens, who had written Forster from Genoa on October 6 to complain that he could not get himself going on the new Christmas book, owing in part to the infernal, never-ending clanging of church bells in the city, wrote only two days later to announce that he had found his title and the "machinery" of his novel at last. "I am in regular, ferocious excitement with the *Chimes*," he told Forster, and proclaimed that he saw "in this little book, a great blow for the poor . . . and if my design be anything at all, it has a grip upon the very throat of time."

He finished the book on November 3, and following his last dot, as he told Forster, had "a real good cry!" He traveled to London in early December to oversee the correction of page proofs and to read the story to groups of friends, including the actor and producer William Charles Macready who—according to the author, at least—burst into tears during Dickens's performance.

There was a stage play mounted at the Adelphi Theatre concurrent with the book's publication on December 16, and most of the first edition of 20,000 copies flew immediately off the shelves. Though it was handsomely packaged, with a gold-stamped red cover, Dickens and his new publishers took a lesson from the Carol and omitted the hand coloring and colored type. As a result, Dickens earned even a bit more than the quick £1,000 he had hoped for on *A Christmas Carol*: £1,065 8s. 2d., to be exact. But there were signs from the beginning that *The Chimes* would not long keep its grip on time's throat. The critical response was decidedly mixed, and the general audience—though drawn to buy the book on the strength of his first holiday tale—found the story far grimmer and more downbeat than its holiday predecessor. An urchin on crutches was one thing, but a mother about to drown herself and her baby?

There were other miscalculations as well: the nondescript goblins of *The Chimes* are far less singular and evocative than the memorably distinct quartet of ghosts who haunt Scrooge's chambers; and Trotty himself is not nearly as swept up by his amazing adventures as was his predecessor. His inclination is to stand at some remove from what is going on around him, and it sometimes seems as if it is the author himself instructing readers on just what to make of it all.

Perhaps most significant, however, was the decision to leave Christmas out of the proceedings. Dickens understandably wanted to achieve the same emotional effect in his audiences without appearing to produce an outright copy of his first holiday tale, but proud as he was to have found the "machinery" of *The Chimes*, he did not take into account the effect of cutting himself off from some two thousand years of mythic power and buried emotion by leaving Christmas behind. In contrast to Christmas, even a Christmas dimmed by the fervor of the Puritans and the need of factory owners to keep their furnaces blazing, the New Year's holiday was a pale afterthought.

Though he remained wedded to the concept of producing an annual Christmas book, the fall of 1845 found Dickens moved back to London, and, along with Bradbury and Evans, mired in preparations for the launch of a new morning newspaper, the *Daily News*. Dickens, lured by the thought of heading up a major liberal-voiced competitor to the *Times*, the *Morning Chronicle*, and the *Morning Post*, and by the prospect of the unlimited backing promised by a group of railway executives who partnered with Bradbury and Evans on the venture, accepted the editorship of the paper, and promised regular contributions to it.

Still, Dickens found time to write a third Christmas book, though this one, *The Cricket on the Hearth*, has nothing overtly to do with the season at all. It is the story of how a young laborer overcomes his irrational suspicions of his lovely young wife, whom he one day spots talking to a mysterious stranger. The eponymous cricket is the agency by which our good man learns the error of his ways, but that bit of surrealism is about all that links the book to its illustrious Christmas predecessor. Still, it reflected what Dickens called "Carol philosophy" in its "jolly good temper" and "vein of glowing hearty, generous, mirthful beaming reference in everything to Home and Fireside."

As with *The Chimes*, the fact that any reference to Christmas was lacking altogether in the story did not prevent its commercial success. A staged version of *Cricket* opened at the Lyceum Theatre on December 20, 1845, simultaneously with the book's publication, and ran for sixty performances. By January, seventeen productions of the story had been mounted in London, and sales of the book's two editions had earned its author £1,022. For the remainder of Dickens's life—and of the nineteenth century, for that matter—the story was adapted far more regularly than was *A Christmas Carol,* and in fact Dickens himself devised a version that he read in public on a number of occasions in the 1850s.

In 1846, while living in Switzerland and finally back to work on an extended fiction in the form of *Dombey and Son,* Dickens forced himself into the writing of a fourth holiday book, *The Battle of Life,* lamenting to Forster that his soul sank at times when he stepped back to consider what was going on in this tale. Once again, Christmas made no appearance in the story—that of a young woman who sacrifices her true love to her sister and cures their father of his cynical attitude in the process. Dickens complained of the strictures of the shortened form, the absence of any supernatural "machinery," and the guilt of spending time away from *Dombey.* He warned his friend as early as September that there might not in fact be a Christmas book in 1846, and when he finished, he admitted to Forster, "I really do not know what this story is worth."

Some of the critics were happy to opine on the matter: "Exaggerated, absurd, impossible sentimentality," is what the *Morning Chronicle* had to say of his efforts in *The Battle of Life,* and the fact that most of the other reviews were equally hostile puts to rest any notion that the *Chronicle*'s editors might have been influenced by Dickens's fling at competition with them. (Overwhelmed by the demands of editing a daily paper, Dickens had resigned his post less than three weeks after the *Daily News* began publication.) Still, *The Battle of Life* sold 23,000 copies on the day of its publication, and though there were but few dramatizations, Dickens did receive £100 for a production staged at the Lyceum by his actor friend Robert Keely (who had also produced versions of *The Chimes* and *The Cricket on the Hearth*).

His preoccupation with *Dombey and Son*, which was selling at as many as 35,000 copies per installment (issues of Thackeray's *Vanity Fair* were selling about 5,000 copies at the same time), kept Dickens from writing a Christmas book in 1847. But, "loath to lose the money," as he put it to Forster, he began work on his fifth and final Christmas book in October of 1848. After a month spent primarily, as he described it, "frowning horribly at a quire of paper," he wrote Miss Burdett Coutts that the logjam had finally broken. "I have hit upon a little notion . . . with a good Christmas tendency," he told his old friend, and finished *The Haunted Man* on November 30, in Brighton, and after "crying my eyes out over it."

The story is that of Redlaw, a depressive academic who has sunk into despair over the contemplation of his many past losses and betrayals, including memories of a miserable childhood. On Christmas Eve, Redlaw receives a visit from a spirit, who not only grants him relief from all his painful memories but also endows Redlaw with the power to do the same for others in turn. The gift proves to be a curse, however, for Redlaw comes to understand that without the memory of painful experiences, human beings have no way to judge what pleasure is by contrast.

When he begs for release, the spirit is indifferent and decrees that he will first have to meet with Milly, wife of the college's lodging house master. Milly, the kindest person

Redlaw knows, proves more than capable of resisting his evil powers, and the encounter transforms Redlaw back into a fully balanced human, capable of gratitude and compassion.

While some modern commentators have praised the psychological accuracy and artistry (and the absence of melodramatic contrivance that marked the middle Christmas books), the darkness and complexity of the tale—with its focus on the inner world and not the outer—was hardly the stuff to set the likes of Mr. Fezziwig and Pickwick and their families into a holiday jig. Dickens wrote bravely to a friend that *The Haunted Man* had sold 18,000 copies upon its December 19 debut, but that number was down nearly a quarter from the sales of *The Battle of Life*. In fact, there were still unsold copies of *The Haunted Man* warehoused at the time of Dickens's death, more than twenty years later.

Dickens never commented on why he never wrote another Christmas book, but there is evidence for speculation. Since he had taken the year off to stay focused on *Dombey* in 1847, and spoke of the "grind" of trying to get moving on *The Haunted Man* in 1848, it is possible that he had simply exhausted himself on the subject and realized that it was more practical to stay focused on the longer works. The sales of the first four installments of *Dombey* were enough to bring him finally out of debt, and, as Forster says, "all embarrassments connected with money" were put to rest.

But there might have been a more provocative reason as well. By the fall of 1849, he was well along on *The Personal History of David Copperfield,* the first number of which had appeared on May 1 of that year, and he would continue publishing installments of that novel until November of 1850. In the story of a young man who survives a miserable and abusive childhood to become a parliamentary reporter and then a novelist, Dickens is clearly making use of autobiographical elements.

In addition, it was just prior to beginning the writing of Copperfield, that most commentators believe that Dickens made an attempt to deal directly with the traumatic events of his own childhood, laying them out in that "autobiographical fragment," which he shared only with Forster. And, in both *The Haunted Man* and *David Copperfield,* we see a preoccupation with the power of childhood unhappiness upon adult life; the glimpse of a young Ebenezer, abandoned at his boarding school, is one of the many touches that transform the miser from stereotype to sympathetic figure, and which in turn gives *A Christmas Carol* such power.

Thus, the common notion that Dickens may have exhausted himself on the subject of Christmas might be replaced by the speculation that beginning with *A Christmas Carol* and culminating in *David Copperfield,* Dickens had finally dragged up the powerful demons of his past and wrestled them away, to the extent that successful literature allows, at least. If that is true, then the engine that had driven him down this path in the first place was at last stilled.

In any case, while sales of its installments dropped down to 20,000 or so, the critical response of his peers to *David Copperfield* was universally positive, and to this day, some find it the very best of all his works. Dickens himself proclaimed the book to be "a very complicated interweaving of truth and fiction," and was happily consumed by the writing of it. As Forster put it, "Once fairly in it, the story bore him irresistibly along . . . and he was probably never less harassed by interruptions or breaks in his invention."

Whatever the reasons, Dickens would go to his grave calling *David Copperfield* his own "favorite child." In his preface to the 1867 edition, he said, "Of all my books, I like this the best."

At the same time that he was consumed with *David Copperfield*, Dickens was also involved in another significant undertaking, one that would in its own way lead him back to Christmas. In late March of 1850, he had begun—in partnership with Bradbury and Evans, who took a quarter-share, and Forster, who held an eighth—the publication of a weekly magazine called *Household Words*. A collection of journalism, sketches, poetry, and short stories, the publication, with Dickens as its editor, would continue until he died.

Priced at tuppence, and with an editorial by Dickens in every issue and contributions from himself and his friends—the leading literati of the day—the magazine, which was aimed at what might be described as *The New Yorker* audience of its day, became a resounding success. The first issue sold 100,000 copies, and though those were not the numbers of a penny rag for the masses, which could reach as high as 300,000, Dickens and his partners were quite happy. *Household Words* settled in at around 40,000 thereafter, and the magazine would provide Dickens with a stable income (he received a yearly salary of £500 as well as his half-share in the profits) and a satisfying ancillary focus for the rest of his life and career.

But if the editorship of the magazine, combined with the race to finish *David Copperfield* in November, made the writing of a Christmas book practically impossible, his new undertaking also allowed Dickens to do the next best thing. If he could not publish a Christmas book, at the very least he could bring out a holiday-themed issue of his new magazine, and he would of course contribute something to it.

The first Christmas issue of *Household Words* was published on December 21, 1850, and among the nine pieces included was Dickens's masterwork of nonfiction, "A Christmas Tree." In this blend of essay and reminiscence and pure paean to life, Dickens sets down the great depth of his feeling for the season directly and without pretense. He manages, without a false note and in essay form, to convey the same blend of childhood wonder, fantasy, humor, celebration, and solemnity that distinguishes *A Christmas Carol* in narrative form.

Dickens closes his piece with a reminder of the tree as the centerpiece of the season's celebratory nature: "Now, the tree is decorated with bright merriment, and song, and dance, and cheerfulness. And they are welcome. Innocent and welcome be they ever held, beneath the branches of the Christmas Tree, which cast no gloomy shadow!"

And while he might have left it there, with a reminder of good cheer and goodwill and fellowship that marked the season so indelibly for him, he adds a postscript—"But, as it sinks into the ground, I hear a whisper going through the leaves. 'This, in commemoration of the law of love and kindness, mercy and compassion. This, in remembrance of Me!'"—and in this reference to the words of Jesus and the Eucharist, he ties together the holy reason for the celebration and the act of celebration itself. Though the clergy of the Anglican Church might be troubled by the concept of a Christmas tree as sacrament, for Dickens it was the perfect union of the cloister and the hearth.

17.

Even if it is true that, from the inception of *A Christmas Carol* through the completion of *David Copperfield,* Dickens was unconsciously wrestling with the demons from his childhood, and even if the publication of "A Christmas Tree" in 1850 was the final punctuation mark in that process, there was much to come from Dickens, both in life and art, and also as regards his beloved holiday.

Sales of the 1850 Christmas issue of *Household Words* soared to 80,000, and subsequent holiday numbers of the magazine published through 1858 would hold steady at that number. And such halcyon days might have continued for the magazine, save for the fact that in that year, Dickens separated from his wife, Catherine, with whom he had raised ten children and from whom he had grown increasingly estranged over the decade. The dissolution of this marriage of twenty-two years became so acrimonious that, in an attempt to discredit rumors floated by the Hogarth family that he was having an illicit affair, Dickens used the front page of *Household Words* to print a statement protesting his innocence.

The action might seem mind-boggling enough—imagine Benjamin Bradlee taking over the front page of the *Washington Post* to explain some delicate matter from his personal life—but Dickens compounded the awkward situation by asking Bradbury and Evans to reprint his statement in *Punch,* which they had published since its inception. When Bradbury and Evans suggested that this was perhaps not the sort of thing to be published in a magazine of social commentary and satire, Dickens exploded and tried to force the publishers from their quarter-share of *Household Words.*

When Bradbury and Evans went to court, claiming exclusive rights to the title of the magazine, Dickens countered by simply dissolving *Household Words* and announcing the formation of a successor, *All the Year Round.* As if to prove the adage that there is no such thing as bad publicity, sales of the new magazine soared immediately above 100,000 copies; for the holiday numbers, sales rose to 300,000 and more, though it would not sustain those rates forever.

The 1850s were in fact an up-and-down period for Dickens. He followed *David Copperfield* with *Bleak House* (1852–53), an ambitious novel that received mixed reviews in its day (Forster faulted it for its didactic approach toward social institutions, including the chancery courts), but which modern critics have hailed as his masterpiece. Despite its rather downbeat story line and the disdain of many contemporary critics, *Bleak House* nonetheless proved popular, with its sales averaging 34,000 per issue, well up from those for *David Copperfield.* As a result, Dickens realized a profit of more than £11,000, sending him into previously uncharted financial realms for a writer. Robert C. Patten, a biographer who has meticulously tallied the economics of Dickens's career, says that *Bleak House* made the author "the literary Croesus" of his time.

In 1854 Dickens began the serial publication of *Hard Times* as part of a strategy to boost the suddenly sagging sales of *Household Words*. It was the first time Dickens had published a novel in weekly rather than monthly installments since the days of *Barnaby Rudge*, and while he lamented the tight deadlines and strictures of space, the strategy worked insofar as *Household Words* was concerned. Published in twenty weekly installments between April 1 and August 12 of 1854, the novel raised the net profits of the magazine by 237 percent. Critics of the day found the book all but impossible to read, however, and indeed the characters in the book are little more than ciphers for Dickens's scathing commentary on an industrialized society. By this time the author was in his forties, and as *Hard Times* seemed to make clear, something of his youthful optimism had burned away, and his hopeful stance replaced by a decidedly critical one.

In late 1855 Dickens began the monthly publication of *Little Dorrit,* his eleventh novel, under the terms of a new contract with Bradbury and Evans. The eight-year term of their original agreement having expired, Dickens negotiated a new contract that reduced the publishers' share of profits slightly and gave Dickens the opportunity to walk away whenever he chose. Though once again the critics found the rise of the Dorrit family from abject poverty to wealth overly didactic, with the sixth installment featuring the family's incarceration in the Marshalsea debtors' prison, monthly sales of the book rose as high as 40,000 copies per month. "It is a brilliant triumph," Dickens proclaimed to his publishers, and in the preface to the collected edition he wrote, "I have never had so many readers."

Nor had he ever had so many admirers, it would seem. In the fallow period that followed the completion of *Little Dorrit* in June of 1857, Dickens busied himself with the production of several benefit performances of a play by his friend Wilkie Collins, *The Frozen Deep,* to aid the family of a writer friend, Douglas Jerrold, who had died unexpectedly. Dickens himself took the part of a noble Arctic explorer who dies while attempting to save the life of a rival. Several preliminary presentations, including a command performance before the queen, had produced the lachrymose effects on the audience that always signaled success to Dickens. But when they were booked into the vast new Free Trade Hall in Manchester, he realized that his troupe of amateurs would need to be bolstered by professionals who could project to the far reaches of the theater.

Thus began, with the hiring of the Ternan family, including mother Frances and her three comely daughters, Fanny, Maria, and Ellen, the last momentous chapter of Dickens's life. The final scene of the play, in which the lovely Maria Ternan dissolved into unscripted tears as she held the dying Dickens in her arms, "electrified" the audience in Manchester, according to one critic. And while the reviewer did not note the sparks that also flew between youngest sister Ellen Ternan and Mr. Dickens during the performance—or the coincidence that his life was once again taking a momentous turn upon a Manchester stage—

talk of Dickens and "Nelly" Ternan was soon the gossip of London literary society.

The story of the affair between Dickens and Miss Ternan is a difficult one to trace, owing largely to the fact that the author, who until that moment had lived his life in full public view, began thereafter an abrupt turnabout, one of the most marked in the history of celebrity. Formerly, Dickens's personal and private lives had been virtually indistinguishable, and his conduct the very emblem of the Fezziwigian hail-fellow-well-met, more-the-merrier way of life. But after his introduction to Miss Ternan, and his subsequent divorce from Catherine, Dickens simply slammed the door on his private life, a fact that has given modern biographers no end of grief.

The story has its sad and tawdry aspect and is perhaps a bit familiar to the jaded modern reader: noted celebrity fathers several children to devoted wife, and then, finding her turned unaccountably bovine and dull, runs off with a beautiful wisp of an actress less than half his age (Ellen Ternan was all of eighteen when they met, he forty-five). One surmises, however, that from Dickens's point of view—and at his age—it may have seemed that he had miraculously been given a second chance at the sort of rapture he was denied in his youth, when Maria Beadnell rejected him for better prospects.

He had previously written on this subject to Forster, lamenting in 1855 that passion was the "one happiness" he had missed out on in life. In a twist of fate that might be termed Dickensian, a few weeks after he had written to Forster, he received a letter from the former Miss Beadnell, who wanted to let him know that she had been following his career these many years, and was quite proud of what he had accomplished.

She also told Dickens that she was married, of course, and that she was also "toothless, fat, old and ugly." Such caveats seemed like a coquette's protests to Dickens, however, and he persisted in his entreaties until Miss Beadnell, now Mrs. Winter, agreed to bring her husband (a sawmill manager) along to lunch, provided Dickens would escort his wife as well.

At that meeting, it turned out that Mrs. Winter was as accurate as a Victorian novelist in her self-description, and Dickens walked away from the encounter perfectly dazed by the loss of the dream he had borne within him for more than twenty years. No fairy-tale prince who'd dragged himself up a hundred feet of princess hair only to find a hag's face beaming at him could have been more disheartened.

In any case, the fact that the image of the ineffable Miss Beadnell had vanished forever did not relieve Dickens of his sense that he had made a terrible mistake a long time ago. In September 1857, Dickens would write to Forster, "Poor Catherine and I are not made for each other, and there is no help for it. . . . She is exactly what you know, in the way of being amiable and complying; but we are strangely ill-assorted for the bond that lays between us." Soon thereafter, Dickens moved his bed into his dressing room and hired a carpenter to close the door that connected it to Catherine's chambers with a set of shelves.

Whether or not Dickens and Ellen Ternan ever became lovers is a topic that fuels entire volumes to this day, but—beyond such circumstantial evidence as receipts for jewelry and other gifts sent by him to her, and occasional public sightings of the two together, and the fact that Dickens left Ternan £1,000 in his will—inquiring minds must eternally wait in their quest to know. It can be stated, however, that in the year following his meeting Ellen Ternan, Dickens did leave Catherine, and provide his ex-wife with a home and a yearly stipend of £600, and with access to their children as she chose.

Following his divorce, and the break with Bradbury and Evans, and the reconfiguring of his magazine into *All the Year Round,* Dickens entered into a new relationship with his old publishers Chapman and Hall (perhaps encouraged by the fact that Edward Chapman—one of the original partners who had considered docking Dickens £50 from his monthly draw—had been bought out by his cousin Frederic). The first undertaking in his new business was the weekly serialization of *A Tale of Two Cities* in *All the Year Round,* beginning in April of 1859, followed by its publication in volume form by Chapman and Hall in December. Weekly sales of the rather humorless saga, set against the backdrop of the French Revolution, exceeded 100,000 copies for many issues, but critical opinion of Dickens's strength as a historical novelist was divided, then as now. It remains one of Dickens's most popular works, even if one wonders whether its brevity and the resultant assignment to schoolchildren has something to do with that. If it has no other distinction, its immortal first line, "It was the best of times, it was the worst of times," likely rivals Bulwer-Lytton's "dark and stormy night" as the best known in the language.

Dickens published *Great Expectations,* his thirteenth novel, in weekly installments of *All the Year Round* from December 1860 to August 1861; these also appeared more or less simultaneously in *Harper's Weekly* in the United States, from whom the author—much to his satisfaction—had managed to negotiate a £1,000 licensing fee. The complicated story of Pip's encounters with Miss Havisham and his rise from urchin to successful businessman constitutes perhaps the best-rounded of Dickens's works in its combination of narrative sweep, juggling of plot, complex characterization, and social commentary. Certainly it was popular in its day, selling above 100,000 copies of each number. The book also spawned what is arguably the most accomplished film version of Dickens to date, the 1946 adaptation directed by David Lean, starring John Mills, Alec Guinness, and Jean Simmons. Of that adaptation, James Agee said it was "almost never less than graceful, tasteful and intelligent, and some of it better than that."

Dickens's last completed novel, *Our Mutual Friend,* was written between May 1864 and November 1865, and though the composition of it exasperated him, Dickens ultimately wove its materials—the chase of a fortune by a complexly intertwined group of Londoners—into what is often called his most expertly plotted work. Though sales for the first installment surpassed 30,000, the numbers had dropped to just under 20,000 by the end of its run, but Dickens was not particularly daunted. He had his work on the magazine to distract him, and there is little doubt that he continued a quite active relationship with Ellen Ternan as well.

Over the ten years prior to the publication of *Our Mutual Friend,* Dickens had also devoted more and more time to the avocation of public reading, an activity that led him back to his "little Carol." In 1854, as he took a rest from his labors on *Hard Times,* Dickens agreed to make a benefit appearance in Birmingham on behalf of the cause of the education of workingmen, not unlike that appearance he had agreed to in Manchester so many years before. As he pondered just what to do with his time on stage, it occurred to Dickens that—it being December—he might as well read from *A Christmas Carol.* He had practiced such a thing on his friends plenty of times in the past, after all, and if he could bring a sophisticated group such as that to tears, why not take his act to provincial Birmingham?

It proved to be an inspired decision. Dickens read three nights in Birmingham, and on the last evening more than 2,000 paid their sixpence to hear and be blessed by Tiny Tim, every one. Dickens, who had never lost his love of the theater, relished every moment of it, and in 1855 he read *A Christmas Carol* at charitable events in London, Reading, Sherboune, and Bradford, where 3,700 turned out. As the author Jane Smiley notes in her brief biography of Dickens, the intoxicating effect of eliciting tears while acting in a play and reciting the words of another is one thing, but to see some 4,000 people bursting simultaneously into sobs as you read your own words to them is something else again. And as he discovered, there was no shortage of persons willing to pay good money for the experience.

It was not long, then, before Dickens had begun to give public readings on a regular and commercial basis, a practice he would continue—at considerable gain—until his death. During the winter of 1867–68, in fact, he undertook a triumphant return tour of the United States, where he read in seventy-six cities, to audiences eventually totaling more than 100,000 (including Mark Twain, who wrote of taking his wife-to-be on a first date to hear Dickens perform), and earned himself £19,000 in the process.

Though he enjoyed public reading immensely and had allowed the practice to distract him from writing following the publication of *Our Mutual Friend,* Dickens was also getting along in years, and his health—he was plagued now by gout and high blood pressure—had generally begun to fail. The demands of touring and performing exhausted him, and often even ordinary colds would lay him up for days. In April of 1869, following another serious bout of illness, his doctors ordered him to put an end to the readings to which he gave himself so eagerly, but which taxed him in equal measure.

Somewhat reluctantly, he turned away from those dramatic renditions of the murder scene in *Oliver Twist* and the intonations of Marley frightening Scrooge near to death, and back to the lonely work of writing at his desk. He struggled along through the late months of 1869 at what he had settled on as *The Mystery of Edwin Drood,* then took time off—against the vehement opposition of his doctors—for a series of a dozen readings from January to mid-March of 1870.

Then back to the desk he went, and by June 8—and though one suspects he would have rather been playacting at Sykes slaying Nancy—he managed to complete the sixth installment of his new tale-in-progress. *The Mystery of Edwin Drood* was conceived as a murder mystery inspired by the works of his friend Wilkie Collins, concerning the exploits of one John Jasper, pious choirmaster of Cloisterham Cathedral, who wakes up one morning to find himself, unaccountably, in a London opium den.

The generally accepted account of what happened next says that on that evening of June 8, during dinner, Dickens began to complain that he felt out of sorts. Quickly his speech began to slur, then turned to gibberish, and his frantic housekeeper rushed to help him to the floor.

As became clear, he was suffering a massive stroke, and was soon unconscious. Doctors were summoned and Ellen Ternan was called, but it was all to no avail. By the following morning, Charles Dickens was dead at the age of fifty-eight.

It might be said, however, that there is an alternative version to the story of Dickens's last hours. In it, Dickens finishes his day's work on *Edwin Drood* and takes a carriage to Peckham, where Ellen Ternan lives. It is at Ellen Ternan's home that Dickens falls ill, and it is she who cradles him to the floor, much as her sister did on a stage in Manchester nearly fourteen years before.

And there is in fact some evidence for this scenario, as impossibly pat as it might seem. A Ternan family caretaker has sworn that—to avoid the scandal that Dickens had spent years steadfastly avoiding—he carried the unconscious

Dickens from the Ternan house and bore him back to Gad's Hill, where Dickens lived at the time. Adding some credence to this account is also the fact that Dickens cashed a check for a considerable sum earlier on the day that he collapsed, yet he was found with almost nothing in his pockets when he died. Since his housekeeper had to seek funds for necessities from his attorneys in the wake of Dickens's passing, it is certain that the money was not given to her.

All is speculation, of course, but there seems little doubt which version of his passing that Dickens, as a novelist, would have favored. Students of history will simply have to choose for themselves.

18.

No one was more intensely fond than Dickens of old nursery tales," his friend Forster would write, "and he had a secret delight in feeling that he was here only giving them a higher form. The social and manly virtues he desired to teach were to him not less the charm of the ghost, the goblin, and the fairy fancies of his childhood."

This description of the nature and the intent of Dickens's efforts explains as well their enduring charm. The Naturalists who would follow in Dickens's footsteps—Crane, Dreiser, the later Twain—came to sneer at his hopefulness. The thought that a real-life Scrooge could be changed by four ghosts or a thousand—were there such things as "ghosts"—was balderdash. And as for the Deconstructionists who came along in the later part of the next century, any meaning to be found in such a fable as *A Christmas Carol* was as relative to the reader, and as illusory, as the messages in tea leaves.

Yet, despite such cynicism, Dickens and his oeuvre persist. Doubt shadows the contemporary psyche, to be sure, but it might be pointed out that there are few living nihilists. And, for the most part, the only place where readers consume fictions that do not stir their emotions is in a high school or college classroom.

In an elegy, Theodore Watts-Dunton, English poet and

critic and a contemporary of the generation of writers following Dickens, illustrates the profound impact of the great
writer on his times. In an epigraph to his poem, Watts-
Dunton relates the story of a Cockney produce vendor who
had just been given the news of Dickens's passing: "Dickens
dead?" the young woman cried. "Then will Father Christmas die too?"

She needn't have worried, of course, for the holiday
has only burgeoned in the wake of Dickens's passing. Next
Christmas, Anytown Elementary and thousands of its counterparts, great and small, will stage their "re-originations" of
A Christmas Carol, and perhaps the new Hollywood version
and the one after that will have been completed too.

Millions of ordinary people continue to experience
Scrooge's impossible transformation in one form or
another. Some of them will learn of the story of the industrialist who heard Dickens deliver one of his public readings
and ran out of the hall on the spot to purchase turkeys for all
his employees for Christmas. Odd, a few might think, I got a
turkey from my boss just today.

Such tales abound of Dickens's power to suggest and
to prod to action. Another factory owner was said to pro-
claim—in the wake of a Dickens reading—that Christmas
would ever after be a holiday in his shop. Today, the Grinch
who volunteers to work on Christmas will often enjoy double and triple time for his trouble.

In 1874 Robert Louis Stevenson would write of his great

affection for Dickens and his Christmas books: "I feel so good after them and would do anything, yes, and shall do anything, to make it a little better for people." Some modern critics have faulted books that arouse these positive but aimless impulses in readers—the very desire to be charitable makes one feel good about oneself, the argument goes, and once one feels good, the need to do anything more is dispensed with. And it is true that the world awaits the publication of the study that will prove any direct correlation between the number of times experiencing *A Christmas Carol* and annual household giving.

Still—for all the melodrama and the unlikely plot development, and for the impossible notions of goodwill toward men that seem so quaint in an era of mushroom clouds and airport screenings—on any given December 25, when we gather with our families, rich or poor, in homes huge or humble, in an excess of big-ticket gift-giving or a modest homemade something, with a prize-winning turkey on a groaning table or the best we can manage under the circumstances, there is no gainsaying those words of Nephew Fred to his uncle Scrooge as to the nature of Christmastime: "the only time . . . in the long calendar of the year, when men and women seem by one consent to open their shut-up hearts."

The house on Devonshire Terrace where Dickens wrote those words is gone, as is the blacking house where he tied tops to tiny pots of boot polish. Dickens too is long gone. But still with us, as the turn of every season proves, is the immutable, eternal story.

Eliminate ignorance, Dickens dreamed in his *Carol*.

Eliminate want. A tall order then, and a tall order now. But one does not need to be a social scientist to know that he identifies the true sources of misery in this world. And it is a mark of Dickens's genius that we return eagerly to his hopeful vision—millions of us now—year after year. And vow to do the best we can.

NOTES

Many before me have been compelled to write of Dickens, of the Christmas season, and of *A Christmas Carol* in particular. My intent in writing this book has not been to catalog, analyze, or chronicle a life—but rather to weave some rather familiar, if sometimes disparate, elements into a narrative that might enliven the historical facts attendant to it.

And though I have made use of the same research techniques here that I have employed for many years in academic pursuits, I intend this volume to be a fireside pleasure of the Fezziwigian type, and not a formal work of scholarship. Thus, I have set aside the typical convention of footnotes.

Where I have included information that seemed to me the unique contribution of an individual, I have endeavored to give the credit due, either in the text or in the notes that follow.

For the reader who may be interested in tracing an inquiry along some line I have opened in this book, I am hopeful that these notes and the list of sources that were of great interest and help to me as I wrote will be of value to the reader in turn.

Nativity

The particulars of young Dickens's time at Warren's blacking factory have been reported and analyzed by many commentators. But the essential details in this re-creation of his experience are drawn from the autobiographical fragment composed by Dickens sometime in the 1840s—prior to the writing of *David*

Copperfield, according to the author—later shared with Forster and first published in the latter's intimate and informative biography, *The Life of Charles Dickens,* four years after the author's death.

One of those to rank Dickens's tale at the penultimate position of readership is J. H. McNulty, writing nearly a century after the book's publication. In "Our Carol" (*The Dickensian* 34: 15–19) McNulty describes *A Christmas Carol* as "the one perfect short story Dickens wrote," and goes on to add—as Macaulay said of Boswell—"Eclipse is first and the rest nowhere."

1.

The career-context of Dickens's invitation to Manchester is discussed by Forster in Book 4 of *The Life,* "The First Year of Martin Chuzzlewit."

The general course of Dickens's career comes from Forster, Peter Ackroyd's *Dickens,* and the invaluable twelve-volume Pilgrim Edition of *The Letters of Charles Dickens,* edited by House and Storey (Oxford, 1965–2002). A quick and authoritative tour is available in Paul Schlicke's encyclopedic *Oxford Reader's Companion* (1999).

Sales figures for Dickens's work cited throughout this volume are drawn from Robert C. Patten's exhaustive study of the subject, *Charles Dickens and His Publishers.*

For more on Wellerisms, see George B. Bryan and Wolfgang Mieder, "As Sam Weller Said, When Finding Himself on the Stage," *De Proverbio* 3, no. 1 (1997).

An interesting history of British publishing in general, including the transformation attendant to the rise of the novel in the eighteenth and nineteenth centuries, with Dickens's part in the latter, may be found in John Feather's *A History of British Publishing* (New York: Routledge, 1991).

2.

Walter C. Phillips describes the Victorian era as witnessing a complete remaking of the trade in printed matter and the transformation of the earning power of popular writers. "No single figure was more influential in this revolution than Dickens," he adds. In *Dickens, Reade and Collins: Sensation Novelists.*

For a contemporary view of Victorian publishing and the nature of the reading public of the day, see the final volume of Charles Knight's illustrated *The Popular History of England* (London: Warne, 1856–62). Knight, the son of a bookseller and publisher, published his comprehensive eight-volume set, he said, in an effort to tie up social history with the standard account of the country's political history.

The tenor and the details of Dickens's 1842 visit to the United States are of course best rendered in the author's own words—in his letters to friends and in *American Notes for General Circulation.* The edition of the latter referred to here is from St. Martin's Press, 1985.

3.

The edition of *Martin Chuzzlewit* cited here is Penguin, 1986.

4.

Watkin's account of Dickens's 1843 visit to Manchester, "Peeps at Dickens," is collected in *The Dickensian* 34: 37–39.

A discussion of Dickens's associates in Manchester, along with a summary of all his visits to the city, is found in F. R. Dean's "Dickens and Manchester," in *The Dickensian* 34: 111–18.

5.

For more on Cobden, see Nicholas C. Edsall, *Richard Cobden: Independent Radical* (Cambridge, Mass.: Harvard University Press, 1987).

Sorrentino's quite lovely story is "The Moon in Its Flight" (1971), collected recently in a volume of the same name (Minneapolis: Coffee House Press, 2004).

An incisive portrait of Manchester and its influence on the work of Marx and Engels may be found in Boyer's "The Historical Background of the Communist Manifesto," in *Journal of Economic Perspectives,* Autumn, 1998: 151–74.

This author has expanded on Carnegie in *Meet You in Hell* (New York: Crown Publishers, 2005).

References to Dickens's remarks before the Athenaeum come from Fielding's *The Speeches of Charles Dickens* (Oxford, 1960).

6.

The process by which *A Christmas Carol* came to consume Dickens in the wake of his visit to the Saffron Hill school and to Manchester is extrapolated from *The Letters,* esp. vol. 3, and from Forster, Book 4 of *The Life,* "Chuzzlewit Disappointments and Christmas Carol."

7.

Forster is the principal source for Dickens's dealings with Chapman and Hall. As an adviser to both the publishing house and the author, Forster fulfilled the role of editor and agent simultaneously, and at a time long before either position had even been formalized in the industry. Despite the delicacy of such a position, both Dickens's letters and Forster's reminiscences suggest that he was able to carry off the dual assignment without alienating either side.

8.

The facsimile of Dickens's manuscript of *A Christmas Carol* published by the Pierpont Morgan Library offers the next best experience to holding the original copy in one's hands. Dickens gave his manuscript to his attorney Mitton shortly after he finished it, and Mitton sold it shortly after Dickens's death. J. Pierpont Morgan acquired the manuscript in London in 1902 and brought it back to his library, where it has remained since, along with the original manuscript of Milton's *Paradise Lost,* Thoreau's journals, and much more. Commentators have noted that Dickens's handwriting in this manuscript is smaller and more careful when compared to earlier works, with the greater number of corrections also attesting to the care with which the story was produced.

Among the many pleasures of Michael Patrick Hearn's exhaustive companion, *The Annotated Christmas Carol,* is his description of Dickens's relationship with illustrator Leech and the impact of the latter's work on the finished book. The quantity and breadth of Hearn's research on Dickens's slender volume constitute the most significant work on the novel to date.

9.

A version of "The Story of the Goblins Who Stole a Sexton" is included, along with an adroit introduction to several other Dickens pieces, in Michael Slater, ed., *A Christmas Carol and Other Christmas Writings.*

The summary of *A Christmas Carol* is based upon Ackroyd's edition of *The Christmas Books,* vol. 1 (London: Mandarin, 1991) as well as the Facsimile Edition from the Morgan Library (1993).

10.

History of Christmas: Everything that a reader might wish to know about the historical antecedents of the Christmas holiday is to be found in University of Massachusetts historian Nissenbaum's *The Battle for Christmas.*

An interesting discussion of Puritan influences on holiday celebration in the early United States is found in Leigh Eric Schmidt, *Consumer Rites: The Buying and Selling of American Holidays* (Princeton, N.J.: Princeton University Press, 1995).

The definitive edition of Pepys's diary is an eleven-volume set compiled by Robert Latham and William Matthews (London: Bell & Hyman, 1970–83). Highlights are collected by Latham in *The Diary of Samuel Pepys: A Selection* (New York: Penguin, 2003).

The reconstruction of the mummers' play is by Roderick Marshall, quoted by noted actor Simon Callow in *Dickens' Christmas.*

Besides Callow's lively account, other works linking Dickens and his literary forebears with the season include *The Lives and Times of Ebenezer Scrooge* by Paul Davis, and *Christmas and Charles Dickens* by David Parker.

Dickens's essay "A Christmas Tree" is included in the collection compiled by Michael Slater, mentioned earlier.

The discussion of the financial pressures that impinged on Dickens is extrapolated primarily from the letters of the author and the commentary of Forster.

11.

The lines are from Wordsworth's "My Heart Leaps Up," published in 1807, reprinted in *The Norton Anthology of English Literature,* vol. 2 (New York: Norton, 1968).

Hearn (*The Annotated Christmas Carol*) provides an exhaustive summary of the contemporary press and magazine response at the time of publication and after.

Mrs. Carlyle's letter of December 28, 1844, is to her cousin Jeannie Welsh, and is found in *The Collected Letters of Thomas and Jane Welsh Carlyle,* vol. 17 (Durham, N.C.: Duke University Press, 1970–93).

12.

By way of contrast to the five-shilling ($1.25) cover price of the novel, a first edition of *A Christmas Carol* today might fetch anywhere from $10,000 to $40,000, depending upon its condition.

For an informative and provocative commentary on the history of copyright law, see Harry Hillman Chartrand, "Copyright C.P.U.: Creators, Proprietors & Users," in *Journal of Arts Management, Law & Society* 30, no. 3 (Fall 2000).

The story of Dickens's ill-fated suit against Lee & Haddock is told in engaging style by E. T. Jaques, "Solicitor of the Supreme Court," in his *Charles Dickens in Chancery*.

Ancillary to Jaques's account is an annotated time line of the case by S. J. Rust in "At the Dickens House: Legal Documents Relating to the Piracy of *A Christmas Carol*," *The Dickensian*, 41–44. Rust appends a note from Talfourd to Mitton lamenting the outcome of their victory: "I hope . . . that some means may be found to deliver our friend [Dickens] from the penalty which will await on success—the payment of his own cost of an action against Bankrupt Robbers."

13.

The balance sheet from Chapman and Hall that Dickens so woefully pored over is extrapolated from Patten, *Charles Dickens and His Publishers*.

The Letters and Forster's *Life* provide the basis for the state of Dickens's mind in the aftermath of the publication of *A Christmas Carol*.

14.

The definitive account of the history of the myriad adaptations of Dickens is found in Philip Bolton, *Dickens Dramatized*.

Also of note in this regard is Fred Guida, *A Christmas Carol and Its Adaptations*.

John Irving's observations on Dickens's modus operandi are more fully drawn in his essay "The King of the Novel" (in *Trying to Save Peggy Sneed*, 1996).

15.

For the discussion of the impact of Christmas on Dickens and of Dickens's impact on the holiday, the author is indebted to a number of sources previously named. An incisive and accurate treatment of the subject is found in Christine Lalumia, "Scrooge and Albert: Christmas in the 1840s."

Without Michelle Persell's "Dickensian Disciple," this writer may well have gone a lifetime without an appreciation of the works of Benjamin Farjeon, Jewish writer of Christmas.

16.

Davis's is a most readable study of the influence of *A Christmas Carol* on contemporary culture: *The Lives and Times of Ebenezer Scrooge* (Yale University Press, 1990).

In his introduction to the first volume of *The Christmas Books,* Ackroyd points out that while Dickens intended to profit from these seasonable fables, he was anything but cynical about the enterprise. In fact, for the social themes embedded in *The Chimes* he suffered vituperative criticism from some who found him a revolutionary in a romantic's clothing, too fond of the "felon" and the "rick-burner."

Patten (1978) is the source of the information regarding the unsold copies of *The Haunted Mansion.*

Over time, Dickens's Christmas books not only moved away from any reference to the season but also became less tied to specific social issues and more concerned with the general nature of man. As he put it in his Preface to the first Cheap Edition published in 1852, his purpose in the stories was less "great elaboration of detail" (which he believed could not be achieved within such narrow confines) than it was the construction of "a whimsical kind of masque which the good humor of the season justified, to awaken some loving and forbearing thoughts, never out of season in a Christian land."

17.

In his *Dickens and Popular Entertainment,* Paul Schlicke quotes one of Dickens's advisers who estimates that the author earned as much as £45,000 from the readings he gave between April of 1858 and his death in 1870. And Forster suggests that in those later years, it was by his readings as much as by his books that the world came to know him. As any number of commentators have pointed out, however, he threw his energies into the performances to such a degree that they as much as anything can be said to have killed him.

Dickens began his readings by assuring audiences that it was quite all right to "give vent to any feeling of emotion." Cheers or sobs would not disturb him in the slightest, he said. For the typical two-hour performance, everyone should "make themselves as much as possible like a group of friends, listening to a tale told by a winter fire." It is testament, says Schlicke, that Dickens saw himself first and foremost as a popular entertainer.

Jane Smiley's observations on the pleasure of reading one's works aloud are contained within her fine short study, *Charles Dickens.* Smiley's work is particularly valuable for the insight she brings as an accomplished novelist in her own right. Of Dickens's later years she says, "A novelist's late, eccentric life is analogous to his late eccentric novels. His ties to the mainstream have loosened. His primary job is no longer to be representative, as when he was a young writer looking for a publisher and an audience; it is to be still interesting."

Perhaps the most intriguing view of Dickens's later life comes though the lens of Claire Tomalin in her study of Ellen

Ternan and her relationship with the author, *The Invisible Woman*. Tomalin (1991) is the source for the alternative version of Dickens's passing.

18.

The anecdote of the costermonger's lament on Dickens's death is a favorite of biographers. Watts-Dunton, a contemporary of Tennyson and Swinburne, opened his 1898 poem with a reference to the legend, then closed with a reassurance to Londoners: "City he loved, take courage . . . Dickens returns on Christmas Day." ("Dickens Returns on Christmas Day," in *The Coming of Love and Other Poems* [London and New York: Lane, 1898].)

Robert Louis Stevenson's comments on Dickens's Christmas books are from an undated letter written at Bournemouth, where he was living while working on *Dr. Jekyll and Mr. Hyde* (1886). According to a *New York Times* story of February 5, 1922 ("Stevenson Cried Over Dickens Tale"), the seven-page letter was purchased at auction by William Randolph Hearst, for $1,150. Sold at the same auction was a stuffed raven named Grip that had once belonged to Dickens, for $210.

As proof that in some quarters no good impulse or deed goes uncriticized, Simon Callow passes along accounts of mass feedings of the poor conducted by the Salvation Army in late-nineteenth-century New York, where as many as 25,000 received Christmas dinner. *The Saturday Evening Post* found such charity offensive and laid the blame on Dickens, for, in the opinion of the editors, "A great Christmas dinner, in the minds of many, cancels the charity obligations of the entire year." Callow also quotes Lord Chesterton in response to suggestions that the practice be stopped: "Doubtless he [Dickens] would have regarded the charity as folly, but he would also have regarded the forcible removal of it as theft."

SELECTED BIBLIOGRAPHY

Primary sources

Dickens, Charles. *A Christmas Carol: A Facsimile Edition of the Autograph Manuscript in the Pierpont Morgan Library.* New Haven, Conn.: Pierpont Morgan Library/Yale University Press, 1993.

Fielding, K. J. *The Speeches of Charles Dickens.* Oxford, England: Clarendon Press, 1960.

House, Madeline, and Graham Storey. *The Letters of Charles Dickens,* Pilgrim Edition. 12 vols. Oxford, England: Oxford University Press, 1965–2002.

Other editions

Dickens, Charles. *American Notes for General Circulation.* New York: St. Martin's Press, 1985.

_____. *The Christmas Books,* vol. 1, edited by Peter Ackroyd. London: Mandarin, 1991.

_____. *A Christmas Carol and Other Christmas Writings,* edited by Michael Slater. New York: Penguin, 2002.

_____. *Martin Chuzzlewit.* New York: Penguin, 1986.

Biographies

Of the many biographies of Dickens's life, three distinguish themselves: Forster's for being the first and coming from a friend and lifelong associate; Ackroyd's for its comprehensiveness; and Smiley's for its incisiveness.

Ackroyd, Peter. *Dickens*. New York: HarperCollins, 1990.

Forster, John. *The Life of Charles Dickens*. 3 vols. London: Chapman and Hall, 1872–74.

Smiley, Jane. *Charles Dickens*. New York: Viking, 2002.

Tomalin, Claire. *The Invisible Woman: The Story of Nelly Ternan and Charles Dickens*. New York: Knopf, 1991.

Encyclopedia (sketches of all things pertaining to Dickens, A–Z)

Oxford Reader's Companion to Dickens, edited by Paul Schlicke. Oxford, England: Oxford University Press, 1999.

Dickens adaptations and editions

Bolton, Philip H. *Dickens Dramatized*. Boston: G. K. Hall, 1987.

Feather, John. *A History of British Publishing*. New York: Routledge, 1991.

Patten, Robert C. *Charles Dickens and His Publishers*. Oxford, England: Clarendon Press, 1978.

Dickens and A Christmas Carol and the Christmas season

Callow, Simon. *Dickens' Christmas: A Victorian Celebration*. New York: Abrams, 2003.

Davis, Paul. *The Lives and Times of Ebenezer Scrooge*. New Haven, Conn.: Yale University Press, 1990.

Guida, Fred. *A Christmas Carol and Its Adaptations*. Jefferson, N.C.: McFarland, 1999.

Hearn, Michael Patrick. *The Annotated Christmas Carol*. New York: W. W. Norton, 2004.

Nissenbaum, Stephen. *The Battle for Christmas*. New York: Knopf, 1997.

Parker, David. *Christmas and Charles Dickens*. New York: AMS, 2005.

And other valuable sources

Baker, William, and Kenneth Womack, eds. *A Companion to the Victorian Novel.* Westport, Conn.: Greenwood Press, 2002.

The Dickensian. Journal of the Dickens Fellowship. 1902–present.

Fielding, K. J. *Charles Dickens: A Critical Introduction.* London: Longmans, Green, 1958.

Glavin, John. *After Dickens: Reading, Adaptation, and Performance.* Cambridge, England: Cambridge University Press, 1999.

Hutton, Ronald. *Stations of the Sun: A History of the Ritual Year in Britain.* Oxford, England: Oxford University Press, 1996.

Irving, John. "The King of the Novel," in *Trying to Save Peggy Sneed.* New York: Little Brown/Arcade, 1996.

Jaques, E. T. *Charles Dickens in Chancery.* London: Longmans, Green, 1914.

Knight, Charles. *The Popular History of England, vol. 8: From the Peace with the United States, 1815, to the Final Extinction of the Corn-Laws, 1849.* London: Warne, 1890.

Lalumia, Christine. "Scrooge and Albert: Christmas in the 1840s." *History Today,* December 2001: 23 et seq.

Persell, Michelle. "Dickensian Disciple: Anglo-Jewish Identity in the Christmas Tales of Benjamin Farjeon." *Philological Quarterly* 73.4 (1994): 451 et seq.

Phillips, Walter C. *Dickens, Reade and Collins: Sensation Novelists.* New York: Columbia University Press, 1919.

Rogers, Byron. "The Man Who Invented Christmas." *Sunday Telegraph* (London), December 18, 1988: 16.

Schlicke, Paul. *Dickens and Popular Entertainment.* London: Unwin Hyman, 1988.

ACKNOWLEDGMENTS

VERY SPECIAL THANKS are due to several individuals who helped make this book possible: If I could not find what I was looking for, Addis Beesting, Educational Reference Librarian at Florida International University, could, and in a trice; James W. Hall, my ever-patient friend and literary compass, encouraged me and—as usual—helped me stay on track; bless Rachel Klayman, my editor, for carrying the flag for this book at Crown, and Lucinda Bartley, also at Crown, for her close eye and many helpful suggestions, and Kim Witherspoon, at Inkwell Management, for helping me collect my thoughts and battle plan. And, as always, many thanks to my wife, Kimberly, for her support and understanding—these days I am coming to dinner when it is called.

ABOUT THE AUTHOR

LES STANDIFORD is the author of the *New York Times* bestselling books *Bringing Adam Home, Last Train to Paradise,* and *Meet You in Hell,* along with ten novels and the recent critically acclaimed *Water to the Angels.* He is director of the Creative Writing Program at Florida International University in Miami, where he lives with his wife, Kimberly, a psychotherapist and artist. Visit his website at Les-Standiford.com.

A READER'S GUIDE

FOR

The Man Who Invented CHRISTMAS

How Charles Dickens's

A Christmas Carol

Rescued His Career and Revived

Our Holiday Spirits

BY LES STANDIFORD

1. How did the immense popularity of Dickens's writings affect the emerging publishing and bookselling industries of nineteenth-century England? Who do you think was more responsible for his dizzying sales figures, Dickens or his publisher?

2. Dickens never spoke publicly about the miserable conditions of his childhood. What do you make of the fact that abused and deprived children feature prominently in his work, especially *Oliver Twist* and *A Christmas Carol*?

3. Dickens's 1842 tour of the United States had its positive moments, but was in the end such a disappointment that he canceled the final portion of the trip, a swing through the American South. Who do you think was more at fault, the author or his hosts? Why?

4. At the time when Dickens appeared before the Manchester Athenaeum in the fall of 1842, his career was on the downslide, his marriage—with a fifth child on the way—teetering, and his finances in disarray. What happened during that speech in Manchester to turn things around?

5. Dickens's publishers, Chapman and Hall, famously turned him down when he first proposed *A Christmas Carol*.

How do you explain their rejection of it? Do you think that it ended up benefitting or hurting the book?

6. Do you find Scrooge's monumental transformation credible? Does the fact that this is a "ghost story" add to or take away from its thematic impact?

7. Do you think that, in writing the story of Scrooge, Dickens was on some level writing about himself? Why or why not?

8. At the time of the book's publication, Christmas was a decidedly "second-tier" holiday in both England and the United States. What social, political, and religious factors accounted for that?

9. Dickens's enthusiasm for Christmas does not seem to have had much basis in traditional religious practice. What do you think accounts for his enthusiasm?

10. Immediately following its publication, unscrupulous people began to print and sell pirated editions of *A Christmas Carol*, without paying Dickens a cent in royalties. These days, pirated editions of many books are available for download on the Internet rather than as physical books. What effects do you think Internet pirating has had on the publishing industry? Is there any difference between today's theft of intellectual property and the theft that took place in Dickens's era?

11. *A Christmas Carol* is one of the most frequently adapted literary works of all time. What is it that attracts so many dramatists and filmmakers? Can you think of other works that are often adapted? What do they have in common with—and how do they differ from—*A Christmas Carol*?

12. Compared to the Christmas of Dickens's era, Christmas is now an extravaganza. Dickens writes: "I have always thought of Christmas time as . . . the only time I know of, in the long calendar of the year when men and women seem by one consent to open their shut-up hearts freely, and to think of people below them as if they really were fellow-passengers to the grave." Is there any way in which you see this attitude reflected in the modern celebration of Christmas? If you celebrate Christmas, is there anything you might resolve to do next Christmas season to bring Dickens's words to life?

13. Dickens went on to write many more successful books, including *David Copperfield, Bleak House,* and *Great Expectations.* However, the four Christmas stories he wrote after *A Christmas Carol* never found a wide readership. Why do you think *A Christmas Carol* resonated so uniquely with readers?

A Christmas Carol

PREFACE

I HAVE ENDEAVOURED in this Ghostly little book, to raise the Ghost of an Idea, which shall not put my readers out of humour with themselves, with each other, with the season, or with me. May it haunt their house pleasantly, and no one wish to lay it.

Their faithful Friend and Servant,
C.D.
December 1843.

Marley's Ghost

Marley was dead: to begin with. There is no doubt whatever about that. The register of his burial was signed by the clergyman, the clerk, the undertaker, and the chief mourner. Scrooge signed it: and Scrooge's name was good upon 'Change, for anything he chose to put his hand to. Old Marley was as dead as a door-nail.

Mind! I don't mean to say that I know, of my own knowledge, what there is particularly dead about a door-nail. I might have been inclined, myself, to regard a coffin-nail as the deadest piece of ironmongery in the trade. But the wisdom of our ancestors is in the simile; and my unhallowed hands shall not disturb it, or the Country's done for. You will therefore permit me to repeat, emphatically, that Marley was as dead as a door-nail.

Scrooge knew he was dead? Of course he did. How could it be otherwise? Scrooge and he were partners for I don't know how many years. Scrooge was his sole executor, his sole administrator, his sole assign, his sole residuary legatee, his sole friend and sole mourner. And even Scrooge was not so dreadfully cut up by the sad event, but that he was an excellent man of business on the very day of the funeral, and solemnised it with an undoubted bargain.

The mention of Marley's funeral brings me back to the point I started from. There is no doubt that Marley was dead. This must be distinctly understood, or nothing wonderful can come of the story I am going to relate. If we were not perfectly convinced that Hamlet's Father died before the play began, there would be nothing more remarkable in his taking a stroll at night, in an easterly wind, upon his own ramparts, than there would be in any other middle-aged gentleman rashly turning out after dark in a breezy spot—say Saint Paul's Churchyard for instance—literally to astonish his son's weak mind.

Scrooge never painted out Old Marley's name. There it stood, years afterwards, above the warehouse door: Scrooge and Marley. The firm was known as Scrooge and Marley. Sometimes people new to the business called Scrooge Scrooge, and sometimes Marley, but he answered to both names: it was all the same to him.

Oh! but he was a tight-fisted hand at the grindstone, Scrooge! a squeezing, wrenching, grasping, scraping, clutching, covetous old sinner! Hard and sharp as flint, from which no steel had ever struck out generous fire; secret, and self-contained, and solitary as an oyster. The cold within him froze his old features, nipped his pointed nose, shrivelled his cheek, stiffened his gait; made his eyes red, his thin lips blue; and spoke out shrewdly in his grating voice. A frosty rime was on his head, and on his eyebrows, and his wiry chin. He carried his own low temperature always about with him; he iced his office in the dog-days; and didn't thaw it one degree at Christmas.

External heat and cold had little influence on Scrooge. No warmth could warm, nor wintry weather chill him. No wind that blew was bitterer than he, no falling snow was more intent upon its purpose, no pelting rain less open to entreaty. Foul weather didn't know where to have him. The heaviest rain, and snow, and hail, and sleet, could boast of the advantage over him in only one respect. They often "came down" handsomely, and Scrooge never did.

Nobody ever stopped him in the street to say, with gladsome looks, "My dear Scrooge, how are you? when will you come to see me?" No beggars implored him to bestow a trifle, no children asked him what it was o'clock, no man or woman ever once in all his life inquired the way to such and such a place, of Scrooge. Even the blindmen's dogs appeared to know him; and when they saw him coming on, would tug their owners into doorways and up courts; and then would wag their tails as though they said, "no eye at all is better than an evil eye, dark master!"

But what did Scrooge care? It was the very thing he liked. To edge his way along the crowded paths of life, warning all human sympathy to keep its distance, was what the knowing ones call "nuts" to Scrooge.

Once upon a time—of all the good days in the year, on Christmas Eve—old Scrooge sat busy in his counting-house. It was cold, bleak, biting weather: foggy withal: and he could hear the people in the court outside, go wheezing up and down, beating their hands upon their breasts, and stamping their feet upon the pavement-stones to warm them. The city clocks had only just gone three, but it was quite dark already: it had not been light all day: and candles were flaring in the windows of the neighbouring offices, like ruddy smears upon the palpable brown air. The fog came pouring in at every chink and keyhole, and was so dense without, that although the court was of the narrowest, the houses opposite were mere phantoms. To see the dingy cloud come drooping down, obscuring everything, one might have thought that Nature lived hard by, and was brewing on a large scale.

The door of Scrooge's counting-house was open that he might keep his eye upon his clerk, who in a dismal little cell beyond, a sort of tank, was copying letters. Scrooge had a very small fire, but the clerk's fire was so very much smaller that it looked like one coal. But he couldn't replenish it, for Scrooge kept the coal-box in his own room; and so surely as the clerk came in with the shovel, the master predicted that it would be necessary for them to part. Wherefore the clerk put on his white comforter, and tried to warm himself at the candle; in which effort, not being a man of a strong imagination, he failed.

"A merry Christmas, uncle! God save you!" cried a cheerful voice. It was the voice of Scrooge's nephew, who came upon him so quickly that this was the first intimation he had of his approach.

"Bah!" said Scrooge, "Humbug!"

He had so heated himself with rapid walking in the fog and frost, this nephew of Scrooge's, that he was all in a glow;

his face was ruddy and handsome; his eyes sparkled, and his breath smoked again.

"Christmas a humbug, uncle!" said Scrooge's nephew. "You don't mean that, I am sure?"

"I do," said Scrooge. "Merry Christmas! What right have you to be merry? what reason have you to be merry? You're poor enough."

"Come, then," returned the nephew gaily. "What right have you to be dismal? what reason have you to be morose? You're rich enough."

Scrooge having no better answer ready on the spur of the moment, said, "Bah!" again; and followed it up with "Humbug."

"Don't be cross, uncle," said the nephew.

"What else can I be" returned the uncle, "when I live in such a world of fools as this? Merry Christmas! Out upon merry Christmas! What's Christmas time to you but a time for paying bills without money; a time for finding yourself a year older, and not an hour richer; a time for balancing your books and having every item in 'em through a round dozen of months presented dead against you? If I could work my will," said Scrooge, indignantly, "every idiot who goes about with 'Merry Christmas,' on his lips, should be boiled with his own pudding, and buried with a stake of holly through his heart. He should!"

"Uncle!" pleaded the nephew.

"Nephew!" returned the uncle, sternly, "keep Christmas in your own way, and let me keep it in mine."

"Keep it!" repeated Scrooge's nephew. "But you don't keep it."

"Let me leave it alone, then," said Scrooge. "Much good may it do you! Much good it has ever done you!"

"There are many things from which I might have derived good, by which I have not profited, I dare say," returned the nephew: "Christmas among the rest. But I am sure I have always thought of Christmas time, when it has come round—apart from the veneration due to its sacred name and origin, if anything belonging to it can be apart from that—as a good time: a kind, forgiving, charitable, pleasant time: the only time I know of, in the long calendar of the year, when men and women seem by one consent to open their shut-up hearts freely, and to think of people below them as if they really were fellow-passengers to the grave, and not another race of creatures bound on other journeys. And therefore, uncle, though it has never put a scrap of gold or silver in my pocket, I believe that it *has* done me good, and *will* do me good; and I say, God bless it!"

The clerk in the tank involuntarily applauded: becoming immediately sensible of the impropriety, he poked the fire, and extinguished the last frail spark for ever.

"Let me hear another sound from *you*," said Scrooge, "and you'll keep your Christmas by losing your situation. You're quite a powerful speaker, sir," he added, turning to his nephew. "I wonder you don't go into Parliament."

"Don't be angry, uncle. Come! Dine with us to-morrow."

Scrooge said that he would see him—yes, indeed he did.

He went the whole length of the expression, and said that he would see him in that extremity first.

"But why?" cried Scrooge's nephew. "Why?"

"Why did you get married?" said Scrooge.

"Because I fell in love."

"Because you fell in love!" growled Scrooge, as if that were the only one thing in the world more ridiculous than a merry Christmas. "Good afternoon!"

"Nay, uncle, but you never came to see me before that happened. Why give it as a reason for not coming now?"

"Good afternoon," said Scrooge.

"I want nothing from you; I ask nothing of you; why cannot we be friends?"

"Good afternoon," said Scrooge.

"I am sorry, with all my heart, to find you so resolute. We have never had any quarrel, to which I have been a party. But I have made the trial in homage to Christmas, and I'll keep my Christmas humour to the last. So A Merry Christmas, uncle!"

"Good afternoon!" said Scrooge.

"And A Happy New Year!"

"Good afternoon!" said Scrooge.

His nephew left the room without an angry word, notwithstanding. He stopped at the outer door to bestow the greetings of the season on the clerk, who, cold as he was, was warmer than Scrooge; for he returned them cordially.

"There's another fellow," muttered Scrooge; who overheard him: "my clerk, with fifteen shillings a-week, and a wife and family, talking about a merry Christmas. I'll retire to Bedlam."

This lunatic, in letting Scrooge's nephew out, had let two other people in. They were portly gentlemen, pleasant to behold, and now stood, with their hats off, in Scrooge's office. They had books and papers in their hands, and bowed to him.

"Scrooge and Marley's, I believe," said one of the gentlemen, referring to his list. "Have I the pleasure of addressing Mr. Scrooge, or Mr. Marley?"

"Mr. Marley has been dead these seven years," Scrooge replied. "He died seven years ago, this very night."

"We have no doubt his liberality is well represented by his surviving partner," said the gentleman, presenting his credentials.

It certainly was; for they had been two kindred spirits. At the ominous word "liberality," Scrooge frowned, and shook his head, and handed the credentials back.

"At this festive season of the year, Mr. Scrooge," said the gentleman, taking up a pen, "it is more than usually desirable that we should make some slight provision for the poor and destitute, who suffer greatly at the present time. Many thousands are in want of common necessaries; hundreds of thousands are in want of common comforts, sir."

"Are there no prisons?" asked Scrooge.

"Plenty of prisons," said the gentleman, laying down the pen again.

"And the Union workhouses?" demanded Scrooge. "Are they still in operation?"

"They are. Still," returned the gentleman, "I wish I could say they were not."

"The Treadmill and the Poor Law are in full vigour, then?" said Scrooge.

"Both very busy, sir."

"Oh! I was afraid, from what you said at first, that something had occurred to stop them in their useful course," said Scrooge. "I'm very glad to hear it."

"Under the impression that they scarcely furnish Christian cheer of mind or body to the multitude," returned the gentleman, "a few of us are endeavoring to raise a fund to buy the Poor some meat and drink, and means of warmth. We choose this time because it is a time, of all others, when Want is keenly felt, and Abundance rejoices. What shall I put you down for?"

"Nothing!" Scrooge replied.

"You wish to be anonymous?"

"I wish to be left alone," said Scrooge. "Since you ask me what I wish, gentlemen, that is my answer. I don't make merry myself at Christmas, and I can't afford to make idle people merry. I help to support the establishments I have mentioned: they cost enough: and those who are badly off must go there."

"Many can't go there; and many would rather die."

"If they would rather die," said Scrooge, "they had better do it, and decrease the surplus population. Besides—excuse me—I don't know that."

"But you might know it," observed the gentleman.

"It's not my business," Scrooge returned. "It's enough

for a man to understand his own business, and not to interfere with other people's. Mine occupies me constantly. Good afternoon, gentlemen!"

Seeing clearly that it would be useless to pursue their point, the gentlemen withdrew. Scrooge resumed his labours with an improved opinion of himself, and in a more facetious temper than was usual with him.

Meanwhile the fog and darkness thickened so, that people ran about with flaring links, proffering their services to go before horses in carriages, and conduct them on their way. The ancient tower of a church, whose gruff old bell was always peeping slily down at Scrooge out of a gothic window in the wall, became invisible, and struck the hours and quarters in the clouds, with tremulous vibrations afterwards, as if its teeth were chattering in its frozen head up there. The cold became intense. In the main street, at the corner of the court, some labourers were repairing the gas-pipes, and had lighted a great fire in a brazier, round which a party of ragged men and boys were gathered: warming their hands and winking their eyes before the blaze in rapture. The water-plug being left in solitude, its overflowings sullenly congealed, and turned to misanthropic ice. The brightness of the shops where holly sprigs and berries crackled in the lamp-heat of the windows, made pale faces ruddy as they passed. Poulterers' and grocers' trades became a splendid joke: a glorious pageant, with which it was next to impossible to believe that such dull principles as bargain and sale had anything to do. The Lord Mayor, in the stronghold of the mighty Mansion House, gave orders to his fifty cooks and butlers to keep

Christmas as a Lord Mayor's household should; and even the little tailor, whom he had fined five shillings on the previous Monday for being drunk and blood-thirsty in the streets, stirred up to-morrow's pudding in his garret, while his lean wife and the baby sallied out to buy the beef.

Foggier yet, and colder! Piercing, searching, biting cold. If the good Saint Dunstan had but nipped the Evil Spirit's nose with a touch of such weather as that, instead of using his familiar weapons, then indeed he would have roared to lusty purpose. The owner of one scant young nose, gnawed and mumbled by the hungry cold as bones are gnawed by dogs, stooped down at Scrooge's keyhole to regale him with a Christmas carol: but at the first sound of—

> *"God bless you, merry gentleman!*
> *May nothing you dismay!"*

Scrooge seized the ruler with such energy of action, that the singer fled in terror, leaving the keyhole to the fog and even more congenial frost.

At length the hour of shutting up the counting-house arrived. With an ill-will Scrooge dismounted from his stool, and tacitly admitted the fact to the expectant clerk in the Tank, who instantly snuffed his candle out, and put on his hat.

"You'll want all day to-morrow, I suppose?" said Scrooge.

"If quite convenient, sir."

"It's not convenient," said Scrooge, "and it's not fair.

If I was to stop half-a-crown for it, you'd think yourself ill used, I'll be bound?"

The clerk smiled faintly.

"And yet," said Scrooge, "you don't think *me* ill used, when I pay a day's wages for no work."

The clerk observed that it was only once a year.

"A poor excuse for picking a man's pocket every twenty-fifth of December!" said Scrooge, buttoning his great-coat to the chin. "But I suppose you must have the whole day. Be here all the earlier next morning!"

The clerk promised that he would; and Scrooge walked out with a growl. The office was closed in a twinkling, and the clerk, with the long ends of his white comforter dangling below his waist (for he boasted no great-coat), went down a slide on Cornhill, at the end of a lane of boys, twenty times, in honour of its being Christmas-eve, and then ran home to Camden Town as hard as he could pelt, to play at blind-man's-buff.

Scrooge took his melancholy dinner in his usual melancholy tavern; and having read all the newspapers, and beguiled the rest of the evening with his banker's-book, went home to bed. He lived in chambers which had once belonged to his deceased partner. They were a gloomy suite of rooms, in a lowering pile of building up a yard, where it had so little business to be, that one could scarcely help fancying it must have run there when it was a young house, playing at hide-and-seek with other houses, and have forgotten the way out again. It was old enough now, and dreary enough, for nobody lived in it but Scrooge, the other rooms being all let out as offices. The yard was so dark that even Scrooge, who knew its every stone, was fain to grope with his hands. The fog and frost so hung about the black old gateway of the house, that it seemed as if the Genius of the Weather sat in mournful meditation on the threshold.

Now, it is a fact, that there was nothing at all particular about the knocker on the door, except that it was very large. It is also a fact, that Scrooge had seen it night and morning during his whole residence in that place; also that Scrooge had as little of what is called fancy about him as any man in the City of London, even including—which is a bold word—the corporation, aldermen, and livery. Let it also be borne in mind that Scrooge had not bestowed one thought on Marley, since his last mention of his seven-years' dead partner that afternoon. And then let any man explain to me, if he can, how it happened that Scrooge, having his key in the lock of the door, saw in the knocker, without its undergoing any intermediate process of change: not a knocker, but Marley's face.

Marley's face. It was not in impenetrable shadow as the other objects in the yard were, but had a dismal light about it, like a bad lobster in a dark cellar. It was not angry or ferocious, but looked at Scrooge as Marley used to look: with ghostly spectacles turned up upon its ghostly forehead. The hair was curiously stirred, as if by breath or hot-air; and though the eyes were wide open, they were perfectly motionless. That, and its livid colour, made it horrible; but its horror seemed to be, in spite of the face and beyond its control, rather than a part of its own expression.

As Scrooge looked fixedly at this phenomenon, it was a knocker again.

To say that he was not startled, or that his blood was not conscious of a terrible sensation to which it had been a stranger from infancy, would be untrue. But he put his hand upon the key he had relinquished, turned it sturdily, walked in, and lighted his candle.

He *did* pause, with a moment's irresolution, before he shut the door; and he *did* look cautiously behind it first, as if he half-expected to be terrified with the sight of Marley's pig-tail sticking out into the hall. But there was nothing on the back of the door, except the screws and nuts that held the knocker on; so he said "Pooh, pooh!" and closed it with a bang.

The sound resounded through the house like thunder. Every room above, and every cask in the wine-merchant's cellars below, appeared to have a separate peal of echoes of its own. Scrooge was not a man to be frightened by echoes. He fastened the door, and walked across the hall, and up the stairs: slowly too: trimming his candle as he went.

You may talk vaguely about driving a coach-and-six up a good old flight of stairs, or through a bad young Act of Parliament; but I mean to say you might have got a hearse up that staircase, and taken it broadwise, with the splinter-bar towards the wall, and the door towards the balustrades: and done it easy. There was plenty of width for that, and room to spare; which is perhaps the reason why Scrooge thought he saw a locomotive hearse going on before him in the gloom. Half a dozen gas-lamps out of the street wouldn't have lighted the entry too well, so you may suppose that it was pretty dark with Scrooge's dip.

Up Scrooge went, not caring a button for that: darkness is cheap, and Scrooge liked it. But before he shut his heavy door, he walked through his rooms to see that all was right. He had just enough recollection of the face to desire to do that.

Sitting room, bed-room, lumber-room. All as they should be. Nobody under the table, nobody under the sofa; a small fire in the grate; spoon and basin ready; and the little sauce-pan of gruel (Scrooge had a cold in his head) upon the hob. Nobody under the bed; nobody in the closet; nobody in his dressing-gown, which was hanging up in a suspicious atti-tude against the wall. Lumber-room as usual. Old fire-guard, old shoes, two fish-baskets, washing-stand on three legs, and a poker.

Quite satisfied, he closed his door, and locked himself in; double-locked himself in, which was not his custom. Thus secured against surprise, he took off his cravat; put on his dressing-gown and slippers, and his night-cap; and sat down before the fire to take his gruel.

It was a very low fire indeed; nothing on such a bitter night. He was obliged to sit close to it, and brood over it, be-fore he could extract the least sensation of warmth from such a handful of fuel. The fireplace was an old one, built by some Dutch merchant long ago, and paved all round with quaint Dutch tiles, designed to illustrate the Scriptures. There were Cains and Abels; Pharaoh's daughters, Queens of Sheba, Angelic messengers descending through the air on clouds like feather-beds, Abrahams, Belshazzars, Apostles putting off to sea in butter-boats, hundreds of figures to attract his thoughts; and yet that face of Marley, seven years dead, came like the ancient Prophet's rod, and swallowed up the whole. If each smooth tile had been a blank at first, with power to shape some picture on its surface from the disjointed fragments of his thoughts, there would have been a copy of old Marley's head on every one.

"Humbug!" said Scrooge; and walked across the room.

After several turns, he sat down again. As he threw his head back in the chair, his glance happened to rest upon a bell, a disused bell, that hung in the room, and communicated for some purpose now forgotten with a chamber in the highest story of the building. It was with great astonishment, and with a strange, inexplicable dread, that as he looked, he saw this bell begin to swing. It swung so softly in the outset that it scarcely made a sound; but soon it rang out loudly, and so did every bell in the house.

This might have lasted half a minute, or a minute, but it seemed an hour. The bells ceased as they had begun, together. They were succeeded by a clanking noise, deep down below; as if some person were dragging a heavy chain over the casks in the wine-merchant's cellar. Scrooge then remembered to have heard that ghosts in haunted houses were described as dragging chains.

The cellar-door flew open with a booming sound, and then he heard the noise much louder, on the floors below; then coming up the stairs; then coming straight towards his door.

"It's humbug still!" said Scrooge. "I won't believe it."

His colour changed though, when, without a pause, it came on through the heavy door, and passed into the room before his eyes. Upon its coming in, the dying flame leaped up, as though it cried "I know him! Marley's Ghost!" and fell again.

The same face: the very same. Marley in his pig-tail, usual waistcoat, tights, and boots; the tassels on the latter bristling, like his pig-tail, and his coat-skirts, and the hair upon his head. The chain he drew was clasped about his middle. It was long, and wound about him like a tail; and it was made (for Scrooge observed it closely) of cash-boxes, keys, padlocks, ledgers, deeds, and heavy purses wrought in steel. His body was transparent: so that Scrooge, observing him, and looking through his waistcoat, could see the two buttons on his coat behind.

Scrooge had often heard it said that Marley had no bowels, but he had never believed it until now.

No, nor did he believe it even now. Though he looked the phantom through and through, and saw it standing before him; though he felt the chilling influence of its death-cold eyes; and marked the very texture of the folded kerchief bound about its head and chin, which wrapper he had not observed before: he was still incredulous, and fought against his senses.

"How now!" said Scrooge, caustic and cold as ever. "What do you want with me?"

"Much!"—Marley's voice, no doubt about it.

"Who are you?"

"Ask me who I *was*."

"Who were you then?" said Scrooge, raising his voice. "You're particular—for a shade." He was going to say *"to* a shade," but substituted this, as more appropriate.

"In life I was your partner, Jacob Marley."

"Can you—can you sit down?" asked Scrooge, looking doubtfully at him.

"I can."

"Do it then."

Scrooge asked the question, because he didn't know whether a ghost so transparent might find himself in a condition to take a chair; and felt that in the event of its being impossible, it might involve the necessity of an embarrassing explanation. But the ghost sat down on the opposite side of the fireplace, as if he were quite used to it.

"You don't believe in me," observed the Ghost.

"I don't," said Scrooge.

"What evidence would you have of my reality, beyond that of your senses?"

"I don't know," said Scrooge.

"Why do you doubt your senses?"

"Because," said Scrooge, "a little thing affects them. A slight disorder of the stomach makes them cheats. You may be an undigested bit of beef, a blot of mustard, a crumb of cheese, a fragment of an underdone potato. There's more of gravy than of grave about you, whatever you are!"

Scrooge was not much in the habit of cracking jokes, nor did he feel, in his heart, by any means waggish then. The truth is, that he tried to be smart, as a means of distracting his own attention, and keeping down his terror; for the spectre's voice disturbed the very marrow in his bones.

To sit, staring at those fixed, glazed eyes, in silence for a moment, would play, Scrooge felt, the very deuce with him. There was something very awful, too, in the spectre's being provided with an infernal atmosphere of its own. Scrooge could not feel it himself, but this was clearly the case; for though the Ghost sat perfectly motionless, its hair, and skirts, and tassels, were still agitated as by the hot vapour from an oven.

"You see this toothpick?" said Scrooge, returning quickly to the charge, for the reason just assigned; and wishing, though it were only for a second, to divert the vision's stony gaze from himself.

"I do," replied the Ghost.

"You are not looking at it," said Scrooge.

"But I see it," said the Ghost, "notwithstanding."

"Well!" returned Scrooge. "I have but to swallow this, and be for the rest of my days persecuted by a legion of goblins, all of my own creation. Humbug, I tell you—humbug!"

At this, the spirit raised a frightful cry, and shook its chain with such a dismal and appalling noise, that Scrooge held on tight to his chair, to save himself from falling in a swoon. But how much greater was his horror, when the phantom taking off the bandage round its head, as if it were too warm to wear in-doors, its lower jaw dropped down upon its breast!

Scrooge fell upon his knees, and clasped his hands before his face.

"Mercy!" he said. "Dreadful apparition, why do you trouble me?"

"Man of the worldly mind!" replied the Ghost, "do you believe in me or not?"

"I do," said Scrooge. "I must. But why do spirits walk the earth, and why do they come to me?"

"It is required of every man," the Ghost returned, "that the spirit within him should walk abroad among his fellow-men, and travel far and wide; and if that spirit goes not forth in life, it is condemned to do so after death. It is doomed to wander through the world—oh, woe is me!—and witness what it cannot share, but might have shared on earth, and turned to happiness!"

Again the spectre raised a cry, and shook its chain and wrung its shadowy hands.

"You are fettered," said Scrooge, trembling. "Tell me why?"

"I wear the chain I forged in life," replied the Ghost. "I made it link by link, and yard by yard; I girded it on of my own free will, and of my own free will I wore it. Is its pattern strange to *you*?"

Scrooge trembled more and more.

"Or would you know," pursued the Ghost, "the weight and length of the strong coil you bear yourself? It was full as heavy and as long as this, seven Christmas Eves ago. You have laboured on it, since. It is a ponderous chain!"

Scrooge glanced about him on the floor, in the expectation of finding himself surrounded by some fifty or sixty fathoms of iron cable: but he could see nothing.

"Jacob," he said, imploringly. "Old Jacob Marley, tell me more. Speak comfort to me, Jacob."

"I have none to give," the Ghost replied. "It comes from other regions, Ebenezer Scrooge, and is conveyed by other ministers, to other kinds of men. Nor can I tell you what I would. A very little more is all permitted to me. I cannot rest, I cannot stay, I cannot linger anywhere. My spirit never walked beyond our counting-house—mark me!—in life my spirit never roved beyond the narrow limits of our money-changing hole; and weary journeys lie before me!"

It was a habit with Scrooge, whenever he became thoughtful, to put his hands in his breeches pockets. Pondering on what the Ghost had said, he did so now, but without lifting up his eyes, or getting off his knees.

"You must have been very slow about it, Jacob," Scrooge observed, in a business-like manner, though with humility and deference.

"Slow!" the Ghost repeated.

"Seven years dead," mused Scrooge. "And travelling all the time?"

"The whole time," said the Ghost. "No rest, no peace. Incessant torture of remorse."

"You travel fast?" said Scrooge.

"On the wings of the wind," replied the Ghost.

"You might have got over a great quantity of ground in seven years," said Scrooge.

The Ghost, on hearing this, set up another cry, and

clanked its chain so hideously in the dead silence of the night, that the Ward would have been justified in indicting it for a nuisance.

"Oh! captive, bound, and double-ironed," cried the phantom, "not to know, that ages of incessant labour by immortal creatures, for this earth must pass into eternity before the good of which it is susceptible is all developed. Not to know that any Christian spirit working kindly in its little sphere, whatever it may be, will find its mortal life too short for its vast means of usefulness. Not to know that no space of regret can make amends for one life's opportunity misused! Yet such was I! Oh! such was I!"

"But you were always a good man of business, Jacob," faultered Scrooge, who now began to apply this to himself.

"Business!" cried the Ghost, wringing its hands again. "Mankind was my business. The common welfare was my business; charity, mercy, forbearance, and benevolence, were, all, my business. The dealings of my trade were but a drop of water in the comprehensive ocean of my business!"

It held up its chain at arm's length, as if that were the cause of all its unavailing grief, and flung it heavily upon the ground again.

"At this time of the rolling year," the spectre said, "I suffer most. Why did I walk through crowds of fellow-beings with my eyes turned down, and never raise them to that blessed Star which led the Wise Men to a poor abode? Were there no poor homes to which its light would have conducted *me*!"

Scrooge was very much dismayed to hear the spectre going on at this rate, and began to quake exceedingly.

"Hear me!" cried the Ghost. "My time is nearly gone."

"I will," said Scrooge. "But don't be hard upon me! Don't be flowery, Jacob! Pray!"

"How it is that I appear before you in a shape that you can see, I may not tell. I have sat invisible beside you many and many a day."

It was not an agreeable idea. Scrooge shivered, and wiped the perspiration from his brow.

"That is no light part of my penance," pursued the Ghost. "I am here to-night to warn you, that you have yet a chance and hope of escaping my fate. A chance and hope of my procuring, Ebenezer."

"You were always a good friend to me," said Scrooge. "Thank'ee!"

"You will be haunted," resumed the Ghost, "by Three Spirits."

Scrooge's countenance fell almost as low as the Ghost's had done.

"Is that the chance and hope you mentioned, Jacob?" he demanded, in a faultering voice.

"It is."

"I—I think I'd rather not," said Scrooge.

"Without their visits," said the Ghost, "you cannot hope to shun the path I tread. Expect the first to-morrow, when the bell tolls one."

"Couldn't I take 'em all at once, and have it over, Jacob?" hinted Scrooge.

"Expect the second on the next night at the same hour. The third upon the next night when the last stroke of twelve has ceased to vibrate. Look to see me no more; and look that, for your own sake, you remember what has passed between us!"

When it had said these words, the spectre took its wrapper from the table, and bound it round its head, as before. Scrooge knew this, by the smart sound its teeth made, when the jaws were brought together by the bandage. He ventured to raise his eyes again, and found his supernatural visitor confronting him in an erect attitude, with its chain wound over and about its arm.

The apparition walked backward from him; and at every step it took, the window raised itself a little, so that when the spectre reached it, it was wide open. It beckoned Scrooge to approach, which he did. When they were within two paces of each other, Marley's Ghost held up its hand, warning him to come no nearer. Scrooge stopped.

Not so much in obedience, as in surprise and fear: for on the raising of the hand, he became sensible of confused noises in the air; incoherent sounds of lamentation and regret; wailings inexpressibly sorrowful and self-accusatory. The spectre, after listening for a moment, joined in the mournful dirge; and floated out upon the bleak, dark night.

Scrooge followed to the window: desperate in his curiosity. He looked out.

The air filled with phantoms, wandering hither and thither in restless haste, and moaning as they went. Every one of them wore chains like Marley's Ghost; some few (they might be guilty governments) were linked together; none were free. Many had been personally known to Scrooge in their lives. He had been quite familiar with one old ghost, in a white waistcoat, with a monstrous iron safe attached to its ankle, who cried piteously at being unable to assist a wretched woman with an infant, whom it saw below, upon a door-step. The misery with them all was, clearly, that they sought to interfere, for good, in human matters, and had lost the power for ever.

Whether these creatures faded into mist, or mist enshrouded them, he could not tell. But they and their spirit voices faded together; and the night became as it had been when he walked home.

Scrooge closed the window, and examined the door by which the Ghost had entered. It was double-locked, as he had locked it with his own hands, and the bolts were undisturbed. He tried to say "Humbug!" but stopped at the first syllable. And being, from the emotion he had undergone, or the fatigues of the day, or his glimpse of the Invisible World, or the dull conversation of the Ghost, or the lateness of the hour, much in need of repose; went straight to bed, without undressing, and fell asleep upon the instant.

The First of the Three Spirits

When Scrooge awoke, it was so dark, that looking out of bed, he could scarcely distinguish the transparent window from the opaque walls of his chamber. He was endeavouring to pierce the darkness with his ferret eyes, when the chimes of a neighbouring church struck the four quarters. So he listened for the hour.

To his great astonishment the heavy bell went on from six to seven, and from seven to eight, and regularly up to twelve; then stopped. Twelve! It was past two when he went to bed. The clock was wrong. An icicle must have got into the works. Twelve!

He touched the spring of his repeater, to correct this most preposterous clock. Its rapid little pulse beat twelve; and stopped.

"Why, it isn't possible," said Scrooge, "that I can have slept through a whole day and far into another night. It isn't possible that anything has happened to the sun, and this is twelve at noon!"

The idea being an alarming one, he scrambled out of bed, and groped his way to the window. He was obliged to rub the frost off with the sleeve of his dressing-gown before he could see anything; and could see very little then. All he could make out was, that it was still very foggy and extremely cold, and that there was no noise of people running to and fro, and making a great stir, as there unquestionably would have been if night had beaten off bright day, and taken possession of the world. This was a great relief, because "three days after sight of this First of Exchange pay to Mr. Ebenezer Scrooge or his order," and so forth, would have become a mere United States' security if there were no days to count by.

Scrooge went to bed again, and thought, and thought, and thought it over and over and over, and could make nothing of it. The more he thought, the more perplexed he was; and the more he endeavoured not to think, the more he thought. Marley's Ghost bothered him exceedingly. Every time he resolved within himself, after mature inquiry, that it was all a dream, his mind flew back again, like a strong spring released, to its first position, and presented the same problem to be worked all through, "Was it a dream or not?"

Scrooge lay in this state until the chimes had gone three quarters more, when he remembered, on a sudden, that the Ghost had warned him of a visitation when the bell tolled one. He resolved to lie awake until the hour was passed; and, considering that he could no more go to sleep than go to Heaven, this was perhaps the wisest resolution in his power.

The quarter was so long, that he was more than once convinced he must have sunk into a doze unconsciously, and missed the clock. At length it broke upon his listening ear.

"Ding, dong!"

"A quarter past," said Scrooge, counting.

"Ding, dong!"

"Half past!" said Scrooge.

"Ding, dong!"

"A quarter to it," said Scrooge.

"Ding, dong!"

"The hour itself," said Scrooge, triumphantly, "and nothing else!"

He spoke before the hour bell sounded, which it now did with a deep, dull, hollow, melancholy ONE. Light flashed up in the room upon the instant, and the curtains of his bed were drawn.

The curtains of his bed were drawn aside, I tell you, by a hand. Not the curtains at his feet, nor the curtains at his back, but those to which his face was addressed. The curtains of his bed were drawn aside; and Scrooge, starting up into a half-recumbent attitude, found himself face to face with the unearthly visitor who drew them: as close to it as I am now to you, and I am standing in the spirit at your elbow.

It was a strange figure—like a child: yet not so like a child as like an old man, viewed through some supernatural medium, which gave him the appearance of having receded from the view, and being diminished to a child's proportions. Its hair, which hung about its neck and down its back, was white as if with age; and yet the face had not a wrinkle in it, and the tenderest bloom was on the skin. The arms were very long and muscular; the hands the same, as if its hold were of uncommon strength. Its legs and feet, most delicately formed, were, like those upper members, bare. It wore a tunic of the purest white; and round its waist was bound a lustrous belt, the sheen of which was beautiful. It held a branch of fresh green holly in its hand; and, in singular contradiction of that wintry emblem, had its dress trimmed with summer flowers. But the strangest thing about it was, that from the crown of its head there sprung a bright clear jet of light, by which all this was visible; and which was doubtless the occasion of its using, in its duller moments, a great extinguisher for a cap, which it now held under its arm.

Even this, though, when Scrooge looked at it with increasing steadiness, was *not* its strangest quality. For as its belt sparkled and glittered now in one part and now in another, and what was light one instant, at another time was dark, so the figure itself fluctuated in its distinctness: being now a thing with one arm, now with one leg, now with twenty legs, now a pair of legs without a head, now a head without a body: of which dissolving parts, no outline would be visible in the dense gloom wherein they melted away. And in the very wonder of this, it would be itself again; distinct and clear as ever.

"Are you the Spirit, sir, whose coming was foretold to me?" asked Scrooge.

"I am!"

The voice was soft and gentle. Singularly low, as if instead of being so close beside him, it were at a distance.

"Who, and what are you?" Scrooge demanded.

"I am the Ghost of Christmas Past."

"Long Past?" inquired Scrooge: observant of its dwarfish stature.

"No. Your past."

Perhaps, Scrooge could not have told anybody why, if anybody could have asked him; but he had a special desire to see the Spirit in his cap; and begged him to be covered.

"What!" exclaimed the Ghost, "would you so soon put out, with worldly hands, the light I give? Is it not enough that you are one of those whose passions made this cap, and force me through whole trains of years to wear it low upon my brow!"

Scrooge reverently disclaimed all intention to offend, or any knowledge of having wilfully "bonneted" the Spirit at any period of his life. He then made bold to inquire what business brought him there.

"Your welfare!" said the Ghost.

Scrooge expressed himself much obliged, but could not help thinking that a night of unbroken rest would have been more conducive to that end. The Spirit must have heard him thinking for it said immediately:

"Your reclamation, then. Take heed!"

It put out its strong hand as it spoke, and clasped him gently by the arm.

"Rise! and walk with me!"

It would have been in vain for Scrooge to plead that the weather and the hour were not adapted to pedestrian purposes; that bed was warm, and the thermometer a long way below freezing; that he was clad but lightly in his slippers, dressing-gown, and nightcap; and that he had a cold upon him at that time. The grasp, though gentle as a woman's hand, was not to be resisted. He rose: but finding that the Spirit made towards the window, clasped its robe in supplication.

"I am a mortal," Scrooge remonstrated, "and liable to fall."

"Bear but a touch of my hand *there*," said the Spirit, laying it upon his heart, "and you shall be upheld in more than this!"

As the words were spoken, they passed through the wall, and stood upon an open country road, with fields on either hand. The city had entirely vanished. Not a vestige of it was to be seen. The darkness and the mist had vanished with it, for it was a clear, cold, winter day, with snow upon the ground.

"Good Heaven!" said Scrooge, clasping his hands together, as he looked about him. "I was bred in this place. I was a boy here!"

The Spirit gazed upon him mildly. Its gentle touch, though it had been light and instantaneous, appeared still present to the old man's sense of feeling. He was conscious of a thousand odours floating in the air, each one connected with a thousand thoughts, and hopes, and joys, and cares long, long, forgotten!

"Your lip is trembling," said the Ghost. "And what is that upon your cheek?"

Scrooge muttered, with an unusual catching in his voice, that it was a pimple; and begged the Ghost to lead him where he would.

"You recollect the way?" inquired the Spirit.

"Remember it!" cried Scrooge with fervour—"I could walk it blindfold."

"Strange to have forgotten it for so many years!" observed the Ghost. "Let us go on."

They walked along the road; Scrooge recognising every gate, and post, and tree; until a little market-town appeared in the distance, with its bridge, its church, and winding river. Some shaggy ponies now were seen trotting towards them with boys upon their backs, who called to other boys in country gigs and carts, driven by farmers. All these boys were in great spirits, and shouted to each other, until the broad fields were so full of merry music, that the crisp air laughed to hear it.

"These are but shadows of the things that have been," said the Ghost. "They have no consciousness of us."

The jocund travellers came on; and as they came, Scrooge knew and named them every one. Why was he rejoiced beyond all bounds to see them! Why did his cold eye glisten, and his heart leap up as they went past! Why was he filled with gladness when he heard them give each other Merry Christmas, as they parted at cross-roads and byeways, for their several homes! What was merry Christmas to Scrooge? Out upon merry Christmas! What good had it ever done to him?

"The school is not quite deserted," said the Ghost. "A solitary child, neglected by his friends, is left there still."

Scrooge said, he knew it. And he sobbed.

They left the high-road, by a well remembered lane,

and soon approached a mansion of dull red brick, with a little weathercock-surmounted cupola on the roof, and a bell hanging in it. It was a large house, but one of broken fortunes; for the spacious offices were little used, their walls were damp and mossy, their windows broken, and their gates decayed. Fowls clucked and strutted in the stables; and the coach-houses and sheds were over-run with grass. Nor was it more retentive of its ancient state, within; for entering the dreary hall, and glancing through the open doors of many rooms, they found them poorly furnished, cold, and vast. There was an earthy savour in the air, a chilly bareness in the place, which associated itself somehow with too much getting up by candle-light, and not too much to eat.

They went, the Ghost and Scrooge, across the hall, to a door at the back of the house. It opened before them, and disclosed a long, bare, melancholy room, made barer still by lines of plain deal forms and desks. At one of these a lonely boy was reading near a feeble fire; and Scrooge sat down upon a form, and wept to see his poor forgotten self as he had used to be.

Not a latent echo in the house, not a squeak and scuffle from the mice behind the panelling, not a drip from the half-thawed water-spout in the dull yard behind, not a sigh among the leafless boughs of one despondent poplar, not the idle swinging of an empty store-house door, no, not a clicking in the fire, but fell upon the heart of Scrooge with a softening influence, and gave a freer passage to his tears.

The Spirit touched him on the arm, and pointed to his younger self, intent upon his reading. Suddenly a man, in foreign garments: wonderfully real and distinct to look at: stood outside the window, with an axe stuck in his belt, and leading an ass laden with wood by the bridle.

"Why, it's Ali Baba!" Scrooge exclaimed in ecstasy. "It's dear old honest Ali Baba! Yes, yes, I know! One Christmas time, when yonder solitary child was left here all alone, he *did* come, for the first time, just like that. Poor boy! And Valentine," said Scrooge, "and his wild brother, Orson; there they go! And what's his name, who was put down in his drawers, asleep, at the Gate of Damascus; don't you see him! And the Sultan's Groom turned upside-down by the Genii; there he is upon his head! Serve him right. I'm glad of it. What business had *he* to be married to the Princess!"

To hear Scrooge expending all the earnestness of his nature on such subjects, in a most extraordinary voice between laughing and crying; and to see his heightened and excited face; would have been a surprise to his business friends in the city, indeed.

"There's the Parrot!" cried Scrooge. "Green body and yellow tail, with a thing like a lettuce growing out of the top of his head; there he is! Poor Robin Crusoe, he called him, when he came home again after sailing round the island. 'Poor Robin Crusoe, where have you been, Robin Crusoe?' The man thought he was dreaming, but he wasn't. It was the Parrot, you know. There goes Friday, running for his life to the little creek! Halloa! Hoop! Halloo!"

Then, with a rapidity of transition very foreign to his usual character, he said, in pity for his former self, "Poor boy!" and cried again.

"I wish," Scrooge muttered, putting his hand in his pocket, and looking about him, after drying his eyes with his cuff: "but it's too late now."

"What is the matter?" asked the Spirit.

"Nothing," said Scrooge. "Nothing. There was a boy singing a Christmas Carol at my door last night. I should like to have given him something: that's all."

The Ghost smiled thoughtfully, and waved its hand: saying as it did so, "Let us see another Christmas!"

Scrooge's former self grew larger at the words, and the room became a little darker and more dirty. The panels shrunk, the windows cracked; fragments of plaster fell out of the ceiling, and the naked laths were shown instead; but how all this was brought about, Scrooge knew no more than you do. He only knew that it was quite correct; that everything had happened so; that there he was, alone again, when all the other boys had gone home for the jolly holidays.

He was not reading now, but walking up and down despairingly. Scrooge looked at the Ghost, and with a mournful shaking of his head, glanced anxiously towards the door.

It opened; and a little girl, much younger than the boy, came darting in, and putting her arms about his neck, and often kissing him, addressed him as her "Dear, dear brother."

"I have come to bring you home, dear brother!" said the child, clapping her tiny hands, and bending down to laugh. "To bring you home, home, home!"

"Home, little Fan?" returned the boy.

"Yes!" said the child, brimful of glee. "Home, for good

and all. Home, for ever and ever. Father is so much kinder
than he used to be, that home's like Heaven! He spoke so
gently to me one dear night when I was going to bed, that
I was not afraid to ask him once more if you might come
home; and he said Yes, you should; and sent me in a coach to
bring you. And you're to be a man!" said the child, opening
her eyes, "and are never to come back here; but first, we're
to be together all the Christmas long, and have the merriest
time in all the world."

"You are quite a woman, little Fan!" exclaimed the boy.

She clapped her hands and laughed, and tried to touch
his head; but being too little, laughed again, and stood on
tiptoe to embrace him. Then she began to drag him, in her
childish eagerness, towards the door; and he, nothing loth
to go, accompanied her.

A terrible voice in the hall cried, "Bring down Master
Scrooge's box, there!" and in the hall appeared the schoolmaster himself, who glared on Master Scrooge with a ferocious condescension, and threw him into a dreadful state
of mind by shaking hands with him. He then conveyed him
and his sister into the veriest old well of a shivering best-par-
lour that ever was seen, where the maps upon the wall, and
the celestial and terrestrial globes in the windows were waxy
with cold. Here he produced a decanter of curiously light
wine, and a block of curiously heavy cake, and administered
instalments of those dainties to the young people: at the
same time, sending out a meagre servant to offer a glass of
"something" to the postboy, who answered that he thanked
the gentleman, but if it was the same tap as he had tasted be-

fore, he had rather not. Master Scrooge's trunk being by this time tied on to the top of the chaise, the children bade the schoolmaster good-bye right willingly; and getting into it, drove gaily down the garden-sweep: the quick wheels dashing the hoar-frost and snow from off the dark leaves of the evergreens like spray.

"Always a delicate creature, whom a breath might have withered," said the Ghost. "But she had a large heart!"

"So she had," cried Scrooge. "You're right. I'll not gainsay it, Spirit. God forbid!"

"She died a woman," said the Ghost, "and had, as I think, children."

"One child," Scrooge returned.

"True," said the Ghost. "Your nephew!"

Scrooge seemed uneasy in his mind; and answered briefly, "Yes."

Although they had but that moment left the school behind them, they were now in the busy thoroughfares of a city, where shadowy passengers passed and repassed; where shadowy carts and coaches battled for the way, and all the strife and tumult of a real city were. It was made plain enough, by the dressing of the shops, that here too it was Christmas time again; but it was evening, and the streets were lighted up.

The Ghost stopped at a certain warehouse door, and asked Scrooge if he knew it.

"Know it!" said Scrooge. "Was I apprenticed here?"

They went in. At sight of an old gentleman in a Welch wig, sitting behind such a high desk, that if he had been two inches taller he must have knocked his head against the ceiling, Scrooge cried in great excitement:

"Why, it's old Fezziwig! Bless his heart; it's Fezziwig alive again!"

Old Fezziwig laid down his pen, and looked up at the clock, which pointed to the hour of seven. He rubbed his hands; adjusted his capacious waistcoat; laughed all over himself, from his shoes to his organ of benevolence; and called out in a comfortable, oily, rich, fat, jovial voice:

"Yo ho, there! Ebenezer! Dick!"

Scrooge's former self, now grown a young man, came briskly in, accompanied by his fellow-'prentice.

"Dick Wilkins, to be sure!" said Scrooge to the Ghost. "Bless me, yes. There he is. He was very much attached to me, was Dick. Poor Dick! Dear, dear!"

"Yo ho, my boys!" said Fezziwig. "No more work tonight. Christmas Eve, Dick. Christmas, Ebenezer! Let's have the shutters up," cried old Fezziwig, with a sharp clap of his hands, "before a man can say, Jack Robinson!"

You wouldn't believe how those two fellows went at it! They charged into the street with the shutters—one, two, three—had 'em up in their places—four, five, six—barred 'em and pinned 'em—seven, eight, nine—and came back before you could have got to twelve, panting like race-horses.

"Hilli-ho!" cried old Fezziwig, skipping down from the high desk, with wonderful agility. "Clear away, my lads, and let's have lots of room here! Hilli-ho, Dick! Chirrup, Ebenezer!"

Clear away! There was nothing they wouldn't have

cleared away, or couldn't have cleared away, with old Fez-ziwig looking on. It was done in a minute. Every movable was packed off, as if it were dismissed from public life for evermore; the floor was swept and watered, the lamps were trimmed, fuel was heaped upon the fire; and the warehouse was as snug, and warm, and dry, and bright a ball-room, as you would desire to see upon a winter's night.

In came a fiddler with a music-book, and went up to the lofty desk, and made an orchestra of it, and tuned like fifty stomach-aches. In came Mrs. Fezziwig, one vast substan-tial smile. In came the three Miss Fezziwigs, beaming and lovable. In came the six young followers whose hearts they broke. In came all the young men and women employed in the business. In came the housemaid, with her cousin, the baker. In came the cook, with her brother's particular friend, the milkman. In came the boy from over the way, who was suspected of not having board enough from his master; try-ing to hide himself behind the girl from next door but one, who was proved to have had her ears pulled by her Mistress. In they all came, one after another; some shyly, some boldly, some gracefully, some awkwardly, some pushing, some pull-ing; in they all came, anyhow and everyhow. Away they all went, twenty couple at once, hands half round and back again the other way; down the middle and up again; round and round in various stages of affectionate grouping; old top couple always turning up in the wrong place; new top couple starting off again, as soon as they got there; all top couples at last, and not a bottom one to help them. When this re-sult was brought about, old Fezziwig, clapping his hands to stop the dance, cried out, "Well done!" and the fiddler plunged his hot face into a pot of porter, especially provided for that purpose. But scorning rest upon his reappearance, he instantly began again, though there were no dancers yet, as if the other fiddler had been carried home, exhausted, on a shutter; and he were a bran-new man resolved to beat him out of sight, or perish.

There were more dances, and there were forfeits, and more dances, and there was cake, and there was negus, and there was a great piece of Cold Roast, and there was a great piece of Cold Boiled, and there were mince-pies, and plenty of beer. But the great effect of the evening came after the Roast and Boiled, when the fiddler (an artful dog, mind! The sort of man who knew his business better than you or I could have told it him!) struck up "Sir Roger de Coverley." Then old Fezziwig stood out to dance with Mrs. Fezziwig. Top couple, too; with a good stiff piece of work cut out for them; three or four and twenty pair of partners; people who were not to be trifled with; people who *would* dance, and had no notion of walking.

But if they had been twice as many: ah, four times: old Fezziwig would have been a match for them, and so would Mrs. Fezziwig. As to *her,* she was worthy to be his partner in every sense of the term. If that's not high praise, tell me higher, and I'll use it. A positive light appeared to issue from Fezziwig's calves. They shone in every part of the dance like moons. You couldn't have predicted, at any given time, what would become of 'em next. And when old Fezziwig and Mrs. Fezziwig had gone all through the dance; advance and retire, hold hands with your partner; bow and curtsey; corkscrew; thread-the-needle, and back again to your place; Fezziwig "cut"—cut so deftly, that he appeared to wink with his legs, and came upon his feet again without a stagger.

When the clock struck eleven, this domestic ball broke up. Mr. and Mrs. Fezziwig took their stations, one on either side the door, and shaking hands with every person individually as he or she went out, wished him or her a Merry Christmas. When everybody had retired but the two 'prentices, they did the same to them; and thus the cheerful voices died away, and the lads were left to their beds; which were under a counter in the back-shop.

During the whole of this time, Scrooge had acted like a man out of his wits. His heart and soul were in the scene, and with his former self. He corroborated everything, remembered everything, enjoyed everything, and underwent the strangest agitation. It was not until now, when the bright faces of his former self and Dick were turned from them, that he remembered the Ghost, and became conscious that it was looking full upon him, while the light upon its head burnt very clear.

"A small matter," said the Ghost, "to make these silly folks so full of gratitude."

"Small!" echoed Scrooge.

The Spirit signed to him to listen to the two apprentices, who were pouring out their hearts in praise of Fezziwig: and when he had done so, said,

"Why! Is it not? He has spent but a few pounds of your

mortal money: three or four, perhaps. Is that so much that he deserves this praise?"

"It isn't that," said Scrooge, heated by the remark, and speaking unconsciously like his former, not his latter, self. "It isn't that, Spirit. He has the power to render us happy or unhappy; to make our service light or burdensome; a pleasure or a toil. Say that his power lies in words and looks; in things so slight and insignificant that it is impossible to add and count 'em up: what then? The happiness he gives, is quite as great as if it cost a fortune."

He felt the Spirit's glance, and stopped.

"What is the matter?" asked the Ghost.

"Nothing particular," said Scrooge.

"Something, I think?" the Ghost insisted.

"No," said Scrooge, "No. I should like to be able to say a word or two to my clerk just now! That's all."

His former self turned down the lamps as he gave utterance to the wish; and Scrooge and the Ghost again stood side by side in the open air.

"My time grows short," observed the Spirit. "Quick!"

This was not addressed to Scrooge, or to any one whom he could see, but it produced an immediate effect. For again Scrooge saw himself. He was older now; a man in the prime of life. His face had not the harsh and rigid lines of later years; but it had begun to wear the signs of care and avarice. There was an eager, greedy, restless motion in the eye, which showed the passion that had taken root, and where the shadow of the growing tree would fall.

He was not alone, but sat by the side of a fair young girl

in a mourning-dress: in whose eyes there were tears, which sparkled in the light that shone out of the Ghost of Christmas Past.

"It matters little," she said, softly. "To you, very little. Another idol has displaced me; and if it can cheer and comfort you in time to come, as I would have tried to do, I have no just cause to grieve."

"What Idol has displaced you?" he rejoined.

"A golden one."

"This is the even-handed dealing of the world!" he said. "There is nothing on which it is so hard as poverty; and there is nothing it professes to condemn with such severity as the pursuit of wealth!"

"You fear the world too much," she answered, gently. "All your other hopes have merged into the hope of being beyond the chance of its sordid reproach. I have seen your nobler aspirations fall off one by one, until the master-passion, Gain, engrosses you. Have I not?"

"What then?" he retorted. "Even if I have grown so much wiser, what then? I am not changed towards you."

She shook her head.

"Am I?"

"Our contract is an old one. It was made when we were both poor and content to be so, until, in good season, we could improve our worldly fortune by our patient industry. You *are* changed. When it was made, you were another man."

"I was a boy," he said impatiently.

"Your own feeling tells you that you were not what you

are," she returned. "I am. That which promised happiness when we were one in heart, is fraught with misery now that we are two. How often and how keenly I have thought of this, I will not say. It is enough that I *have* thought of it, and can release you."

"Have I ever sought release?"

"In words. No. Never."

"In what, then?"

"In a changed nature; in an altered spirit; in another atmosphere of life; another Hope as its great end. In every-thing that made my love of any worth or value in your sight. If this had never been between us," said the girl, looking mildly, but with steadiness, upon him; "tell me, would you seek me out and try to win me now? Ah, no!"

He seemed to yield to the justice of this supposition, in spite of himself. But he said, with a struggle, "You think not."

"I would gladly think otherwise if I could," she an-swered, "Heaven knows! When *I* have learned a Truth like this, I know how strong and irresistible it must be. But if you were free to-day, to-morrow, yesterday, can even I believe that you would choose a dowerless girl—you who, in your very confidence with her, weigh everything by Gain: or, choosing her, if for a moment you were false enough to your one guiding principle to do so, do I not know that your re-pentance and regret would surely follow? I do; and I release you. With a full heart, for the love of him you once were."

He was about to speak; but with her head turned from him, she resumed.

"You may—the memory of what is past half makes me hope you will—have pain in this. A very, very brief time, and you will dismiss the recollection of it, gladly, as an unprofitable dream, from which it happened well that you awoke. May you be happy in the life you have chosen!"

She left him; and they parted.

"Spirit!" said Scrooge, "show me no more! Conduct me home. Why do you delight to torture me?"

"One shadow more!" exclaimed the Ghost.

"No more!" cried Scrooge. "No more. I don't wish to see it. Show me no more!"

But the relentless Ghost pinioned him in both his arms, and forced him to observe what happened next.

They were in another scene and place: a room, not very large or handsome, but full of comfort. Near to the winter fire sat a beautiful young girl, so like the last that Scrooge believed it was the same, until he saw *her*, now a comely matron, sitting opposite her daughter. The noise in this room was perfectly tumultuous, for there were more children there, than Scrooge in his agitated state of mind could count; and, unlike the celebrated herd in the poem, they were not forty children conducting themselves like one, but every child was conducting itself like forty. The consequences were uproarious beyond belief; but no one seemed to care; on the contrary, the mother and daughter laughed heartily, and enjoyed it very much, and the latter, soon beginning to mingle in the sports, got pillaged by the young brigands most ruthlessly. What would I not have given to be one of them! Though I never could have been so rude, no, no! I wouldn't for the wealth of all the world have crushed that braided hair, and torn it down; and for the precious little shoe, I wouldn't have plucked it off, God bless my soul! to save my life. As to measuring her waist in sport, as they did, bold young brood, I couldn't have done it; I should have expected my arm to have grown round it for a punishment, and never come straight again. And yet I should have dearly liked, I own, to have touched her lips; to have questioned her, that she might have opened them; to have looked upon the lashes of her downcast eyes, and never raised a blush; to have let loose waves of hair, an inch of which would be a keepsake beyond price: in short, I should have liked, I do confess, to have had the lightest licence of a child, and yet been man enough to know its value.

But now a knocking at the door was heard, and such a rush immediately ensued that she with laughing face and plundered dress was borne towards it the centre of a flushed and boisterous group, just in time to greet the father, who came home attended by a man laden with Christmas toys and presents. Then the shouting and the struggling, and the onslaught that was made on the defenceless porter! The scaling him with chairs for ladders, to dive into his pockets, despoil him of brown-paper parcels, hold on tight by his cravat, hug him round the neck, pommel his back, and kick his legs in irrepressible affection! The shouts of wonder and delight with which the development of every package was received! The terrible announcement that the baby had been taken in the act of putting a doll's frying-pan into his mouth, and was more than suspected of having swallowed a fictitious turkey, glued on a wooden platter! The immense relief of finding this a false alarm! The joy, and gratitude, and ecstasy! They are all indescribable alike. It is enough that by degrees the children and their emotions got out of the parlour and by one stair at a time, up to the top of the house; where they went to bed, and so subsided.

And now Scrooge looked on more attentively than ever, when the master of the house, having his daughter leaning fondly on him, sat down with her and her mother at his own fireside; and when he thought that such another creature, quite as graceful and as full of promise, might have called him father, and been a spring-time in the haggard winter of his life, his sight grew very dim indeed.

"Belle," said the husband, turning to his wife with a smile, "I saw an old friend of yours this afternoon."

"Who was it?"

"Guess!"

"How can I? Tut, don't I know," she added in the same breath, laughing as he laughed. "Mr. Scrooge."

"Mr. Scrooge it was. I passed his office window; and as it was not shut up, and he had a candle inside, I could scarcely help seeing him. His partner lies upon the point of death, I hear; and there he sat alone. Quite alone in the world, I do believe."

"Spirit!" said Scrooge in a broken voice, "remove me from this place."

"I told you these were shadows of the things that have been," said the Ghost. "That they are what they are, do not blame me!"

"Remove me!" Scrooge exclaimed. "I cannot bear it!"

He turned upon the Ghost, and seeing that it looked upon him with a face, in which in some strange way there were fragments of all the faces it had shown him, wrestled with it.

"Leave me! Take me back. Haunt me no longer!"

In the struggle, if that can be called a struggle in which the Ghost with no visible resistance on its own part was undisturbed by any effort of its adversary, Scrooge observed that its light was burning high and bright; and dimly connecting that with its influence over him, he seized the extinguisher-cap, and by a sudden action pressed it down upon its head.

The Spirit dropped beneath it, so that the extinguisher covered its whole form; but though Scrooge pressed it down with all his force, he could not hide the light: which streamed from under it, in a unbroken flood upon the ground.

He was conscious of being exhausted, and overcome by an irresistible drowsiness; and, further, of being in his own bedroom. He gave the cap a parting squeeze, in which his hand relaxed; and had barely time to reel to bed, before he sank into a heavy sleep.

The Second of the Three Spirits

A WAKING in the middle of a prodigiously tough snore, and sitting up in bed to get his thoughts together, Scrooge had no occasion to be told that the bell was again upon the stroke of One. He felt that he was restored to consciousness in the right nick of time, for the especial purpose of holding a conference with the second messenger despatched to him through Jacob Marley's intervention. But, finding that he turned uncomfortably cold when he began to wonder which of his curtains this new spectre would draw back, he put them every one aside with his own hands; and lying down again, established a sharp look-out all round the bed. For he wished to challenge the Spirit on the moment of its appearance, and did not wish to be taken by surprise and made nervous.

Gentlemen of the free-and-easy sort, who plume themselves on being acquainted with a move or two, and being usually equal to the time-of-day, express the wide range of their capacity for adventure by observing that they are good for anything from pitch-and-toss to manslaughter; between which opposite extremes, no doubt, there lies a tolerably wide and comprehensive range of subjects. Without venturing for Scrooge quite as hardily as this, I don't mind calling on you to believe that he was ready for a good broad field of strange appearances, and that nothing between a baby and a rhinoceros would have astonished him very much.

Now, being prepared for almost anything, he was not by any means prepared for nothing; and, consequently, when the Bell struck One, and no shape appeared, he was taken with a violent fit of trembling. Five minutes, ten minutes, a quarter of an hour went by, yet nothing came. All this time, he lay upon his bed, the very core and centre of a blaze of ruddy light, which streamed upon it when the clock proclaimed the hour; and which being only light, was more alarming than a dozen ghosts, as he was powerless to make out what it meant, or would be at; and was sometimes apprehensive that he might be at that very moment an interesting case of spontaneous combustion, without having the consolation of knowing it. At last, however, he began to think—as you or I would have thought at first; for it is always the person not in the predicament who knows what ought to have been done in it, and would unquestionably have done it too—at last, I say, he began to think that the source and secret of this ghostly light might be in the adjoining room: from whence, on further tracing it, it seemed to shine. This idea taking full possession of his mind, he got up softly and shuffled in his slippers to the door.

The moment Scrooge's hand was on the lock, a strange voice called him by his name, and bade him enter. He obeyed.

It was his own room. There was no doubt about that. But it had undergone a surprising transformation. The walls and ceiling were so hung with living green, that it looked a perfect grove, from every part of which, bright gleaming berries glistened. The crisp leaves of holly, mistletoe, and ivy reflected back the light, as if so many little mirrors had been scattered there; and such a mighty blaze went roaring up the chimney, as that dull petrification of a hearth had never known in Scrooge's time, or Marley's, or for many and many a winter season gone. Heaped up on the floor, to form a kind of throne, were turkeys, geese, game, poultry, brawn, great joints of meat, sucking-pigs, long wreaths of sausages, mince-pies, plum-puddings, barrels of oysters, red-hot chestnuts, cherry-cheeked apples, juicy oranges, luscious pears, immense twelfth-cakes, and seething bowls of punch, that made the chamber dim with their delicious steam. In easy state upon this couch, there sat a jolly Giant, glorious to see; who bore a glowing torch, in shape not unlike Plenty's horn, and held it up, high up, to shed its light on Scrooge, as he came peeping round the door.

"Come in!" exclaimed the Ghost. "Come in! and know me better, man!"

Scrooge entered timidly, and hung his head before this Spirit. He was not the dogged Scrooge he had been; and though the Spirit's eyes were clear and kind, he did not like to meet them.

"I am the Ghost of Christmas Present," said the Spirit. "Look upon me!"

Scrooge reverently did so. It was clothed in one simple

deep green robe, or mantle, bordered with white fur. This garment hung so loosely on the figure, that its capacious breast was bare, as if disdaining to be warded or concealed by any artifice. Its feet, observable beneath the ample folds of the garment, were also bare; and on its head it wore no other covering than a holly wreath, set here and there with shining icicles. Its dark brown curls were long and free: free as its ge-nial face, its sparkling eye, its open hand, its cheery voice, its unconstrained demeanour, and its joyful air. Girded round its middle was an antique scabbard; but no sword was in it, and the ancient sheath was eaten up with rust.

"You have never seen the like of me before!" exclaimed the Spirit.

"Never," Scrooge made answer to it.

"Have never walked forth with the younger members of my family; meaning (for I am very young) my elder brothers born in these later years?" pursued the Phantom.

"I don't think I have," said Scrooge. "I am afraid I have not. Have you had many brothers, Spirit?"

"More than eighteen hundred," said the Ghost.

"A tremendous family to provide for!" muttered Scrooge. The Ghost of Christmas Present rose.

"Spirit," said Scrooge submissively, "conduct me where you will. I went forth last night on compulsion, and I learnt a lesson which is working now. To-night, if you have aught to teach me, let me profit by it."

"Touch my robe!"

Scrooge did as he was told, and held it fast.

Holly, mistletoe, red berries, ivy, turkeys, geese, game,

poultry, brawn, meat, pigs, sausages, oysters, pies, pud-dings, fruit, and punch, all vanished instantly. So did the room, the fire, the ruddy glow, the hour of night, and they stood in the city streets on Christmas morning, where (for the weather was severe) the people made a rough, but brisk and not unpleasant kind of music, in scraping the snow from the pavement in front of their dwellings, and from the tops of their houses: whence it was mad delight to the boys to see it come plumping down into the road below, and splitting into artificial little snow-storms.

The house fronts looked black enough, and the windows blacker, contrasting with the smooth white sheet of snow upon the roofs, and with the dirtier snow upon the ground; which last deposit had been ploughed up in deep furrows by the heavy wheels of carts and wagons; furrows that crossed and re-crossed each other hundreds of times where the great streets branched off, and made intricate channels, hard to trace, in the thick yellow mud and icy water. The sky was gloomy, and the shortest streets were choked up with a dingy mist, half thawed, half frozen, whose heavier particles descended in a shower of sooty atoms, as if all the chimneys in Great Britain had, by one consent, caught fire, and were blazing away to their dear hearts' content. There was noth-ing very cheerful in the climate or the town, and yet was there an air of cheerfulness abroad that the clearest summer air and brightest summer sun might have endeavoured to diffuse in vain.

For the people who were shovelling away on the house-tops were jovial and full of glee; calling out to one another from the parapets, and now and then exchanging a facetious snowball—better-natured missile far than many a wordy jest—laughing heartily if it went right, and not less heartily if it went wrong. The poulterers' shops were still half open, and the fruiterers' were radiant in their glory. There were great round, pot-bellied baskets of chestnuts, shaped like the waist-coats of jolly old gentlemen, lolling at the doors, and tumbling out into the street in their apoplectic opulence. There were ruddy, brown-faced, broad-girthed Spanish Onions, shining in the fatness of their growth like Spanish Friars; and winking from their shelves in wanton slyness at the girls as they went by, and glanced demurely at the hung-up mistletoe. There were pears and apples, clustered high in blooming pyramids; there were bunches of grapes, made in the shopkeepers' benevolence to dangle from conspicuous hooks, that people's mouths might water gratis as they passed; there were piles of filberts, mossy and brown, recalling, in their fragrance, ancient walks among the woods, and pleasant shufflings ankle deep through withered leaves; there were Norfolk Biffins, squab and swarthy, setting off the yellow of the oranges and lemons, and, in the great compactness of their juicy persons, urgently entreating and beseeching to be carried home in paper bags and eaten after dinner. The very gold and silver fish, set forth among these choice fruits in a bowl, though members of a dull and stagnant-blooded race, appeared to know that there was something going on; and, to a fish, went gasping round and round their little world in slow and passionless excitement.

The Grocers'! oh the Grocers'! nearly closed, with perhaps two shutters down, or one; but through those gaps such glimpses! It was not alone that the scales descending on the counter made a merry sound, or that the twine and roller parted company so briskly, or that the canisters were rattled up and down like juggling tricks, or even that the blended scents of tea and coffee were so grateful to the nose, or even that the raisins were so plentiful and rare, the almonds so extremely white, the sticks of cinnamon so long and straight, the other spices so delicious, the candied fruits so caked and spotted with molten sugar as to make the coldest lookers-on feel faint and subsequently bilious. Nor was it that the figs were moist and pulpy, or that the French plums blushed in modest tartness from their highly-decorated boxes, or that everything was good to eat and in its Christmas dress: but the customers were all so hurried and so eager in the hopeful promise of the day, that they tumbled up against each other at the door, clashing their wicker baskets wildly, and left their purchases upon the counter, and came running back to fetch them, and committed hundreds of the like mistakes in the best humour possible; while the Grocer and his people were so frank and fresh that the polished hearts with which they fastened their aprons behind might have been their own, worn outside for general inspection, and for Christmas daws to peck at if they chose.

But soon the steeples called good people all, to church and chapel, and away they came, flocking through the streets in their best clothes, and with their gayest faces. And at the same time there emerged from scores of bye streets, lanes, and nameless turnings, innumerable people, carrying their

"You would deprive them of their means of dining every seventh day, often the only day on which they can be said to dine at all," said Scrooge. "Wouldn't you?"

"I!" cried the Spirit.

"You seek to close these places on the Seventh Day?" said Scrooge. "And it comes to the same thing."

"*I* seek!" exclaimed the Spirit.

"Forgive me if I am wrong. It has been done in your name, or at least in that of your family," said Scrooge.

"There are some upon this earth of yours," returned the Spirit, "who lay claim to know us, and who do their deeds of passion, pride, ill-will, hatred, envy, bigotry, and selfishness in our name, who are as strange to us and all our kith and kin, as if they had never lived. Remember that, and charge their doings on themselves, not us."

Scrooge promised that he would; and they went on, invisible, as they had been before, into the suburbs of the town. It was a remarkable quality of the Ghost (which Scrooge had observed at the baker's) that notwithstanding his gigantic size, he could accommodate himself to any place with ease; and that he stood beneath a low roof quite as gracefully and like a supernatural creature, as it was possible he could have done in any lofty hall.

And perhaps it was the pleasure the good Spirit had in showing off this power of his, or else it was his own kind, generous, hearty nature, and his sympathy with all poor men, that led him straight to Scrooge's clerk's; for there he went, and took Scrooge with him, holding to his robe; and on the threshold of the door the Spirit smiled, and stopped to bless Bob Cratchit's dwelling with the sprinkling of his torch. Think of that! Bob had but fifteen "Bob" a-week himself; he pocketed on Saturdays but fifteen copies of his Christian name; and yet the Ghost of Christmas Present blessed his four-roomed house!

Then up rose Mrs. Cratchit, Cratchit's wife, dressed out but poorly in a twice-turned gown, but brave in ribbons, which are cheap and make a goodly show for sixpence; and she laid the cloth, assisted by Belinda Cratchit, second of her daughters, also brave in ribbons; while Master Peter Cratchit plunged a fork into the saucepan of potatoes, and getting the corners of his monstrous shirt-collar (Bob's private property, conferred upon his son and heir in honour of the day) into his mouth, rejoiced to find himself so gallantly attired, and yearned to show his linen in the fashionable Parks. And now two smaller Cratchits, boy and girl, came tearing in, scream-ing that outside the baker's they had smelt the goose, and known it for their own; and basking in luxurious thoughts of sage and onion, these young Cratchits danced about the table, and exalted Master Peter Cratchit to the skies, while he (not proud, although his collars nearly choked him) blew the fire, until the slow potatoes bubbling up, knocked loudly at the saucepan-lid to be let out and peeled.

"What has ever got your precious father then," said Mrs. Cratchit. "And your brother, Tiny Tim; and Martha warn't as late last Christmas Day by half-an-hour!"

"Here's Martha, mother!" said a girl, appearing as she spoke.

"Here's Martha, mother!" cried the two young Cratchits.

"Hurrah! There's *such* a goose, Martha!"

"Why, bless your heart alive, my dear, how late you are!" said Mrs. Cratchit, kissing her a dozen times, and taking off her shawl and bonnet for her, with officious zeal.

"We'd a deal of work to finish up last night," replied the girl, "and had to clear away this morning, mother!"

"Well! Never mind so long as you are come," said Mrs. Cratchit. "Sit ye down before the fire, my dear, and have a warm, Lord bless ye!"

"No no! There's father coming," cried the two young Cratchits, who were everywhere at once. "Hide Martha, hide!"

So Martha hid herself, and in came little Bob, the father, with at least three feet of comforter exclusive of the fringe, hanging down before him; and his thread-bare clothes darned up and brushed, to look seasonable; and Tiny Tim upon his shoulder. Alas for Tiny Tim, he bore a little crutch, and had his limbs supported by an iron frame!

"Why, where's our Martha?" cried Bob Cratchit looking round.

"Not coming," said Mrs. Cratchit.

"Not coming!" said Bob, with a sudden declension in his high spirits; for he had been Tim's blood horse all the way from church, and had come home rampant. "Not coming upon Christmas Day!"

Martha didn't like to see him disappointed, if it were only in joke; so she came out prematurely from behind the closet door, and ran into his arms, while the two young Cratchits hustled Tiny Tim, and bore him off into the wash-house, that he might hear the pudding singing in the copper.

"And how did little Tim behave?" asked Mrs. Cratchit, when she had rallied Bob on his credulity and Bob had hugged his daughter to his heart's content.

"As good as gold," said Bob, "and better. Somehow he gets thoughtful sitting by himself so much, and thinks the strangest things you ever heard. He told me, coming home, that he hoped the people saw him in the church, because he was a cripple, and it might be pleasant to them to remember upon Christmas Day, who made lame beggars walk and blind men see."

Bob's voice was tremulous when he told them this, and trembled more when he said that Tiny Tim was growing strong and hearty.

His active little crutch was heard upon the floor, and back came Tiny Tim before another word was spoken, escorted by his brother and sister to his stool before the fire; and while Bob, turning up his cuffs—as if, poor fellow, they were capable of being made more shabby—compounded some hot mixture in a jug with gin and lemons, and stirred it round and round and put it on the hob to simmer; Master Peter, and the two ubiquitous young Cratchits went to fetch the goose, with which they soon returned in high procession.

Such a bustle ensued that you might have thought a goose the rarest of all birds; a feathered phenomenon, to which a black swan was a matter of course; and in truth it was something very like it in that house. Mrs. Cratchit made the gravy (ready beforehand in a little saucepan) hissing hot;

Master Peter mashed the potatoes with incredible vigour; Miss Belinda sweetened up the apple-sauce; Martha dusted the hot plates; Bob took Tiny Tim beside him in a tiny corner at the table; the two young Cratchits set chairs for everybody, not forgetting themselves, and mounting guard upon their posts, crammed spoons into their mouths, lest they should shriek for goose before their turn came to be helped. At last the dishes were set on, and grace was said. It was succeeded by a breathless pause, as Mrs. Cratchit, looking slowly all along the carving-knife, prepared to plunge it in the breast; but when she did, and when the long expected gush of stuffing issued forth, one murmur of delight arose all round the board, and even Tiny Tim, excited by the two young Cratchits, beat on the table with the handle of his knife, and feebly cried Hurrah!

There never was such a goose. Bob said he didn't believe there ever was such a goose cooked. Its tenderness and flavour, size and cheapness, were the themes of universal admiration. Eked out by the apple-sauce and mashed potatoes, it was a sufficient dinner for the whole family; indeed, as Mrs. Cratchit said with great delight (surveying one small atom of a bone upon the dish), they hadn't ate it all at last! Yet every one had had enough, and the youngest Cratchits in particular, were steeped in sage and onion to the eyebrows! But now, the plates being changed by Miss Belinda, Mrs. Cratchit left the room alone—too nervous to bear witnesses—to take the pudding up, and bring it in.

Suppose it should not be done enough! Suppose it should break in turning out! Suppose somebody should have got over the wall of the back-yard, and stolen it, while they were merry with the goose: a supposition at which the two young Cratchits became livid! All sorts of horrors were supposed.

Hallo! A great deal of steam! The pudding was out of the copper. A smell like a washing-day! That was the cloth. A smell like an eating-house, and a pastry cook's next door to each other, with a laundress's next door to that! That was the pudding. In half a minute Mrs. Cratchit entered: flushed, but smiling proudly: with the pudding, like a speckled cannon-ball, so hard and firm, blazing in half of half-a-quartern of ignited brandy, and bedight with Christmas holly stuck into the top.

Oh, a wonderful pudding! Bob Cratchit said, and calmly too, that he regarded it as the greatest success achieved by Mrs. Cratchit since their marriage. Mrs. Cratchit said that now the weight was off her mind, she would confess she had had her doubts about the quantity of flour. Everybody had something to say about it, but nobody said or thought it was at all a small pudding for a large family. It would have been flat heresy to do so. Any Cratchit would have blushed to hint at such a thing.

At last the dinner was all done, the cloth was cleared, the hearth swept, and the fire made up. The compound in the jug being tasted, and considered perfect, apples and oranges were put upon the table, and a shovel-full of chestnuts on the fire. Then all the Cratchit family drew round the hearth, in what Bob Cratchit called a circle, meaning half a one; and at Bob Cratchit's elbow stood the family display of glass; two tumblers, and a custard-cup without a handle.

These held the hot stuff from the jug, however, as well as golden goblets would have done; and Bob served it out with beaming looks, while the chestnuts on the fire sputtered and crackled noisily. Then Bob proposed:

"A Merry Christmas to us all, my dears. God bless us!"

Which all the family re-echoed.

"God bless us every one!" said Tiny Tim, the last of all.

He sat very close to his father's side, upon his little stool. Bob held his withered little hand in his, as if he loved the child, and wished to keep him by his side, and dreaded that he might be taken from him.

"Spirit," said Scrooge, with an interest he had never felt before, "tell me if Tiny Tim will live."

"I see a vacant seat," replied the Ghost, "in the poor chimney corner, and a crutch without an owner, carefully preserved. If these shadows remain unaltered by the Future, the child will die."

"No, no," said Scrooge. "Oh no, kind Spirit! say he will be spared."

"If these shadows remain unaltered by the Future, none other of my race," returned the Ghost, "will find him here. What then? If he be like to die, he had better do it, and decrease the surplus population."

Scrooge hung his head to hear his own words quoted by the Spirit, and was overcome with penitence and grief.

"Man," said the Ghost, "if man you be in heart, not adamant, forbear that wicked cant until you have discovered What the surplus is, and Where it is. Will you decide what men shall live, what men shall die? It may be, that in the sight of Heaven, you are more worthless and less fit to live than millions like this poor man's child. Oh God! to hear the Insect on the leaf pronouncing on the too much life among his hungry brothers in the dust!"

Scrooge bent before the Ghost's rebuke, and trembling cast his eyes upon the ground. But he raised them speedily, on hearing his own name.

"Mr. Scrooge!" said Bob; "I'll give you Mr. Scrooge, the Founder of the Feast!"

"The Founder of the Feast indeed!" cried Mrs. Cratchit, reddening. "I wish I had him here. I'd give him a piece of my mind to feast upon, and I hope he'd have a good appetite for it."

"My dear," said Bob, "the children; Christmas Day."

"It should be Christmas Day, I am sure," said she, "on which one drinks the health of such an odious, stingy, hard, unfeeling man as Mr. Scrooge. You know he is, Robert! Nobody knows it better than you do, poor fellow!"

"My dear," was Bob's mild answer, "Christmas Day."

"I'll drink his health for your sake and the Day's," said Mrs. Cratchit, "not for his. Long life to him! A merry Christmas and a happy new year!—he'll be very merry and very happy, I have no doubt!"

The children drank the toast after her. It was the first of their proceedings which had no heartiness in it. Tiny Tim drank it last of all, but he didn't care twopence for it. Scrooge was the Ogre of the family. The mention of his name cast a dark shadow on the party, which was not dispelled for full five minutes.

After it had passed away, they were ten times merrier than before, from the mere relief of Scrooge the Baleful being done with. Bob Cratchit told them how he had a situation in his eye for Master Peter, which would bring in, if obtained, full five-and-sixpence weekly. The two young Cratchits laughed tremendously at the idea of Peter's being a man of business; and Peter himself looked thoughtfully at the fire from between his collars, as if he were deliberating what particular investments he should favour when he came into the receipt of that bewildering income. Martha, who was a poor apprentice at a milliner's, then told them what kind of work she had to do, and how many hours she worked at a stretch, and how she meant to lie a-bed to-morrow morning for a good long rest; to-morrow being a holiday she passed at home. Also how she had seen a countess and a lord some days before, and how the lord "was much about as tall as Peter"; at which Peter pulled up his collars so high that you couldn't have seen his head if you had been there. All this time the chestnuts and the jug went round and round; and bye and bye they had a song, about a lost child travelling in the snow, from Tiny Tim; who had a plaintive little voice, and sang it very well indeed.

There was nothing of high mark in this. They were not a handsome family; they were not well dressed; their shoes were far from being water-proof; their clothes were scanty; and Peter might have known, and very likely did, the inside of a pawnbroker's. But they were happy, grateful, pleased with one another, and contented with the time; and when they faded, and looked happier yet in the bright sprinklings of the Spirit's torch at parting, Scrooge had his eye upon them, and especially on Tiny Tim, until the last.

By this time it was getting dark, and snowing pretty heavily; and as Scrooge and the Spirit went along the streets, the brightness of the roaring fires in kitchens, parlours, and all sorts of rooms, was wonderful. Here, the flickering of the blaze showed preparations for a cosy dinner, with hot plates baking through and through before the fire, and deep red curtains, ready to be drawn, to shut out cold and darkness. There, all the children of the house were running out into the snow to meet their married sisters, brothers, cousins, uncles, aunts, and be the first to greet them. Here, again, were shadows on the window-blind of guests assembling; and there a group of handsome girls, all hooded and fur-booted, and all chattering at once, tripped lightly off to some near neighbour's house; where, woe upon the single man who saw them enter—artful witches: well they knew it—in a glow!

But if you had judged from the numbers of people on their way to friendly gatherings, you might have thought that no one was at home to give them welcome when they got there, instead of every house expecting company, and piling up its fires half-chimney high. Blessings on it, how the Ghost exulted! How it bared its breadth of breast, and opened its capacious palm, and floated on, outpouring, with a generous hand, its bright and harmless mirth on everything within its reach! The very lamplighter, who ran on before dotting the dusky street with specks of light, and who was dressed to spend the evening somewhere, laughed out loudly as the

Spirit passed: though little kenned the lamplighter that he had any company but Christmas!

And now, without a word of warning from the Ghost, they stood upon a bleak and desert moor, where monstrous masses of rude stone were cast about, as though it were the burial-place of giants; and water spread itself wheresoever it listed—or would have done so, but for the frost that held it prisoner; and nothing grew but moss and furze, and coarse, rank grass. Down in the west the setting sun had left a streak of fiery red, which glared upon the desolation for an instant, like a sullen eye, and frowning lower, lower, lower yet, was lost in the thick gloom of darkest night.

"What place is this?" asked Scrooge.

"A place where Miners live, who labour in the bowels of the earth," returned the Spirit. "But they know me. See!"

A light shone from the window of a hut, and swiftly they advanced towards it. Passing through the wall of mud and stone, they found a cheerful company assembled round a glowing fire. An old, old man and woman, with their children and their children's children, and another generation beyond that, all decked out gaily in their holiday attire. The old man, in a voice that seldom rose above the howling of the wind upon the barren waste, was singing them a Christmas song; it had been a very old song when he was a boy; and from time to time they all joined in the chorus. So surely as they raised their voices, the old man got quite blithe and loud; and so surely as they stopped, his vigour sang again.

The Spirit did not tarry here, but bade Scrooge hold his robe, and passing on above the moor, sped whither? Not to sea? To sea. To Scrooge's horror, looking back, he saw the last of the land, a frightful range of rocks, behind them; and his ears were deafened by the thundering of water, as it rolled, and roared, and raged among the dreadful caverns it had worn, and fiercely tried to undermine the earth.

Built upon a dismal reef of sunken rocks, some league or so from shore, on which the waters chafed and dashed, the wild year through, there stood a solitary lighthouse. Great heaps of sea-weed clung to its base, and storm-birds—born of the wind one might suppose, as sea-weed of the water—rose and fell about it, like the waves they skimmed.

But even here, two men who watched the light had made a fire, that through the loophole in the thick stone wall shed out a ray of brightness on the awful sea. Joining their horny hands over the rough table at which they sat, they wished each other Merry Christmas in their can of grog; and one of them: the elder, too, with his face all damaged and scarred with hard weather, as the figure-head of an old ship might be: struck up a sturdy song that was like a Gale in itself.

Again the Ghost sped on, above the black and heaving sea—on, on—until, being far away, as he told Scrooge, from any shore, they lighted on a ship. They stood beside the helmsman at the wheel, the look-out in the bow, the officers who had the watch; dark, ghostly figures in their several stations; but every man among them hummed a Christmas tune, or had a Christmas thought, or spoke below his breath to his companion of some bygone Christmas Day, with homeward hopes belonging to it. And every man on board, waking or sleeping, good or bad, had had a kinder word for another on that day than on any day in the year; and had shared to some extent in its festivities; and had remembered those he cared for at a distance, and had known that they delighted to remember him.

It was a great surprise to Scrooge, while listening to the moaning of the wind, and thinking what a solemn thing it was to move on through the lonely darkness over an unknown abyss, whose depths were secrets as profound as Death: it was a great surprise to Scrooge, while thus engaged, to hear a hearty laugh. It was a much greater surprise to Scrooge to recognise it as his own nephew's, and to find himself in a bright, dry, gleaming room, with the Spirit standing smiling by his side, and looking at that same nephew with approving affability!

"Ha, ha!" laughed Scrooge's nephew. "Ha, ha, ha!"

If you should happen, by any unlikely chance, to know a man more blest in a laugh than Scrooge's nephew, all I can say is, I should like to know him too. Introduce him to me, and I'll cultivate his acquaintance.

It is a fair, even-handed, noble adjustment of things, that while there is infection in disease and sorrow, there is nothing in the world so irresistibly contagious as laughter and good-humour. When Scrooge's nephew laughed in this way: holding his sides, rolling his head, and twisting his face into the most extravagant contortions: Scrooge's niece, by marriage, laughed as heartily as he. And their assembled friends being not a bit behindhand, roared out, lustily.

"Ha, ha! Ha, ha, ha, ha!"

"He said that Christmas was a humbug, as I live!" cried Scrooge's nephew. "He believed it too!"

"More shame for him, Fred!" said Scrooge's niece, indignantly. Bless those women; they never do anything by halves. They are always in earnest.

She was very pretty: exceedingly pretty. With a dimpled, surprised-looking, capital face; a ripe little mouth, that seemed made to be kissed—as no doubt it was; all kinds of good little dots about her chin, that melted into one another when she laughed; and the sunniest pair of eyes you ever saw in any little creature's head. Altogether she was what you would have called provoking, you know; but satisfactory too. Oh, perfectly satisfactory!

"He's a comical old fellow," said Scrooge's nephew, "that's the truth: and not so pleasant as he might be. However, his offences carry their own punishment, and I have nothing to say against him."

"I'm sure he is very rich, Fred," hinted Scrooge's niece. "At least you always tell *me* so."

"What of that, my dear!" said Scrooge's nephew. "His wealth is of no use to him. He don't do any good with it. He don't make himself comfortable with it. He hasn't the satisfaction of thinking—ha, ha, ha!—that he is ever going to benefit Us with it."

"I have no patience with him," observed Scrooge's niece. Scrooge's niece's sisters, and all the other ladies, expressed the same opinion.

"Oh, I have!" said Scrooge's nephew. "I am sorry for him; I couldn't be angry with him if I tried. Who suffers by his ill whims! Himself, always. Here, he takes it into his head to dislike us, and he won't come and dine with us. What's the consequence? He don't lose much of a dinner."

"Indeed, I think he loses a very good dinner," interrupted Scrooge's niece. Everybody else said the same, and they must be allowed to have been competent judges, because they had just had dinner; and, with the dessert upon the table, were clustered round the fire, by lamplight.

"Well! I'm very glad to hear it," said Scrooge's nephew, "because I haven't great faith in these young housekeepers. What do *you* say, Topper?"

Topper had clearly got his eye upon one of Scrooge's niece's sisters, for he answered that a bachelor was a wretched outcast, who had no right to express an opinion on the subject. Whereat Scrooge's niece's sister—the plump one with the lace tucker: not the one with the roses—blushed.

"Do go on, Fred," said Scrooge's niece, clapping her hands. "He never finishes what he begins to say! He is such a ridiculous fellow!"

Scrooge's nephew revelled in another laugh, and as it was impossible to keep the infection off; though the plump sister tried hard to do it with aromatic vinegar; his example was unanimously followed.

"I was going to say," said Scrooge's nephew, "that the consequence of his taking a dislike to us, and not making merry with us, is, as I think, that he loses some pleasant moments, which could do him no harm. I am sure he loses pleasanter companions than he can find in his own thoughts, either in his mouldy old office, or his dusty chambers. I mean to give him the same chance every year, whether he likes it or not, for I pity him. He may rail at Christmas till he dies, but he can't help thinking better of it—I defy him—if he finds me going there, in good temper, year after year, and saying Uncle Scrooge, how are you? If it only puts him in the vein to leave his poor clerk fifty pounds, *that's* something; and I think I shook him, yesterday."

It was their turn to laugh now, at the notion of his shaking Scrooge. But being thoroughly good-natured, and not much caring what they laughed at, so that they laughed at any rate, he encouraged them in their merriment, and passed the bottle, joyously.

After tea, they had some music. For they were a musical family, and knew what they were about, when they sung a Glee or Catch, I can assure you: especially Topper, who could growl away in the bass like a good one, and never swell the large veins in his forehead, or get red in the face over it. Scrooge's niece played well upon the harp; and played among other tunes a simple little air (a mere nothing: you might learn to whistle it in two minutes), which had been familiar to the child who fetched Scrooge from the boarding-school, as he had been reminded by the Ghost of Christmas Past. When this strain of music sounded, all the things that Ghost had shown him, came upon his mind; he softened more and more; and thought that if he could have listened to it often, years ago, he might have cultivated the kindnesses of life for his own happiness with his own hands, without resorting to the sexton's spade that buried Jacob Marley.

But they didn't devote the whole evening to music. After a while they played at forfeits; for it is good to be children sometimes, and never better than at Christmas, when its mighty Founder was a child himself. Stop! There was first a game at blind-man's buff. Of course there was. And I no more believe Topper was really blind than I believe he had eyes in his boots. My opinion is, that it was a done thing between him and Scrooge's nephew; and that the Ghost of Christmas Present knew it. The way he went after that plump sister in the lace tucker, was an outrage on the credulity of human nature. Knocking down the fire-irons, tumbling over the chairs, bumping against the piano, smothering himself among the curtains, wherever she went, there went he. He always knew where the plump sister was. He wouldn't catch anybody else. If you had fallen up against him, as some of them did, and stood there; he would have made a feint of endeavoring to seize you, which would have been an affront to your understanding; and would instantly have sidled off in the direction of the plump sister. She often cried out that it wasn't fair; and it really was not. But when at last, he caught her; when, in spite of all her silken rustlings, and her rapid flutterings past him, he got her into a corner whence there was no escape; then his conduct was the most execrable. For his pretending not to know her; his pretending that it was necessary to touch her head-dress, and further to assure himself of her identity by pressing a certain ring upon her finger, and a certain chain about her neck; was

was exposed, elicited from him that he was thinking of an animal, a live animal, rather a disagreeable animal, a savage animal, an animal that growled and grunted sometimes, and talked sometimes, and lived in London, and walked about the streets, and wasn't made a show of, and wasn't led by anybody, and didn't live in a menagerie, and was never killed in a market, and was not a horse, or an ass, or a cow, or a bull, or a tiger, or a dog, or a pig, or a cat, or a bear. At every fresh question that was put to him, this nephew burst into a fresh roar of laughter; and was so inexpressibly tickled, that he was obliged to get up off the sofa and stamp. At last the plump sister, falling into a similar state, cried out:

"I have found it out! I know what it is, Fred! I know what it is!"

"What is it?" cried Fred.

"It's your Uncle Scro-o-o-o-oge!"

Which it certainly was. Admiration was the universal sentiment, though some objected that the reply to "Is it a bear?" ought to have been "Yes;" inasmuch as an answer in the negative was sufficient to have diverted their thoughts from Mr. Scrooge, supposing they had ever had any tendency that way.

"He has given us plenty of merriment, I am sure," said Fred, "and it would be ungrateful not to drink his health. Here is a glass of mulled wine ready to our hand at the moment; and I say 'Uncle Scrooge!' "

"Well! Uncle Scrooge!" they cried.

"A Merry Christmas and a Happy New Year to the old man, whatever he is!" said Scrooge's nephew. "He wouldn't take it from me, but may he have it, nevertheless. Uncle Scrooge!"

Uncle Scrooge had imperceptibly become so gay and light of heart, that he would have pledged the unconscious company in return, and thanked them in an inaudible speech, if the Ghost had given him time. But the whole scene passed off in the breath of the last word spoken by his nephew; and he and the Spirit were again upon their travels.

Much they saw, and far they went, and many homes they visited, but always with a happy end. The Spirit stood beside sick beds, and they were cheerful; on foreign lands, and they were close at home; by struggling men, and they were patient in their greater hope; by poverty, and it was rich. In alms-house, hospital, and jail, in misery's every refuge, where vain man in his little brief authority had not made fast the door, and barred the Spirit out, he left his blessing, and taught Scrooge his precepts.

It was a long night, if it were only a night; but Scrooge had his doubts of this, because the Christmas Holidays appeared to be condensed into the space of time they passed together. It was strange, too, that while Scrooge remained unaltered in his outward form, the Ghost grew older, clearly older. Scrooge had observed this change, but never spoke of it, until they left a children's Twelfth Night party, when, looking at the Spirit as they stood together in an open place, he noticed that its hair was gray.

"Are spirits' lives so short?" asked Scrooge.

"My life upon this globe, is very brief," replied the Ghost. "It ends to-night."

"To-night!" cried Scrooge.

"To-night at midnight. Hark! The time is drawing near."

The chimes were ringing the three quarters past eleven at that moment.

"Forgive me if I am not justified in what I ask," said Scrooge, looking intently at the Spirit's robe, "but I see something strange, and not belonging to yourself, protruding from your skirts. Is it a foot or a claw!"

"It might be a claw, for the flesh there is upon it," was the Spirit's sorrowful reply. "Look here."

From the foldings of its robe, it brought two children; wretched, abject, frightful, hideous, miserable. They knelt down at its feet, and clung upon the outside of its garment.

"Oh, Man! look here. Look, look, down here!" exclaimed the Ghost.

They were a boy and girl. Yellow, meagre, ragged, scowling, wolfish; but prostrate, too, in their humility. Where graceful youth should have filled their features out, and touched them with its freshest tints, a stale and shrivelled hand, like that of age, had pinched, and twisted them, and pulled them into shreds. Where angels might have sat enthroned, devils lurked; and glared out menacing. No change, no degradation, no perversion of humanity, in any grade, through all the mysteries of wonderful creation, has monsters half so horrible and dread.

Scrooge started back, appalled. Having them shown to him in this way, he tried to say they were fine children, but the words choked themselves, rather than be parties to a lie of such enormous magnitude.

"Spirit! are they yours?" Scrooge could say no more.

"They are Man's," said the Spirit, looking down upon them. "And they cling to me, appealing from their fathers. This boy is Ignorance. This girl is Want. Beware them both, and all of their degree, but most of all beware this boy, for on his brow I see that written which is Doom, unless the writing be erased. Deny it!" cried the Spirit, stretching out its hand towards the city. "Slander those who tell it ye! Admit it for your factious purposes, and make it worse. And bide the end!"

"Have they no refuge or resource?" cried Scrooge.

"Are there no prisons?" said the Spirit, turning on him for the last time with his own words. "Are there no workhouses?"

The bell struck twelve.

Scrooge looked about him for the Ghost, and saw it not. As the last stroke ceased to vibrate, he remembered the prediction of old Jacob Marley, and lifting up his eyes, beheld a solemn Phantom, draped and hooded, coming, like a mist along the ground, towards him.

STAVE IV

The Last of the Spirits

THE Phantom slowly, gravely, silently, approached. When it came near him, Scrooge bent down upon his knee; for in the very air through which this Spirit moved it seemed to scatter gloom and mystery.

It was shrouded in a deep black garment, which concealed its head, its face, its form, and left nothing of it visible save one outstretched hand. But for this it would have been difficult to detach its figure from the night, and separate it from the darkness by which it was surrounded.

He felt that it was tall and stately when it came beside him, and that its mysterious presence filled him with a solemn dread. He knew no more, for the Spirit neither spoke nor moved.

"I am in the presence of the Ghost of Christmas Yet To Come?" said Scrooge.

The Spirit answered not, but pointed onward with its hand.

"You are about to show me shadows of the things that have not happened, but will happen in the time before us," Scrooge pursued. "Is that so, Spirit?"

The upper portion of the garment was contracted for an instant in its folds, as if the Spirit had inclined its head. That was the only answer he received.

Although well used to ghostly company by this time, Scrooge feared the silent shape so much that his legs trembled beneath him, and he found that he could hardly stand when he prepared to follow it. The Spirit paused a moment, as observing his condition, and giving him time to recover.

But Scrooge was all the worse for this. It thrilled him with a vague uncertain horror, to know that behind the dusky shroud, there were ghostly eyes intently fixed upon him, while he, though he stretched his own to the utmost, could see nothing but a spectral hand and one great heap of black.

"Ghost of the Future!" he exclaimed, "I fear you more than any Spectre I have seen. But as I know your purpose is to do me good, and as I hope to live to be another man from what I was, I am prepared to bear you company, and do it with a thankful heart. Will you not speak to me?"

It gave him no reply. The hand was pointed straight before them.

"Lead on!" said Scrooge. "Lead on! The night is waning fast, and it is precious time to me, I know. Lead on, Spirit!"

The Phantom moved away as it had come towards him. Scrooge followed in the shadow of its dress, which bore him up, he thought, and carried him along.

They scarcely seemed to enter the city; for the city rather seemed to spring up about them, and encompass them of its own act. But there they were, in the heart of it; on 'Change, amongst the merchants; who hurried up and down, and chinked the money in their pockets, and conversed in groups, and looked at their watches, and trifled thoughtfully with their great gold seals; and so forth, as Scrooge had seen them often.

The Spirit stopped beside one little knot of business men. Observing that the hand was pointed to them, Scrooge advanced to listen to their talk.

"No," said a great fat man with a monstrous chin, "I don't know much about it, either way. I only know he's dead."

"When did he die?" inquired another.

"Last night, I believe."

"Why, what was the matter with him?" asked a third, taking a vast quantity of snuff out of a very large snuff-box. "I thought he'd never die."

"God knows," said the first, with a yawn.

"What has he done with his money?" asked a red-faced gentleman with a pendulous excrescence on the end of his nose, that shook like the gills of a turkey-cock.

"I haven't heard," said the man with the large chin, yawning again. "Left it to his Company, perhaps. He hasn't left it to *me*. That's all I know."

This pleasantry was received with a general laugh.

"It's likely to be a very cheap funeral," said the same speaker; "for upon my life I don't know of anybody to go to it. Suppose we make up a party and volunteer?"

"I don't mind going if a lunch is provided," observed the gentleman with the excrescence on his nose. "But I must be fed, if I make one."

Another laugh.

"Well, I am the most disinterested among you, after all," said the first speaker, "for I never wear black gloves, and I never eat lunch. But I'll offer to go, if anybody else will. When I come to think of it, I'm not at all sure that I wasn't his most particular friend; for we used to stop and speak whenever we met. Bye, bye!"

Speakers and listeners strolled away, and mixed with other groups. Scrooge knew the men, and looked towards the Spirit for an explanation.

The Phantom glided on into a street. Its finger pointed to two persons meeting. Scrooge listened again, thinking that the explanation might lie here.

He knew these men, also, perfectly. They were men of business: very wealthy, and of great importance. He had made a point always of standing well in their esteem: in a business point of view, that is; strictly in a business point of view.

"How are you?" said one.

"How are you?" returned the other.

"Well!" said the first. "Old Scratch has got his own at last, hey?"

"So I am told," returned the second. "Cold, isn't it?"

"Seasonable for Christmas time. You're not a skaiter, I suppose?"

"No. No. Something else to think of. Good morning!"

Not another word. That was their meeting, their conversation, and their parting.

Scrooge was at first inclined to be surprised that the Spirit should attach importance to conversations apparently so trivial; but feeling assured that they must have some hidden purpose, he set himself to consider what it was likely to be. They could scarcely be supposed to have any bearing on the death of Jacob, his old partner, for that was Past, and this Ghost's province was the Future. Nor could he think of any one immediately connected with himself, to whom he could apply them. But nothing doubting that to whomsoever they applied they had some latent moral for his own improvement, he resolved to treasure up every word he heard, and everything he saw; and especially to observe the shadow of himself when it appeared. For he had an expectation that the conduct of his future self would give him the clue he missed, and would render the solution of these riddles easy.

He looked about in that very place for his own image; but another man stood in his accustomed corner, and though the clock pointed to his usual time of day for being there, he saw no likeness of himself among the multitudes that poured in through the Porch. It gave him little surprise, however; for he had been revolving in his mind a change of life, and thought and hoped he saw his new-born resolutions carried out in this.

Quiet and dark, beside him stood the Phantom, with its outstretched hand. When he roused himself from his thoughtful quest, he fancied from the turn of the hand, and its situation in reference to himself, that the Unseen Eyes were looking at him keenly. It made him shudder, and feel very cold.

They left the busy scene, and went into an obscure part of the town, where Scrooge had never penetrated before although he recognised its situation, and its bad repute. The ways were foul and narrow; the shops and houses wretched; the people half-naked, drunken, slipshod, ugly. Alleys and archways, like so many cesspools, disgorged their offences of smell, and dirt, and life, upon the straggling streets; and the whole quarter reeked with crime, with filth, and misery.

Far in this den of infamous resort, there was a low-browed, beetling shop, below a pent-house roof, where iron, old rags, bottles, bones, and greasy offal, were bought. Upon the floor within, were piled up heaps of rusty keys, nails, chains, hinges, files, scales, weights, and refuse iron of all kinds. Secrets that few would like to scrutinise were bred and hidden in mountains of unseemly rags, masses of corrupted fat, and sepulchres of bones. Sitting in among the wares he dealt in, by a charcoal-stove, made of old bricks, was a gray-haired rascal, nearly seventy years of age; who had screened himself from the cold air without, by a frousy curtaining of miscellaneous tatters, hung upon a line; and smoked his pipe in all the luxury of calm retirement.

Scrooge and the Phantom came into the presence of this man, just as a woman with a heavy bundle slunk into the shop. But she had scarcely entered, when another woman, similarly laden, came in too; and she was closely followed by a man in faded black, who was no less startled by the sight of them, than they had been upon the recognition of each other. After a short period of blank astonishment, in which the old man with the pipe had joined them, they all three burst into a laugh.

"Let the charwoman alone to be the first!" cried she who

had entered first. "Let the laundress alone to be the second; and let the undertaker's man alone to be the third. Look here, old Joe, here's a chance! If we haven't all three met here without meaning it."

"You couldn't have met in a better place," said old Joe, removing his pipe from his mouth. "Come into the parlour. You were made free of it long ago, you know; and the other two an't strangers. Stop till I shut the door of the shop. Ah! How it skreeks! There an't such a rusty bit of metal in the place as its own hinges, I believe; and I'm sure there's no such old bones here, as mine. Ha, ha! We're all suitable to our calling, we're well matched. Come into the parlour. Come into the parlour."

The parlour was the space behind the screen of rags. The old man raked the fire together with an old stair-rod, and having trimmed his smoky lamp (for it was night), with the stem of his pipe, put it in his mouth again.

While he did this, the woman who had already spoken threw her bundle on the floor and sat down in a flaunting manner on a stool; crossing her elbows on her knees, and looking with a bold defiance at the other two.

"What odds then! What odds, Mrs. Dilber?" said the woman. "Every person has a right to take care of themselves. *He* always did!"

"That's true, indeed!" said the laundress. "No man more so."

"Why then, don't stand staring as if you was afraid, woman; who's the wiser? We're not going to pick holes in each other's coats, I suppose?"

"No, indeed!" said Mrs. Dilber and the man together. "We should hope not."

"Very well, then!" cried the woman. "That's enough. Who's the worse for the loss of a few things like these? Not a dead man, I suppose."

"No, indeed," said Mrs. Dilber, laughing.

"If he wanted to keep 'em after he was dead, a wicked old screw," pursued the women, "why wasn't he natural in his lifetime? If he had been, he'd have had somebody to look after him when he was struck with Death, instead of lying gasping out his last there, alone by himself."

"It's the truest word that ever was spoke," said Mrs. Dilber. "It's a judgment on him."

"I wish it was a little heavier one," replied the woman; "and it should have been, you may depend upon it, if I could have laid my hands on anything else. Open that bundle, old Joe, and let me know the value of it. Speak out plain. I'm not afraid to be the first, nor afraid for them to see it. We knew pretty well that we were helping ourselves, before we met here, I believe. It's no sin. Open the bundle, Joe."

But the gallantry of her friends would not allow of this; and the man in faded black, mounting the breach first, produced *his* plunder. It was not extensive. A seal or two, a pencil-case, a pair of sleeve-buttons, and a brooch of no great value, were all. They were severally examined and appraised by old Joe, who chalked the sums he was disposed to give for each, upon the wall, and added them up into a total when he found there was nothing more to come.

"That's your account," said Joe, "and I wouldn't give another sixpence, if I was to be boiled for not doing it. Who's next?"

Mrs. Dilber was next. Sheets and towels, a little wearing apparel, two old-fashioned silver teaspoons, a pair of sugar-tongs, and a few boots. Her account was stated on the wall in the same manner.

"I always give too much to ladies. It's a weakness of mine, and that's the way I ruin myself," said old Joe. "That's your account. If you asked me for another penny, and made it an open question, I'd repent of being so liberal and knock off half-a-crown."

"And now undo *my* bundle, Joe," said the first woman.

Joe went down on his knees for the greater convenience of opening it, and having unfastened a great many knots, dragged out a large and heavy roll of some dark stuff.

"What do you call this?" said Joe. "Bed-curtains!"

"Ah!" returned the woman, laughing and leaning forward on her crossed arms. "Bed-curtains!"

"You don't mean to say you took 'em down, rings and all, with him lying there?" said Joe.

"Yes I do," replied the woman. "Why not?"

"You were born to make your fortune," said Joe, "and you'll certainly do it."

"I certainly shan't hold my hand, when I get anything in it by reaching it out, for the sake of such a man as He was, I promise you, Joe," returned the woman coolly. "Don't drop that oil upon the blankets, now."

"His blankets?" asked Joe.

"Whose else's do you think?" replied the woman. "He isn't likely to take cold without 'em, I dare say."

"I hope he didn't die of anything catching? Eh?" said old Joe, stopping in his work, and looking up.

"Don't you be afraid of that," returned the woman. "I an't so fond of his company that I'd loiter about him for such things, if he did. Ah! you may look through that shirt till your eyes ache; but you won't find a hole in it, nor a threadbare place. It's the best he had, and a fine one too. They'd have wasted it, if it hadn't been for me."

"What do you call wasting of it?" asked old Joe.

"Putting it on him to be buried in, to be sure," replied the woman with a laugh. "Somebody was fool enough to do it, but I took it off again. If calico an't good enough for such a purpose, it isn't good enough for anything. It's quite as becoming to the body. He can't look uglier than he did in that one."

Scrooge listened to this dialogue in horror. As they sat grouped about their spoil, in the scanty light afforded by the old man's lamp, he viewed them with a detestation and disgust, which could hardly have been greater, though they had been obscene demons, marketing the corpse itself.

"He, ha!" laughed the same woman, when old Joe, producing a flannel bag with money in it, told out their several gains upon the ground. "This is the end of it, you see! He frightened every one away from him when he was alive, to profit us when he was dead! Ha, ha, ha!"

"Spirit!" said Scrooge, shuddering from head to foot. "I see, I see. The case of this unhappy man might be my own. My life tends that way, now. Merciful Heaven, what is this!"

He recoiled in terror, for the scene had changed, and now he almost touched a bed: a bare, uncurtained bed: on which, beneath a ragged sheet, there lay a something covered up, which, though it was dumb, announced itself in awful language.

The room was very dark, too dark to be observed with any accuracy, though Scrooge glanced round it in obedience to a secret impulse, anxious to know what kind of room it was. A pale light, rising in the outer air, fell straight upon the bed; and on it, plundered and bereft, unwatched, unwept, uncared for, was the body of this man.

Scrooge glanced towards the Phantom. Its steady hand was pointed to the head. The cover was so carelessly adjusted that the slightest raising of it, the motion of a finger upon Scrooge's part, would have disclosed the face. He thought of it, felt how easy it would be to do, and longed to do it; but had no more power to withdraw the veil than to dismiss the spectre at his side.

Oh cold, cold, rigid, dreadful Death, set up thine altar here, and dress it with such terrors as thou hast at thy command: for this is thy dominion! But of the loved, revered, and honoured head, thou canst not turn one hair to thy dread purposes, or make one feature odious. It is not that the hand is heavy and will fall down when released; it is not that the heart and pulse are still; but that the hand WAS open, generous, and true; the heart brave, warm, and tender; and the pulse a man's. Strike, Shadow, strike! And see his good deeds springing from the wound, to sow the world with life immortal!

No voice pronounced these words in Scrooge's ears, and yet he heard them when he looked upon the bed. He thought, if this man could be raised up now, what would be his foremost thoughts? Avarice, hard dealing, griping cares? They have brought him to a rich end, truly!

He lay, in the dark empty house, with not a man, a woman, or a child, to say that he was kind to me in this or that, and for the memory of one kind word I will be kind to him. A cat was tearing at the door, and there was a sound of gnawing rats beneath the hearth-stone. What *they* wanted in the room of death, and why they were so restless and disturbed, Scrooge did not dare to think.

"Spirit!" he said, "this is a fearful place. In leaving it, I shall not leave its lesson, trust me. Let us go!"

Still the Ghost pointed with an unmoved finger to the head.

"I understand you," Scrooge returned, "and I would do it, if I could. But I have not the power, Spirit. I have not the power."

Again it seemed to look upon him.

"If there is any person in the town, who feels emotion caused by this man's death," said Scrooge quite agonised, "show that person to me, Spirit, I beseech you!"

The Phantom spread its dark robe before him for a moment, like a wing; and withdrawing it, revealed a room by daylight, where a mother and her children were.

She was expecting some one, and with anxious eagerness; for she walked up and down the room; started at every sound; looked out from the window; glanced at the clock;

tried, but in vain, to work with her needle; and could hardly bear the voices of the children in their play.

At length the long-expected knock was heard. She hurried to the door, and met her husband; a man whose face was care-worn and depressed, though he was young. There was a remarkable expression in it now; a kind of serious delight of which he felt ashamed, and which he struggled to repress.

He sat down to the dinner that had been hoarding for him by the fire; and when she asked him faintly what news (which was not until after a long silence), he appeared embarrassed how to answer.

"Is it good," she said, "or bad?"—to help him.

"Bad," he answered.

"We are quite ruined?"

"No. There is hope yet, Caroline."

"If *he* relents," she said, amazed, "there is! Nothing is past hope, if such a miracle has happened."

"He is past relenting," said her husband. "He is dead."

She was a mild and patient creature if her face spoke truth; but she was thankful in her soul to hear it, and she said so, with clasped hands. She prayed forgiveness the next moment, and was sorry; but the first was the emotion of her heart.

"What the half-drunken woman whom I told you of last night, said to me, when I tried to see him and obtain a week's delay; and what I thought was a mere excuse to avoid me; turns out to have been quite true. He was not only very ill, but dying, then."

"To whom will our debt be transferred?"

"I don't know. But before that time we shall be ready with the money; and even though we were not, it would be bad fortune indeed to find so merciless a creditor in his successor. We may sleep to-night with light hearts, Caroline!"

Yes. Soften it as they would, their hearts were lighter. The children's faces, hushed and clustered round to hear what they so little understood, were brighter; and it was a happier house for this man's death! The only emotion that the Ghost could show him, caused by the event, was one of pleasure.

"Let me see some tenderness connected with a death," said Scrooge; "or that dark chamber, Spirit, which we left just now, will be for ever present to me."

The Ghost conducted him through several streets familiar to his feet; and as they went along, Scrooge looked here and there to find himself, but nowhere was he to be seen. They entered poor Bob Cratchit's house; the dwelling he had visited before; and found the mother and the children seated round the fire.

Quiet. Very quiet. The noisy little Cratchits were as still as statues in one corner, and sat looking up at Peter, who had a book before him. The mother and her daughters were engaged in sewing. But surely they were very quiet!

" 'And He took a child, and set him in the midst of them.' "

Where had Scrooge heard those words? He had not dreamed them. The boy must have read them out, as he and the Spirit crossed the threshold. Why did he not go on?

The mother laid her work upon the table, and put her hand up to her face.

"The colour hurts my eyes," she said.

The colour? Ah, poor Tiny Tim!

"They're better now again," said Cratchit's wife. "It makes them weak by candle-light; and I wouldn't show weak eyes to your father when he comes home, for the world. It must be near his time."

"Past it rather," Peter answered, shutting up his book. "But I think he's walked a little slower than he used, these few last evenings, mother."

They were very quiet again. At last she said, and in a steady, cheerful voice, that only faultered once:

"I have known him walk with—I have known him walk with Tiny Tim upon his shoulder, very fast indeed."

"And so have I," cried Peter. "Often."

"And so have I!" exclaimed another. So had all.

"But he was very light to carry," she resumed, intent upon her work, "and his father loved him so, that it was no trouble—no trouble. And there is your father at the door!"

She hurried out to meet him; and little Bob in his comforter—he had need of it, poor fellow—came in. His tea was ready for him on the hob, and they all tried who should help him to it most. Then the two young Cratchits got upon his knees and laid, each child a little cheek, against his face, as if they said, "Don't mind it, father. Don't be grieved!"

Bob was very cheerful with them, and spoke pleasantly to all the family. He looked at the work upon the table, and praised the industry and speed of Mrs. Cratchit and the girls. They would be done long before Sunday, he said.

"Sunday! You went to-day then, Robert?" said his wife.

"Yes, my dear," returned Bob. "I wish you could have gone. It would have done you good to see how green a place it is. But you'll see it often. I promised him that I would walk there on a Sunday. My little, little child!" cried Bob. "My little child!"

He broke down all at once. He couldn't help it. If he could have helped it, he and his child would have been farther apart perhaps than they were.

He left the room, and went up stairs into the room above, which was lighted cheerfully, and hung with Christmas. There was a chair set close beside the child, and there were signs of some one having been there, lately. Poor Bob sat down in it, and when he had thought a little and composed himself, he kissed the little face. He was reconciled to what had happened, and went down again quite happy.

They drew about the fire, and talked; the girls and mother working still. Bob told them of the extraordinary kindness of Mr. Scrooge's nephew, whom he had scarcely seen but once, and who, meeting him in the street that day, and seeing that he looked a little—"just a little down you know" said Bob, inquired what had happened to distress him. "On which," said Bob, "for he is the pleasantest-spoken gentleman you ever heard, I told him. 'I am heartily sorry for it, Mr. Cratchit,' he said, 'and heartily sorry for your good wife.' By the bye, how he ever knew *that*, I don't know."

"Knew what, my dear?"

"Why, that you were a good wife," replied Bob.

"Everybody knows that!" said Peter.

"Very well observed, my boy!" cried Bob. "I hope they

do. 'Heartily sorry,' he said, 'for your good wife. If I can be of service to you in any way,' he said, giving me his card, 'that's where I live. Pray come to me.' Now, it wasn't," cried Bob, "for the sake of anything he might be able to do for us, so much as for his kind way, that this was quite delightful. It really seemed as if he had known our Tiny Tim, and felt with us."

"I'm sure he's a good soul!" said Mrs. Cratchit.

"You would be surer of it, my dear," returned Bob, "if you saw and spoke to him. I shouldn't be at all surprised, mark what I say, if he got Peter a better situation."

"Only hear that, Peter," said Mrs. Cratchit.

"And then," cried one of the girls, "Peter will be keeping company with some one, and setting up for himself."

"Get along with you!" retorted Peter, grinning.

"It's just as likely as not," said Bob, "one of these days; though there's plenty of time for that, my dear. But however and whenever we part from one another, I am sure we shall none of us forget poor Tiny Tim—shall we—or this first parting that there was among us?"

"Never, father!" cried they all.

"And I know," said Bob, "I know, my dears, that when we recollect how patient and how mild he was; although he was a little, little child; we shall not quarrel easily among ourselves, and forget poor Tiny Tim in doing it."

"No, never, father!" they all cried again.

"I am very happy," said little Bob, "I am very happy!"

Mrs. Cratchit kissed him, his daughters kissed him, the two young Cratchits kissed him, and Peter and himself shook hands. Spirit of Tiny Tim, thy childish essence was from God!

"Spectre," said Scrooge, "something informs me that our parting moment is at hand. I know it, but I know not how. Tell me what man that was whom we saw lying dead?"

The Ghost of Christmas Yet To Come conveyed him, as before—though at a different time, he thought: indeed, there seemed no order in these latter visions, save that they were in the Future—into the resorts of business men, but showed him not himself. Indeed, the Spirit did not stay for anything, but went straight on, as to the end just now desired, until besought by Scrooge to tarry for a moment.

"This court," said Scrooge, "through which we hurry now, is where my place of occupation is, and has been for a length of time. I see the house. Let me behold what I shall be, in days to come."

The Spirit stopped; the hand was pointed elsewhere.

"The house is yonder," Scrooge exclaimed. "Why do you point away?"

The inexorable finger underwent no change.

Scrooge hastened to the window of his office, and looked in. It was an office still, but not his. The furniture was not the same, and the figure in the chair was not himself. The Phantom pointed as before.

He joined it once again, and wondering why and whither he had gone, accompanied it until they reached an iron gate. He paused to look round before entering.

A churchyard. Here, then, the wretched man whose name he had now to learn, lay underneath the ground. It was a worthy place. Walled in by houses; overrun by grass and weeds, the growth of vegetation's death, not life; choked up with too much burying; fat with repleted appetite. A worthy place!

The Spirit stood among the graves, and pointed down to One. He advanced towards it trembling. The Phantom was exactly as it had been, but he dreaded that he saw new meaning in its solemn shape.

"Before I draw nearer to that stone to which you point," said Scrooge, "answer me one question. Are these the shadows of the things that Will be, or are they shadows of things that May be, only?"

Still the Ghost pointed downward to the grave by which it stood.

"Men's courses will foreshadow certain ends, to which, if persevered in, they must lead," said Scrooge. "But if the courses be departed from, the ends will change. Say it is thus with what you show me!"

The Spirit was immovable as ever.

Scrooge crept towards it, trembling as he went; and following the finger, read upon the stone of the neglected grave his own name, EBENEZER SCROOGE.

"Am *I* that man who lay upon the bed?" he cried, upon his knees.

The finger pointed from the grave to him, and back again.

"No, Spirit! Oh, no, no!"

The finger still was there.

"Spirit!" he cried, tight clutching at its robe, "hear me!

327

I am not the man I was. I will not be the man I must have been but for this intercourse. Why show me this, if I am past all hope?"

For the first time the hand appeared to shake.

"Good Spirit," he pursued, as down upon the ground he fell before it: "Your nature intercedes for me, and pities me. Assure me that I yet may change these shadows you have shown me, by an altered life!"

The kind hand trembled.

"I will honour Christmas in my heart, and try to keep it all the year. I will live in the Past, the Present, and the Future. The Spirits of all Three shall strive within me. I will not shut out the lessons that they teach. Oh, tell me I may sponge away the writing on this stone!"

In his agony, he caught the spectral hand. It sought to free itself, but he was strong in his entreaty, and detained it. The Spirit, stronger yet, repulsed him.

Holding up his hands in a last prayer to have his fate reversed, he saw an alteration in the Phantom's hood and dress. It shrunk, collapsed, and dwindled down into a bedpost.

STAVE V

The End of It

Y ES! and the bedpost was his own. The bed was his own, the room was his own. Best and happiest of all, the Time before him was his own, to make amends in!

"I will live in the Past, the Present, and the Future!" Scrooge repeated, as he scrambled out of bed. "The Spirits of all Three shall strive within me. Oh Jacob Marley! Heaven, and the Christmas Time be praised for this! I say it on my knees, old Jacob; on my knees!"

He was so fluttered and so glowing with his good intentions, that his broken voice would scarcely answer to his call. He had been sobbing violently in his conflict with the Spirit, and his face was wet with tears.

"They are not torn down," cried Scrooge, folding one of his bed-curtains in his arms, "they are not torn down, rings and all. They are here: I am here: the shadows of the things that would have been, may be dispelled. They will be. I know they will!"

His hands were busy with his garments all this time: turning them inside out, putting them on upside down, tear-

329

ing them, mislaying them, making them parties to every kind of extravagance.

"I don't know what to do!" cried Scrooge, laughing and crying in the same breath; and making a perfect Laocoön of himself with his stockings. "I am as light as a feather, I am as happy as an angel, I am as merry as a school-boy. I am as giddy as a drunken man. A merry Christmas to everybody! A happy New Year to all the world! Hallo here! Whoop! Hallo!"

He had frisked into the sitting-room, and was now standing there: perfectly winded.

"There's the saucepan that the gruel was in!" cried Scrooge, starting off again, and frisking round the fire-place. "There's the door, by which the Ghost of Jacob Marley entered! There's the corner where the Ghost of Christmas Present, sat! There's the window where I saw the wandering Spirits! It's all right, it's all true, it all happened. Ha ha ha!"

Really, for a man who had been out of practice for so many years, it was a splendid laugh, a most illustrious laugh. The father of a long, long line of brilliant laughs!

"I don't know what day of the month it is!" said Scrooge. "I don't know how long I've been among the Spirits. I don't know anything. I'm quite a baby. Never mind. I don't care. I'd rather be a baby. Hallo! Whoop! Hallo here!"

He was checked in his transports by the churches ringing out the lustiest peals he had ever heard. Clash, clang, hammer, ding, dong, bell. Bell, dong, ding, hammer, clang, clash! Oh, glorious, glorious!

Running to the window, he opened it, and put out his

head. No fog, no mist; clear, bright, jovial, stirring, cold; cold, piping for the blood to dance to; Golden sunlight; Heavenly sky; sweet fresh air; merry bells. Oh, glorious. Glorious!

"What's to-day?" cried Scrooge, calling downward to a boy in Sunday clothes, who perhaps had loitered in to look about him.

"Eh?" returned the boy, with all his might of wonder.

"What's to-day, my fine fellow?" said Scrooge.

"To-day!" replied the boy. "Why, Christmas Day."

"It's Christmas Day!" said Scrooge to himself. "I haven't missed it. The Spirits have done it all in one night. They can do anything they like. Of course they can. Of course they can. Hallo, my fine fellow!"

"Hallo!" returned the boy.

"Do you know the Poulterer's, in the next street but one, at the corner?" Scrooge inquired.

"I should hope I did," replied the lad.

"An intelligent boy!" said Scrooge. "A remarkable boy! Do you know whether they've sold the prize Turkey that was hanging up there? Not the little prize Turkey: the big one?"

"What, the one as big as me?" returned the boy.

"What a delightful boy!" said Scrooge. "It's a pleasure to talk to him. Yes, my buck!"

"It's hanging there now," replied the boy.

"Is it?" said Scrooge. "Go and buy it."

"Walk-er!" exclaimed the boy.

"No, no," said Scrooge, "I am in earnest. Go and buy it, and tell 'em to bring it here, that I may give them the direction where to take it. Come back with the man, and I'll give you a shilling. Come back with him in less than five minutes, and I'll give you half-a-crown!"

The boy was off like a shot. He must have had a steady hand at a trigger who could have got a shot off half so fast.

"I'll send it to Bob Cratchit's!" whispered Scrooge, rubbing his hands, and splitting with a laugh. "He shan't know who sends it. It's twice the size of Tiny Tim. Joe Miller never made such a joke as sending it to Bob's will be!"

The hand in which he wrote the address was not a steady one, but write it he did, somehow, and went down stairs to open the street door, ready for the coming of the poulterer's man. As he stood there, waiting his arrival, the knocker caught his eye.

"I shall love it, as long as I live!" cried Scrooge, patting it with his hand. "I scarcely ever looked at it before. What an honest expression it has in its face! It's a wonderful knocker!—Here's the Turkey. Hallo! Whoop! How are you! Merry Christmas!"

It *was* a Turkey! He never could have stood upon his legs, that bird. He would have snapped 'em short off in a minute, like sticks of sealing-wax.

"Why, it's impossible to carry that to Camden Town," said Scrooge. "You must have a cab."

The chuckle with which he said this, and the chuckle with which he paid for the Turkey, and the chuckle with which he paid for the cab, and the chuckle with which he recompensed the boy, were only to be exceeded by the chuckle with which he sat down breathless in his chair again, and chuckled till he cried.

Shaving was not an easy task, for his hand continued to shake very much; and shaving requires attention, even when you don't dance while you are at it. But if he had cut the end of his nose off, he would have put a piece of sticking-plaister over it, and been quite satisfied.

He dressed himself "all in his best," and at last got out into the streets. The people were by this time pouring forth, as he had seen them with the Ghost of Christmas Present; and walking with his hands behind him, Scrooge regarded every one with a delighted smile. He looked so irresistibly pleasant, in a word, that three or four good-humoured fellows said, "Good morning, sir! A merry Christmas to you!" And Scrooge said often afterwards, that of all the blithe sounds he had ever heard, those were the blithest in his ears.

He had not gone far, when coming on towards him he beheld the portly gentleman, who had walked into his counting-house the day before and said, "Scrooge and Marley's, I believe?" It sent a pang across his heart to think how this old gentleman would look upon him when they met; but he knew what path lay straight before him, and he took it.

"My dear sir," said Scrooge, quickening his pace, and taking the old gentleman by both his hands. "How do you do? I hope you succeeded yesterday. It was very kind of you. A merry Christmas to you, sir!"

"Mr. Scrooge?"

"Yes," said Scrooge. "That is my name, and I fear it may not be pleasant to you. Allow me to ask your pardon. And will you have the goodness"—here Scrooge whispered in his ear.

"Lord bless me!" cried the gentleman, as if his breath were gone. "My dear Mr. Scrooge, are you serious?"

"If you please," said Scrooge. "Not a farthing less. A great many back-payments are included in it, I assure you. Will you do me that favour?"

"My dear sir," said the other, shaking hands with him. "I don't know what to say to such munifi—"

"Don't say anything, please," retorted Scrooge. "Come and see me. Will you come and see me?"

"I will!" cried the old gentleman. And it was clear he meant to do it.

"Thank'ee," said Scrooge. "I am much obliged to you. I thank you fifty times. Bless you!"

He went to church, and walked about the streets, and watched the people hurrying to and fro, and patted children on the head, and questioned beggars, and looked down into the kitchens of houses, and up to the windows; and found that everything could yield him pleasure. He had never dreamed that any walk—that anything—could give him so much happiness. In the afternoon, he turned his steps towards his nephew's house.

He passed the door a dozen times, before he had the courage to go up and knock. But he made a dash, and did it:

"Is your master at home, my dear?" said Scrooge to the girl. Nice girl! Very.

"Yes, sir."

"Where is he, my love?" said Scrooge.

"He's in the dining-room, sir, along with mistress. I'll show you up stairs, if you please."

"Thank'ee. He knows me," said Scrooge, with his hand already on the dining-room lock. "I'll go in here, my dear."

He turned it gently, and sidled his face in, round the door. They were looking at the table (which was spread out in great array); for these young housekeepers are always nervous on such points, and like to see that everything is right.

"Fred!" said Scrooge.

Dear heart alive, how his niece by marriage started! Scrooge had forgotten, for the moment, about her sitting in the corner with the footstool, or he wouldn't have done it, on any account.

"Why bless my soul!" cried Fred, "who's that?"

"It's I. Your uncle Scrooge. I have come to dinner. Will you let me in, Fred?"

Let him in! It is a mercy he didn't shake his arm off. He was at home in five minutes. Nothing could be heartier. His niece looked just the same. So did Topper when *he* came. So did the plump sister, when *she* came. So did every one when *they* came. Wonderful party, wonderful games, wonderful unanimity, won-der-ful happiness!

But he was early at the office next morning. Oh, he was early there. If he could only be there first, and catch Bob Cratchit coming late! That was the thing he had set his heart upon.

And he did it; yes, he did! The clock struck nine. No Bob. A quarter past. No Bob. He was full eighteen minutes and a half, behind his time. Scrooge sat with his door wide open, that he might see him come into the Tank.

His hat was off, before he opened the door; his comforter too. He was on his stool in a jiffy; driving away with his pen, as if he were trying to overtake nine o'clock.

"Hallo!" growled Scrooge, in his accustomed voice as near as he could feign it. "What do you mean by coming here at this time of day?"

"I am very sorry, sir," said Bob. "I *am* behind my time."

"You are?" repeated Scrooge. "Yes. I think you are. Step this way, if you please."

"It's only once a year, sir," pleaded Bob, appearing from the Tank. "It shall not be repeated. I was making rather merry yesterday, sir."

"Now, I'll tell you what, my friend," said Scrooge, "I am not going to stand this sort of thing any longer. And therefore," he continued, leaping from his stool, and giving Bob such a dig in the waistcoat that he staggered back into the Tank again: "and therefore I am about to raise your salary!"

Bob trembled, and got a little nearer to the ruler. He had a momentary idea of knocking Scrooge down with it; holding him; and calling to the people in the court for help and a strait-waistcoat.

"A merry Christmas, Bob!" said Scrooge, with an earnestness that could not be mistaken, as he clapped him on the back. "A merrier Christmas, Bob, my good fellow, than I have given you, for many a year! I'll raise your salary, and endeavour to assist your struggling family, and we will discuss your affairs this very afternoon, over a Christmas bowl of smoking bishop, Bob! Make up the fires, and buy another coal-scuttle before you dot another i, Bob Cratchit!"

Scrooge was better than his word. He did it all, and infinitely more; and to Tiny Tim, who did NOT die, he was a second father. He became as good a friend, as good a master, and as good a man, as the good old city knew, or any other good old city, town, or borough, in the good old world. Some people laughed to see the alteration in him, but he let them laugh, and little heeded them; for he was wise enough to know that nothing ever happened on this globe, for good, at which some people did not have their fill of laughter in the outset; and knowing that such as these would be blind anyway, he thought it quite as well that they should wrinkle up their eyes in grins, as have the malady in less attractive forms. His own heart laughed: and that was quite enough for him.

He had no further intercourse with Spirits, but lived upon the Total Abstinence Principle, ever afterwards; and it was always said of him, that he knew how to keep Christmas well, if any man alive possessed the knowledge. May that be truly said of us, and all of us! And so, as Tiny Tim observed, God bless Us, Every One!